HUMAN RIGHTS
IN THE DIGITAL AGE

KEY TEXT

REFERENCE

D1340340

glasshouse
press

London • Sydney • Portland, Oregon

HUMAN RIGHTS
IN THE DIGITAL AGE

Edited by
Mathias Klang
and
Andrew Murray

Routledge·Cavendish
Taylor & Francis Group

London • Sydney • Portland, Oregon

First published in Great Britain 2005 by
The GlassHouse Press, The Glass House,
Wharton Street, London WC1X 9PX, United Kingdom
Telephone: + 44 (0)20 7278 8000   Facsimile: + 44 (0)20 7278 8080
Email: info@cavendishpublishing.com
Website: www.cavendishpublishing.com

Published by RoutledgeCavendish
2 Park Square, Milton Park, Abingdon, Oxon, OX14 4RN
270 Madison Ave, New York NY 10016

Transferred to Digital Printing 2006

Published in Australia by The GlassHouse Press,
45 Beach Street, Coogee, NSW 2034, Australia
Telephone: + 61 (2)9664 0909   Facsimile: +61 (2)9664 5420
Email: info@cavendishpublishing.com.au
Website: www.cavendishpublishing.com.au

© Cavendish Publishing Ltd 2005

British Library Cataloguing in Publication Data
Human rights in the digital age
1 Human rights – Great Britain
2 Data protection – Law and legislation – Great Britain
I Klang, Mathias II Murray, Andrew
342.4'1085

Library of Congress Cataloguing in Publication Data
Data available

ISBN 1-90438-531-1
ISBN 978-1-904-38531-8

1 3 5 7 9 10 8 6 4 2

Publisher's Note
The publisher has gone to great lengths to ensure the quality of this reprint but
points out that some imperfections in the original may be apparent

To the memory of Douglas Vick (1960–2004)

He was a legal academic of international standing, but, above all, a kind, thoughtful and gentle man

Preface

The idea for this book crystallised during the course of one evening in Gothenburg in summer 2002. Both of us were independently researching the disruptive effects of technology on established principles of Human Rights and Fundamental Freedoms, and both were feeling frustrated at the lack of a cohesive critical analysis in this juncture. We realised that what was needed was a single source that could be used as an initial reference point for both students and researchers in all fields which intersect this juncture. In short, what was needed was a book that would provide coverage of the key aspects of the subject. Over the course of the next few days we sketched out some of the principles of this book. Our first realisation was that the range of specialist knowledge and skills required dictated that we should engage a team of specialist authors, each of whom could bring with them the particular depth required to address their chosen subject. In gathering our team we have tried to blend authors with practical experience of their subject, such as David Christie, James Couser and Brian Esler, with those from an academic background, such as Douglas Vick, Diane Rowland and Gavin Sutter. We have also blended youth with experience, drawing upon young authors such as Rebecca Wong, Marie Eneman and Bela Chatterjee while acknowledging the contribution of expert commentators such as Jon Bing, Roger Brownsword and Robin Mansell. Finally, we attempted to balance European and North American views by inviting contributors from the US and Canada, such as Daniel Paré, Nart Villeneuve, Ronald Deibert and Brian Esler. We asked these authors to give their individual commentaries on subjects within four broad issues that lie at the heart of the human rights/digital technology nexus: Access, Content, Control and Privacy. The resultant text demonstrates a number of unique viewpoints on these issues. Together we hope that these individual contributions fulfil the aims we had at the outset of this project.

We should note that although we relied upon the skill and knowledge of individual authors to decide exactly which topics should be dealt with within their own chapters, our task as editors was to draw these individual strands together to make the book a harmonious whole. As they were writing mostly in ignorance of the precise contents of the other chapters, any responsibility for errors, in particular errors of omission, or a lack of harmony, lies with us alone. We would particularly like to thank them all for all their efforts in producing this book.

Additional thanks go to the *Kungl Vetenskaps- och Vitterhets- Samhället i Göteborg* and the *Nordic Academic Exchange Scheme*, LSE, whose generous funding enabled Mathias to remain in London while carrying out research and planning for this book. Also, thanks to all at GlassHouse Press for their help and guidance.

Finally, our thanks to Marie and Rachel, who patiently assisted us through the last few months when it seemed we were obsessed with the subject of *Human Rights in the Digital Age* and who supported us throughout the editing and proofreading process, providing moral support and sustaining cups of tea.

Mathias Klang & Andrew Murray
November 2004

Contributors

Professor Jon Bing (jon.bing@jus.uio.no)

Jon Bing is Professor in Computers and Law at the Norwegian Research Centre for Computers and Law, University of Oslo. He holds *doctor juris* (Oslo) and *doctor honoris causa* (Stockholm and Copenhagen). He is Chair, Forum for Information Security, Co-Chair, Conference Committee, International Conference on Artificial Intelligence and Law and is Knight first rank, Order of St Olav. Jon is on the editorial board of 13 journals in the IT & Law field, including *Computer und Recht* and the *Yearbook of Law, Computers and Technology*.

Professor Roger Brownsword (Roger.Brownsword@kcl.ac.uk)

Roger Brownsword is a graduate of the London School of Economics (LLB) and was a member of the Department of Law at the University of Sheffield until 2003. In October 2003 he moved from Sheffield to a Chair in Law at Kings College, London. Until recently he was the case-note editor of the *Modern Law Review* and he is the author of many books and articles on contract law, bioethics and biolaw, and jurisprudence. He is particularly interested in the intersection of legal and moral issues and is working on a new book on Consent in the Law. He is co-author (with Deryck Beyleveld) of the leading text, *Human Dignity in Bioethics and Biolaw* (Oxford: OUP, 2002).

Dr Bela Bonita Chatterjee (b.chatterjee@lancaster.ac.uk)

Bela Chatterjee recently completed her PhD on Cyberpornography and Law, and is currently a lecturer at Lancaster University. She has a strong interest in feminist and queer legal theory. In recent years, her research has tried to integrate feminist legal critique with legal discourses on cyberspace.

David Christie (david@proactive-law.co.uk)

David Christie is a solicitor with Proactive Employment Lawyers. He has practised exclusively in employment law for several years and contributes to a range of specialist and legal publications.

James Couser (james@jcouser.netkonect.co.uk)

James Couser (LLB, LLM, BCL) is a practising barrister and Senior Lecturer in Law at Middlesex University, where he teaches an LLM course on the Regulation of Electronic Technologies. He practises principally in property related law, and is particularly interested in the interaction between personal and proprietary remedies.

Dr Ronald J Deibert (r.deibert@utoronto.ca)

Ronald J Deibert (BA, MA, PhD) is associate professor of political science at the University of Toronto, specialising in media, technology and world politics, and a Ford Foundation Research Scholar of Information and Communication Technologies (2002–03). He is the author of the book *Parchment, Printing, and Hypermedia: Communications in World Order Transformation* (New York: Columbia UP, 1997). The book was designated as a finalist in the 1998 Donald McGannon Award Competition for Social and Ethical Relevance in Communications from Fordham University, New York. He is also the director of the Citizen Lab, based at the University of Toronto (www.citizenlab.org). The Citizen Lab sponsors research at the intersection of digital media and world civic politics.

Donald has published articles on topics relating to Internet politics, civil society and global politics, earth remote sensing and space policy, and social science epistemology in the journals *International Organization, The Review of International Studies, Journal of Social Issues, International Studies Perspectives, Intelligence and National Security* and *The European Journal of International Relations*. He currently serves on the editorial board of the journals *International Studies Perspectives, Astropolitics, The Journal of Environmental Peace* and *Explorations in Media Ecology*. Dr Deibert is presently finishing a manuscript on the politics of Internet security, entitled *Networks, Firewalls, and Power: Internet Security and World Order*. He is also doing research on the Internet and citizen networks and the politics of P2P networks.

Marie Eneman (eneman@informatics.gu.se)

Marie Eneman is a Researcher at the Department of Informatics at the University of Göteborg. She is currently researching within the field of child pornography and information communications technology (ICT), to study the effects of ICT on child pornography. Her research interests include social aspects of information technology, human rights, democracy and socio-technical design. She has an MSc from the Computer Science Department at Chalmers Technical University in Sweden.

Brian Esler (brian.esler@millernash.com)

Born and raised in New Jersey, Brian received his Bachelor of Arts degree in Communications from the Annenberg School of Communications at the University of Pennsylvania in 1987, his Juris Doctorate (*cum laude*) from the Georgetown University Law Center in 1992, and his LLM degree (with merit) in intellectual property law from the University of London (London School of Economics) in 2002. He previously taught Intellectual Property Law, Internet Law and Torts at the University of Hertfordshire, where his primary research interest was the emerging right to technological self-help in digital products through the use of technology to enforce contractual and other rights. He is now with Miller Nash LLP in Seattle, WA, where his practice focuses on commercial litigation, intellectual property advice and litigation, and appellate advocacy. His previous publications have appeared in *IDEA: The Journal of Law and Technology, The Hertfordshire Law Journal, The Register* and the *Journal of Internet Law*. He has also presented numerous conference papers and lectures regarding the legal challenges posed by advancing technology. His contribution is dedicated to his newborn son Conor, who loudly exercises his rights of free speech every chance he gets.

Mathias Klang (klang@informatik.gu.se)

Mathias Klang is a lecturer and researcher in legal informatics at the University of Göteborg, where he teaches courses in electronic commerce and computer ethics. His research interests are primarily in the areas of democracy, human rights and ethics in relation to technology and cyberspace. Mathias is currently working on the completion of his PhD thesis on freedom of expression in digital environments.

Professor Robin Mansell (r.mansell@lse.ac.uk)

Robin Mansell (BA (Hons) Psychology, University of Manitoba 1974; MSc Social Psychology LSE 1976; MA Communication 1980, PhD Communication 1984, Simon Fraser University) joined the London School of Economics in 2001 and holds the

Dixons Chair in New Media and the Internet. Her research and teaching are concerned with the social, economic and policy issues associated with information and communication technologies. Her research examines the integration of new technologies into society, interactions between engineering design and the structure of markets, and sources of regulatory effectiveness and failure. She directs the MSc in New Media, Information and Society and supervises PhD students. Recent books include: *Networking Knowledge for Information and Societies: Institutions and Intervention* (with Rohan Samarajiva and Amy Mahan, eds, The Netherlands: Delft University Press, 2002); *Inside the Communication Revolution: Evolving Patterns of Social and Technical Interaction* (ed, Oxford: OUP, 2002); and *Mobilizing the Information Society: Strategies for Growth and Opportunity* (with WE Steinmueller, Oxford: OUP, 2000).

Andrew Murray (a.murray@lse.ac.uk)

Andrew Murray is Lecturer in IT and Internet Law at the Department of Law, London School of Economics. He teaches courses in Information Technology & the Law, Internet & New Media Regulation and Media & Communications Regulation. Andrew is currently working on a book for Glasshouse Press examining the systems of regulatory control within digital environments, entitled *Regulatory Webs and Webs of Regulation: Regulating the Digital Environment*. His recent publications include 'Regulation and rights in networked space' *Journal of Law and Society* (2003) and 'Controlling the new media: hybrid responses to new forms of power' *Modern Law Review* (2002) (with Colin Scott). He is a member of the Editorial Committee of the *Modern Law Review*, and currently serves as Production Editor for the Review. Andrew is an accredited 'Expert' for the Nominet.uk Domain Name Dispute Resolution Service.

Dr Daniel Paré (dpar2@uottawa.ca)

Dr Daniel Paré is an Assistant Professor in Communication at the University of Ottawa, Canada. Prior to taking a position at Ottawa, he was a Research Fellow in the Department of Media and Communications (Media@LSE) at the London School of Economics and Political Science. His research focuses on e-commerce and international development, Internet governance, and issues of scientific and technological innovation. He is the author of *Internet Governance in Transition: Who is the Master of this Domain?* (Lanham, MD: Rowman & Littlefield Publishers, 2003), and a co-author of *The Reality of E-commerce with Developing Countries* available at www.gapresearchorg/production/Report.pdf). His articles have appeared in journals such as *The Information Society* and *International Review of Law, Computers and Technology*.

Professor Diane Rowland (Diane.Rowland@aber.ac.uk)

Diane Rowland is Professor of law at the University of Wales, Aberystwyth with research interests in a variety of aspects of information technology law. She has published widely in academic journals and the third edition of her book, *Information Technology Law*, will be published in 2005 by Cavendish Publishing (co-author Elizabeth Macdonald). She is the IT Law editor of the *Web Journal of Current Legal Issues*, a member of the editorial board of the *Journal of Information Law and Technology* and currently vice-chair of the British and Irish Law, Education and Technology Association (BILETA).

Gavin Sutter (g.p.sutter@qmul.ac.uk)

Gavin Sutter is a Research Fellow at the Institute of Computer & Communications Law, Centre for Commercial Law Studies (Queen Mary, University of London). He manages the ICCL's LLM IT Law course, teaches content regulation issues on the Internet Law course, and is responsible for the Internet Content Regulation module on the Institute's Internet-based LLM distance learning programme. In addition to his teaching duties, Gavin has also played an active role in ICCL research projects, including the ECLIP (Electronic Commerce Legal Issues Platform). He has published various papers in several academic volumes and journals, and is pleased to note that his professional views on Internet pornography and sexual harassment in the workplace have been quoted in *Shine*, a glossy magazine marketed at women in their late twenties. Gavin also sits on the executive committee of BILETA (British and Irish Law, Education and Technology Association). In his spare time, he is undertaking PhD research into issues surrounding the regulation of culturally sensitive content online.

Douglas W Vick

Douglas W Vick was a Senior Lecturer in Law at the University of Stirling and a Visiting Fellow with the Stirling Media Research Institute. Prior to taking a position at Stirling, Mr Vick taught at Temple University School of Law in Philadelphia, and worked as an attorney in Pennsylvania and New York. His research addressed aspects of media policy and regulation (including Internet law) and related constitutional issues. This book is dedicated to Doug who died suddenly and tragically on 1 May 2004.

Rebecca Wong (R.Wong@sheffield.ac.uk)

Rebecca is currently a doctoral researcher at the University of Sheffield, Law Department. She is examining data protection legislation under the guidance of Professor Beyleveld and Mr David Townend. She assisted with a European Commission funded project, PRIVIREAL, which was concerned with the implementation of the Data Protection Directive 95/46/EC within the European Union in relation to medical research. She graduated with an LLB (Derby) in 1998, MSc (Loughborough) in 2000 and LLM in International, Commercial and European Law (Sheffield) in 2001. She is affiliated with the Sheffield Institute of Biotechnology and Law (SIBLE), the Centre for European, Comparative and International Law (CECIL) and the Centre for Criminology and Legal Research (CCLR). These centres are based at the University of Sheffield.

Nart Villeneuve (nart.villeneuve@utoronto.ca)

Nart Villeneuve is the director of technical research at the Citizen Lab, an interdisciplinary laboratory based at the Munk Centre for International Studies at the University of Toronto. He is currently working with the OpenNet Initiative, documenting Internet content filtering and surveillance practices worldwide. His research interests include hacktivism, cyberterrorism and Internet security. He is a graduate of the University of Toronto's Peace and Conflict Studies program.

Contents

Chapter 1
Introduction – Human Rights and Equity in Cyberspace
Robin Mansell

Introduction

Summit meetings and world conferences have been convened on issues ranging from sustainable development to social development, and women and children. In December 2003, the World Summit on the Information Society (WSIS) was convened under the auspices of the United Nations. This meeting aimed to stimulate action to ensure that the information societies emerging today are more, rather than less, equitable than the societies that have preceded them. Summit meetings generally lead to declarations of principles and intended actions. These are the result of lengthy negotiations that seek to find common ground between the disparate interests of government, business and, in the case of the WSIS, civil society representatives from around the world. One important area that engendered considerable debate in the case of this Summit and the necessity for compromise was a core issue that is addressed in this volume: human rights and their legal protection.

Human rights in the digital age are openly being contested today. The text of the WSIS Declaration of Principles espouses a common vision of the information society, particularly with respect to human rights. For example:

> *We reaffirm* the universality, indivisibility, interdependence and interrelation of all human rights and fundamental freedoms, including the right to development, as enshrined in the Vienna Declaration. We also reaffirm that democracy, sustainable development, and respect for human rights and fundamental freedoms as well as good governance at all levels are interdependent and mutually reinforcing. We further resolve to strengthen respect for the rule of law in international as in national affairs. ...

> *We reaffirm*, as an essential foundation of the Information Society, and as outlined in Article 19 of the Universal Declaration of Human Rights, that everyone has the right to freedom of opinion and expression; that this right includes freedom to hold opinions without interference and to seek, receive and impart information and ideas through any media and regardless of frontiers. Communication is a fundamental social process, a basic human need and the foundation of all social organisation. It is central to the information society. Everyone, everywhere should have the opportunity to participate and no one should be excluded from the benefits the Information Society offers.

> Nothing in this Declaration shall be construed as impairing, contradicting, restricting or derogating from the provisions of the Charter of the United Nations and the Universal Declaration of Human Rights, any other international instrument or national laws adopted in furtherance of these instruments.[1]

---

1 World Summit on the Information Society, 'Declaration of Principles', WSIS-03/GENEVA/DOC/4-E, 12 December 2003, at www.itu.int/wsis/docs/geneva/official/dop.html, paras A.3, 4, 18.

The Declaration goes on to emphasise the need to foster an inclusive information society and to ensure the ability not just to access information and to communicate, but also to contribute. Observations are made about the need for capacity building and for an enabling institutional and legal environment. On issues of building confidence and security in the use of information and communication technologies (ICTs), the Declaration has this to say:

> Strengthening the trust framework, including information and network security, authentication, privacy and consumer protection, is a prerequisite for the development of the Information Society. ...
>
> It is necessary to prevent the use of information resources and technologies for criminal and terrorist purposes, while respecting human rights. ...
>
> All actors in the information society should take appropriate actions and preventative measures, as determined by law, against abusive uses of ICTs, such as illegal and other acts motivated by racism, racial discrimination, xenophobia, and related intolerance, hatred, violence, all forms of child abuse, including paedophilia and child pornography, and trafficking in, and exploitation of, human beings.[2]

Issues of trust, protection from criminal behaviour, and the applicability of international and national legal frameworks are clearly signposted in the WSIS Declaration, which is accompanied by a Plan of Action.[3] The actions envisaged are numerous and are aimed at reducing 'digital divides of many different kinds'. However, the documents are silent with respect to how existing and new interpretations of the law should apply nationally or internationally and on whether variations between countries mean that the Internet makes law enforcement virtually impossible.

Following the WSIS, there has been much discussion about whether the Summit simply provided a costly opportunity to foster a hollow rhetoric about the need for 'digital solidarity' or whether it succeeded in mobilising a major step-shift in the priority that will now be given to finding the resources to implement the high ambitions of the authors of the Declaration and Plan of Action. A clear call is made for research to unveil the causes and consequences of developments in all of the facets of the digital age.

An essential prerequisite if the respect for human rights embedded in the WSIS Declaration is to be upheld is investigation of the way that legal institutions, practices and interpretations are influencing today's information societies. An important aspect of this field of inquiry is research on the way cyberspace is being experienced by people in the very disparate contexts of their everyday lives. The contributors to the present volume tackle these issues from a variety of vantage points. Central to this volume is an inquiry into human action and human rights in those instances where they are mediated by the technologies of the digital age. The chapters encompass a wide range of issues including the production and

---

2 *Ibid*, paras 35, 36, 59.
3 World Summit on the Information Society, 'Plan of Action', WSIS-03/GENEVA/DOC/5-E, 12 December 2003, at www.itu.int/wsis/docs/geneva/official/poa.html.

consumption of digital content, the means of control over unwanted intrusions to the individual's privacy, and emerging means of governing in cyberspace.

Globally and locally, today's information societies are underpinned by digital technologies. These technologies enable applications that may be empowering for some people, allowing them to develop new ways of seeing the world around them. Ubiquitous networks are at the heart of the digital age. They are becoming familiar to people in all parts of the world, albeit unevenly so. The Internet allows for use of chatrooms, email and voice communication by people representing numerous interests, values and aspirations. Together with the World Wide Web's enormous repository of information, the Internet is limited in its application only by the limits of human imagination. Within the digital spaces – or cyberspaces – of this century, there are many opportunities for new forms of business and governance as well as for new forms of criminal or unwanted behaviour. Many of these also create the potential for changes in behaviour and perceptions of the non-virtual world.

One of the key findings of recent research on the way digital technologies and the Internet are mediating our lives is that offline conventions and practices do not diminish in importance in the face of new cyberspace developments. In some cases, cyberspace simply offers a complementary space to conduct familiar activities, while in others, the new virtual spaces amplify existing activities or create opportunities for completely new activities and behaviours.[4] While many efforts are underway to foster e-strategies for the development of new forms of electronic commerce and electronic government as well as a host of other applications, the darker side of cyberspace is often shrouded in mystery or revealed only by the media as 'moral panics' over signs that the Internet is untrustworthy or that the riskiness of cyberspace is substantial.[5] This collection of papers offers a research-based assessment of the implications of the law and its evolving institutions for the protection of human rights and greater equity in cyberspace developments.

Consent and possession in cyberspace

The volume opens with Bela Chatterjee's (Chapter 2) examination of the cyber-sex phenomenon. This involves the use of digital technologies including the World Wide Web to provide and exchange information about prostitutes or pornographic materials. She notes that, while cyberspace may enable women to engage in the sex trade on more favourable terms to themselves, there are also new opportunities for cyber-stalking, 'virtual' pimps and an intensification of harm and exploitation. She reviews UK, European and international legislation and protocols intended to deal with these issues. While human rights are being recognised and legal and socio-economic solutions to protect women from sexual exploitation are being devised, she suggests that there is little recognition that civil and political rights are

---

4 See Mansell, R and Steinmueller, W, *Mobilising the Information Society: Strategies for Growth and Opportunity*, 2000, Oxford: OUP; Silverstone, R, *Why Study the Media?*, 1999, London: Sage.

5 See O'Hara, K, *Trust: From Socrates to Spin*, 2004, Cambridge: Icon; Thomas, D and Loader, B (eds), *Cybercrime: Law Enforcement, Security and Surveillance in the Information Age*, 2000, London: Routledge; Wall, D (ed), *Crime and the Internet*, 2001, London: Routledge.

'gendered'. The cyber-sex trade no longer necessarily involves movement and travel, creating new challenges for legislators, and it continues to be unclear as to the circumstances under which consent may be deemed to have been given or not given in cyberspace.

The infringement of children's rights is central to Marie Eneman's chapter (Chapter 3), which tackles the difficult issues of child pornography. She warns that digital technologies not only make it easier and less costly to produce pornographic content, but software can also be used to produce 'morphed' images, which fall uncertainly within the ambit of existing law. Anonymity and closed Internet-based membership communities also protect paedophiles, make content production a potentially lucrative activity, and enable contacts to be made with children on and offline. Although there is a Council of Europe Convention on Cybercrime that deals with child pornography, Eneman highlights gaps in existing legislation such as that the meaning of 'possession' of child pornography is open to question because of the immaterial nature of this form of digital content.

Governance, liability and balance

Vick's (Chapter 4) discussion of the implications of cyberspace for the control of hate speech begins with the observation that 'no society in the world has concluded that free speech is an absolute barrier to state regulation of harmful expression'. The governance of cyberspace is often said to be beyond the capabilities of the nation-state, yet this chapter shows how differences in national law have implications that make it very difficult to achieve a universally applicable definition of how to protect human rights in the face of the propagation of hate speech over the Internet. Vick stresses that, in the US, the prevailing view is that the best way to counter hate speech is rebuttal by others, rather than by sanctions imposed by the state. It is also the case that hate speech laws may be enforced against marginalised members of society, succeeding only in amplifying resentments. Neither hate speech laws nor a *laissez-faire* approach address the underlying problems of poverty, social isolation and ignorance that give rise to group hatred. In this chapter, the difficulties of governing the Internet are posed as matters for social policy as well as for legislators.

Closely related to this issue is the appropriate balance between the protection of reputation from defamatory speech and the right to freedom of expression. In her analysis of this issue, Diane Rowland (Chapter 5) defines defamation as a statement that is 'injurious to the reputation or dignity of the person allegedly defamed [which] must be published or communicated to another who must understand its connection with the person allegedly defamed'. She shows that, in practice, there is a 'hierarchy of speech' protection. Internet-mediated speech raises issues including the standard to be applied, where publication is deemed to occur and the jurisdiction within which action can be taken. Should liability fall only on the originator of an allegedly defamatory statement or on an Internet service provider (ISP)? This chapter draws attention to the potentially 'chilling' effects of imposing liability on the latter, such as that ISPs may remove information even before there is judicial verification that it is defamatory. Despite the potential of the Internet to amplify defamatory speech, Rowland insists that 'the application of existing legal rules and pre-existing tension between rights of reputation and those of free speech' should pertain, notwithstanding the fact that the stability of the law and its enforcement are challenged by the global reach of the Internet and many different local legal and cultural norms.

The problem of ISP liability is taken up again in Chapter 6 by Gavin Sutter, this time specifically with respect to the European Union and UK legislative context of liability for failure to remove potentially harmful content, or failure to offer the required consumer protection. Existing legislation envisages 'a form of notice and take-down procedure', but it remains unclear what constitutes 'knowledge' and what timeframe is applicable for judgments about an ISP's liability or immunity. Sutter asks whether ISPs will take it upon themselves to function as the moral guardians of cyberspace. Again there are issues of balancing rights and obligations. If over-zealous ISPs refuse to host certain types of Internet sites, they may jeopardise free speech rights. Alternatively, ambiguity about ISP liability could mean that ISPs permit the provision of content without regard to its potentially harmful effects.

Digital divides in cyberspace

There is ongoing debate about the unevenness of access to the means of communicating using digital technologies and about whether, and the extent to which, measures should be taken to reduce the effects of various types of digital divides.[6] After all, there are many other major claims on the scarce resources of time and finance to support health care, education, economic development, or democratic governance. In Chapter 7, Daniel Paré provides an empirically-grounded account of why a binary distinction between those with and those without access to the Internet is unhelpful in thinking about what steps should be taken by legislators to address the numerous and differentiated uses of the Internet. Summarising recent research which has examined Internet use to support commercial activity, he finds that, for small and medium-sized enterprises in developing countries particularly, efforts to introduce uniformity in the law governing electronic transactions often embody a 'techno-centric' logic, which runs counter to people's experiences and preferences for how and with whom they choose to trade. As all the chapters in this volume demonstrate, user- and use-centred approaches to analysing behaviour associated with the spread of the Internet have a much greater potential to shed light on the complex and multi-faceted issues that legislators and legal experts face in the digital age.

---

6   See Couldry, N, 'Digital divide or discursive design? On the emerging ethics of information space' (2003) 5 *Ethics and Information Technology* 89; DiMaggio, P and Hargittai, E, 'From the "digital divide" to "digital inequality"', Working Paper No 15, Center for Arts and Cultural Policy Studies, 2001, Princeton University; Gunkel, D, 'Second thoughts: toward a critique of the digital divide' (2003) 5(4) *New Media & Society* 499; Hargittai, E, 'Second-level digital divide: differences in people's online skills' 7(4) *First Monday*, at www.firstmonday.org/issues/issue7_4/hargittai; Mansell, R, 'Digital opportunities and the missing link for developing countries' (2001) 17(2) *Oxford Review of Economic Policy* 282; Norris, P, *Digital Divide?*, 2001, Cambridge: CUP.

The technologies of governing

The foregoing chapters are concerned mainly with choices and actions on the part of human beings who interact with digital technologies. However, the spread of the Internet is encouraging the development of technologies that can be used by individuals, or programmed as software agents, to filter, block and rate content that is available to end-users. While the market for these technologies has not grown nearly as rapidly as initially expected and there is little harmonisation or interoperability of approaches, these technologies raise crucial issues about the nature of the 'public sphere' and about censorship.[7] Brian Esler (Chapter 8) asks 'whether free speech has any value if it cannot be heard'. He reviews experience with filtering technologies and content rating initiatives in the US and Europe. Aimed at limiting access to illegal, harmful and racist content on the Internet, he shows that new technologies can be institutionally mandated for use, for example, in libraries to prevent children's access. As Esler graphically puts it: 'will the Internet remain a true "marketplace of ideas", a blowsy bazaar of the bizarre to the banal, or will filtering technology transform the experience of many users into something akin to a Communist department store, where choice is limited by central governance?' These technologies also make it feasible for end-users' prejudices to become embedded in the technology, making their use and effects anything but transparent over time.

Ronald Deibert and Nart Villeneuve (Chapter 9) take up the theme of state intervention as a form of Internet governance. In this case, the discussion of filtering, self-censorship and the practices of states focuses on efforts to limit access to content for political reasons.[8] Quite apart from the fact that filtering can lead to errors and mistaken or unintended blockages, the notion that the Internet is inherently open because of the nature of its architecture is not one that can be sustained in the light of current technological developments and various methods of fostering self-censorship. These authors consider the experience of China where citizens are encouraged to make 'public pledges' not to publish information of certain kinds. Elsewhere, Internet café owners are often required to block certain kinds of content. In the US (and as also indicated by Esler in Chapter 8), legislation requires libraries and schools to block content to protect children. Deibert and Villeneuve raise the spectre of the 'strangulation' of the open Internet and point to various methods by which Internet filtering software is being used in ways that elude public scrutiny of the types of content and websites that are excluded. This suggests that the new technologies of governance do not always support the empowerment of civil society movements.[9]

The variety of means by which virtual community actors who use the Internet can be controlled with respect to their use of content that is subject to intellectual

---

7   See Habermas, J, *The Structural Transformation of the Public Sphere*, 1989 [1962], Cambridge: Polity.

8   The broader issues involved in this area are discussed in Kalathil, S and Boas, T, *Open Networks: Closed Regimes*, 2003, Washington, DC: Carnegie Endowment for International Peace.

9   See Surman, M and Reilly, K, 'Appropriating the Internet for social change', 2003, New York: prepared for the Social Science Research Council.

property protection are examined by James Couser (Chapter 10). In the case of Napster and subsequent efforts by the music industry to prosecute individuals who download music that is subject to copyright protection, Couser argues that current copyright protection of digital content and software provides a completely inappropriate 'blanket, one-size-fits-all solution'. When software is so protected, creative efforts to develop new applications are suppressed since any effort to re-use or build upon the software code becomes an infringement of the law. Couser suggests that the practice of registration of copyrights before they take effect offers a means of providing appropriate and differentiated levels of protection.[10]

One of the reasons that states seek legal means of intervening in cyberspace is to counter Denial of Service (DoS) attacks on Internet servers. In Chapter 11, Mathias Klang distinguishes between civil disobedience, criminal activity and terrorism, suggesting that each of these has different legal implications. The meaning of the term 'terrorism' is changing so that emphasis is being given to whether fear is engendered rather than to the extent of violence or devastation. Whether they are the result of co-ordinated action or the actions of a single individual, DoS attacks can completely overwhelm Internet servers. In consequence, legislative measures are being put in place. These include the European Union's Cybercrime Convention, European Council Framework Decision on Attacks against Information Systems and the UK Terrorism Act 2000. Although these measures aim to reduce the likelihood of such attacks, Klang suggests that when such attacks represent a form of civil disobedience and democratic protest, they should not be criminalised. The right to free expression should not be limited without evidence of a clear threat to society. Klang argues that current measures are likely to jeopardise human rights.

Privacy and surveillance

Cyberspace raises many issues for privacy protection.[11] Rebecca Wong (Chapter 12) reviews definitions of privacy focusing particularly on control-based definitions emphasising the individual's autonomy to determine what is kept in the private sphere in contrast to those that regard the social importance of transparency as a collective value that should be considered. She raises the issue of whether privacy should be regarded as a unique or a derivative right. Wong's examination of the European Convention on Human Rights, data protection legislation in the UK, and laws on confidentiality highlights the ambiguity of the law. For instance, it is unclear whether the Human Rights Act 1998 in the UK created a right to the protection of privacy via an extension of the law of confidentiality. Similarly, in the case of the UK Data Protection Act 1998, there are unanswered questions about how privacy infringement should be valued and about the meaning of informed consent with respect to the use of information on the Web.

---

10 See also Steinmueller, WE, 'Information society consequences of expanding the intellectual property domain', 2003, Brighton: STAR Issue Report No 38, SPRU, University of Sussex, October.

11 See Bennett, C and Raab, C, *The Governance of Privacy: Policy Instruments in Global Perspective*, 2003, Aldershot: Ashgate.

The digital age has spawned many new techniques of surveillance and these have been applied increasingly extensively within the workplace. David Christie (Chapter 13) discusses how the law in the UK attempts to reconcile employees' perceptions of the right to privacy with employers' interpretations of employment relationships. Common law does not provide employees with a general right to privacy in the workplace, but Christie suggests that the Human Rights Act 1998, together with the European Convention on Human Rights, may have conferred new rights. However, the new legislation on curtailing employee surveillance (monitoring telephone calls and email communications) is likely to be slow to take effect. On balance, Christie concludes that despite numerous legislative measures, UK legislation is neither coherent nor straightforward in protecting employees' privacy in the workplace. In the absence of clarity about how much privacy can be expected, Christie suggests that the balance favours the employer's right to monitor, rather than the employee's right to privacy.

Mathias Klang takes up broader issues of surveillance and privacy in Chapter 14, by considering the 'camera as the unblinking, unforgiving eye in our urban environment'. Facial, pattern and number recognition using digital technology is being deployed increasingly to detect socially undesirable behaviour. Public surveillance using closed circuit television (CCTV) is becoming pervasive despite the absence of empirical evidence on the effectiveness of its use as a means of crime prevention. Klang argues that it is a matter of human choice as to which individuals or groups receive the greatest attention because of the need to select from the huge quantities of data that are being gathered. In the UK, the Data Protection Act 1998 enables the Information Commissioner to set out a CCTV Code of Practice, which is intended to provide acceptable levels of privacy protection. The extent of protection is considered in this chapter in the light of the provisions of Article 8 of the European Convention on Human Rights, which implies that surveillance can be intrusive because of its potential for error, function creep and privacy invasion. Klang concludes that resources would be better devoted to combating crime in ways that are not so reliant on technology.

Individual privacy protection is an important issue in the digital age, but questions also need to be asked about whether states should have a right to privacy. As the Internet spreads, there are increasing calls for informational transparency on the part of the state[12] but, as government services go online, Andrew Murray (Chapter 15) suggests that there are strong arguments in favour of more, rather than less, state secrecy. The convergence of digital technology is providing numerous outlets for digital media. Murray suggests that the growing capacity for information gathering and transmission means that the 'state is paralysed by fear' and its response is 'spin'. Arguing from Edward Shils' contention that modern democracy depends upon a 'state of political civility',[13] he indicates that it is becoming more and more difficult for the state to manage its relationship with the media.

---

12 See Miller, P, 'The see-through society', 2003, London: DEMOS, note prepared for the Foresight Cyber Trust and Crime Prevention Project.
13 Shills, EA, 'Privacy: its constitution and vicissitudes' (1966) 31 *Law and Contemporary Problems* 281.

Individuals who embody the precepts of the state may benefit from a greater emphasis on personal autonomy, emotional release, self-evaluation, and protected communication. In the UK, much emphasis is given to media management and the co-ordination of information as a result of unrelenting media coverage of the government's actions. Murray argues in favour of an open debate about the feasibility of providing privacy protection for the state as an antidote to the politics of 'spin'.

Cyberspace futures

The contributors to this volume highlight many ambiguities with respect to human rights and available legal protections, and the difficulties of their enforcement due to technological inadequacies and human frailties. The future of digital rights management, for instance, depends on choices with respect to the evolution of the law and its interpretation. Jon Bing (Chapter 16) emphasises the interdependence of the evolution of digital technologies, the law as a means of regulation and control, and the potential for inconsistencies between the interpretation of the law and its implementation in computerised code. Once regulations and rules are automated, they are extremely difficult to subject to judicial review. Following Lawrence Lessig's argument that the code of cyberspace becomes the 'regulator', Bing warns that we face a situation in which 'technology [is] implementing the law'. As 'click wrap licensing' for access to intellectual property on the Web becomes more pervasive, Bing suggests that technology could be used by rights holders to restrict the buyer's legal position. Increasing diversity in the bundles of rights offered to users of protected information is likely and differences in the negotiating power of the rights holders and users may lead to a need for new forms of consumer protection. Bing emphasises that the buyer is, in effect, purchasing a legal position, rather than an immaterial service. Software agents will become negotiators of legal positions and be guided by formalisms in the software code that may not be consistent with the offline position. In the future, 'rights themselves are defined in the terms of programming language', raising many challenges for legal policy and practice.

Chapter 17 by Roger Brownsword considers issues associated with developments in biotechnology and human rights alongside those raised by digital technologies. He suggests that there are three main ethical positions on these issues: a utilitarian pragmatic stance based on assessments of risk and cost, a defence of human rights based on respect for human dignity, and a 'dignitarian alliance' that permits no compromise of human dignity. Brownsword argues that the first position is problematic because it is subject to the erosion of rights. The second rights-based position puts respect for human dignity at the centre of ethical choices about the development of technology, indicating that individuals must have the capacity to make free and informed choices. In the case of the 'dignitarian alliance', which is informed by a Kantian claim that human dignity has no price, developments in biotechnology are ruled out if they do not uphold a duty of self-esteem. Of the three positions, Brownsword indicates that the first two are gaining ground in the UK. He suggests that 'techno-regulation' is eroding the contexts in which the dignity of individual choice, responsibility and achievement are respected, with the result that technologies are being developed which treat human subjects as though they lack the capacity to choose.

Conclusion

This book demonstrates the value of considering the evolution of cyberspace law and the interpretative flexibility of that law from one jurisdiction to another. It is increasingly difficult to unambiguously define human rights and responsibilities in cyberspace. The contributors to this volume take the question of human rights not as an absolute, but as a social construct that is subject to interpretation in the light of changing values. They highlight how many of the judgments and social values that appear to have achieved a consensus are subject to misapplication as we come to rely on technology to implement the law.

There is clearly a growing need for critical assessments of the 'less glamorous' aspects of cyberspace. The chapters in this volume demonstrate why the issues of consent, governance, privacy and surveillance and technology need to be coupled with analysis of ethical positions and legal positions and practices. Only in this way will there be a chance of protecting basic human rights and of fostering responsibility in the digital age.

Chapter 2

Pixels, Pimps and Prostitutes: Human Rights and the Cyber-Sex Trade
Bela Bonita Chatterjee[1]

pixel /'piksel/ *noun* 1 one of thousands of tiny spots on a computer display that together can be manipulated to form an image or character. [blend of PIX + the first syllable of ELEMENT]

pimp /pimp/ *noun* 1a a man who solicits clients for a prostitute or brothel and takes some of their earnings. b a person who supplies or procures whatever is needed to satisfy another person's lusts or vices.[2] prostitute as used by feminists, often not clearly distinct from *woman, lady,* and other terms for female ...[3]

Introduction

In a recent article, Professor Donna Hughes argued that 'the sexual exploitation of women and children is a *global human rights crisis* that is being escalated by the use of new technologies'.[4] Her employment of the language and discourse of human rights is remarkable, in that from a legal point of view, commentaries on the detrimental uses of new information and communication technologies (ICTs) are usually framed in terms of criminality rather than human rights, and are also rarely gendered.[5] Hughes' argument is that ICTs are being used as facilitators for the trafficking and sexual exploitation of women and children in various ways, and her article is devoted to uncovering and cataloguing these digitally mediated abuses.[6] In this chapter, I wish to use Hughes' arguments as a point of departure for my own

---

1 With thanks to the librarians at Lancaster at inter-library loans. Thanks also to Sarah Beresford, Beverley Brown, Alison Diduck, Georgina Firth, Gary Hammond, Mathias Klang, Madeleine Jowett, Steven Riley, Marcus Petz, David Seymour, Sigrun Skogly and my Gender and Law class of 2003.

2 Definitions of 'pixel' and 'pimp' from Allen, R, *The New Penguin English Dictionary*, 2000, Harmondsworth: Penguin.

3 Definition of 'prostitute' from Kramarae, C and Treichler, PA, *A Feminist Dictionary*, 1985, London: Pandora (no entry for 'pimp' or 'pixel').

4 Hughes, D, 'The use of new communications and information technologies for sexual exploitation of women and children' (2002) 13(1) *Hastings Women's LJ* 129, p 129 (emphasis added). See also Hughes, D 'The Internet and sex industries: partners in global sexual exploitation' (2000) *IEEE Technology and Society Magazine*, Spring; Hughes, D, 'The Internet and the global prostitution industry', in Hawthorne, S and Klein, R (eds), *Cyberfeminism: Connectivity, Critique and Creativity*, 1999, Melbourne: Spinifex.

5 See, eg, the recent Convention on Cybercrime (2001, Treaty no 185), which does not mention trafficking or prostitution. In an attempt to recognise the 'human' dimension of cybercrime, an additional Protocol to the Convention on Cybercrime Concerning the Criminalisation of Acts of a Racist and Xenophobic Nature Committed through Computer Systems' (2003, Treaty no 189) is now open for signature. However, whilst this Protocol asserts human rights, it does not mention damaging acts based on gender, sex or sexuality.

6 See Hughes, 2002, *op cit* fn 4. See also Council of Europe, *Group of Specialists on the Impact of the Use of New Information Technologies on Trafficking in Human Beings for the Purpose of Sexual Exploitation – Final Report (EG-S-NT) (2000)* 9, Strasbourg, 17 February 2003 (hereinafter CoE 2003).

analysis, considering the possible human rights issues arising from the use of ICTs in the cyber-sex trade, from a feminist legal perspective.[7] Such an engagement is useful because there is a paucity of critical commentary in this area, and also because Hughes states that comment on the law is outside the scope of her article. Her work, she argues:

> is not about strict legal definitions, nor is it about the law. In fact, many experiences of women and children fall into gray areas, rather than conform to existing legal definitions. Also, much of the research on sexual exploitation and the Internet focuses on images, and the people in the images are rarely available for interviews to describe their experiences, their consent or coercion, their freedom or slavery.[8]

Writing a chapter on the human rights impacts of ICTs in the cyber-sex trade from a feminist perspective therefore immediately raises some problems and questions.[9] As mentioned, there is little explicitly feminist work on *any* aspect of cyberlaw.[10] Whereas there is an established body of feminist commentary on the sex trade and sex workers, including the global aspect,[11] this work tends to pre-date the emergence of cyberspace as a significant arena for sexual discourse and exploitation. The status and role of women in the sex trade is also a contentious

---

7 Whereas Hughes looks at women and children in her work, for the purposes of this chapter I focus solely on women. I feel that consideration of children along with women obscures the fact that, regarding sexual exploitation, they are often subject to different legal regimes. Whilst this difference is in itself an interesting point of comparison, comparison, I feel, is outside the scope of this article. Also, literature on women, children and sexual exploitation can tend to conflate the two, and I consider that this can lead to the 'infantilisation' of women, and obscure the different capacities for agency that women and children have. Men in the cyber-sex trade, along with the queer cyber-sex trade, are also outside the scope of this article; see further Ryan, C and Hall, CM (eds), *Sex Tourism*, 2001, London/New York: Routledge; Oppermann, M (ed), *Sex Tourism and Prostitution: Aspects of Leisure, Recreation, and Work*, 1998, New York: Cognizant Communication Corporation, for discussions of these issues (not always in a cyber context).

8 See Hughes, 2002, *op cit* fn 4, pp 129–30.

9 With reference to Hughes' comments that the voices of sex workers are rarely heard (Hughes, 2002, *op cit* fn 4, pp 129–30) and feminist criticisms that talking *about* sex workers as opposed to talking *to* them can serve to reinforce their objectification (eg, Bell, L (ed), *Good Girls/Bad Girls*, 1987, Toronto: The Women's Press), it could be seen as a criticism or weakness of this chapter that I have not sought to speak to sex workers and include their comments. However, I decided that to organise interviews would not only be beyond the scope of my resources but would also carry moral and legal implications. Methodological difficulties arise, in that it is unlikely that I could set up interviews with sex workers as easily as I could for other 'researchees'. Further, ethical issues come to the fore: as Kempadoo and Doezema point out (*Global Sex Workers*, 1998, London: Routledge, p 2), in many countries prostitution is a criminal act. Despite the fact that my chapter focuses on those forced into the sex trade, I believe that to attempt interviews could lead not only to further stigmatisation, but also to risk of exposure, and the damage that could arise as a consequence. I do, however, draw on material that is based on empirical evidence.

10 See, eg, Kramer, J and Kramarae, C, 'Legal snarls for women in cyberspace' (1995) 5(2) *Internet Research: Electronic Networking Application and Policy* 14; Adam, A (ed), *Artificial Knowing: Gender and the Thinking Machine*, 1998, London: Routledge; Edwards, L, 'Pornography and the Internet', in Edwards, L and Waelde, C (eds), *Law and the Internet*, 2000, Oxford: Hart; Chatterjee, B, 'Razorgirls and cyberdykes: tracing cyberfeminism and thoughts on its use in a legal context' (2002) 7(2/3) *International Journal of Sexuality and Gender Studies* 197.

11 See, eg, Goldman, E, *The Traffic in Women and Other Essays on Feminism*, 1970 [1917], Washington, DC: Times Change Press; Kempadoo and Doezema, *op cit* fn 9; Pateman, C, *The Sexual Contract*, 1988, Cambridge: Polity; Bell, *op cit* fn 9; Skrobanek, S, Boonpakdi, N and Janthakeero, C (eds), *The Traffic in Women*, 1997, London/New York: Zed.

issue, and there is no clear consensus amongst feminist work on this point.[12] With regard to human rights, questions of gender have not always been recognised as having any bearing on human rights discourse, where human rights tend to be seen as 'universal', and therefore inherently equal.[13]

My use of the term 'cyber-sex trade' itself requires some explaining. I broadly take the phrase to mean any use of ICTs to facilitate the sexual exploitation of women. As stated in the Council of Europe's specialist report on the use of ICTs in trafficking:

> the Internet offers unprecedented advantages, which traffickers have been quick to exploit. The Internet and other types of telecommunication provide the sex industry and individual users with new ways of finding, marketing and delivering women ... into appalling conditions of sexual slavery and exploitation.[14]

Although the Council of Europe's report is framed in the terms of the Internet, in the context of this chapter, the 'cyber' aspect denotes rather more than the Internet alone, to include any digital media or combination of digital with traditional media that is used in the sex trade. The cyber-sex trade here refers to the use of websites and/or digital cameras to advertise prostitutes or pornographic images, the use of web conferencing technology, DVDs and web TV/video in the creation and use of 'interactive' prostitution and pornography, or email, bulletin boards and chatrooms used by 'sex tourists' to exchange information about prostitutes either at home or abroad.[15]

The 'sex trade' can be taken to mean any sexual transaction as a form of work, but this description must come with some caveats. It is important to acknowledge that women's agency and freedom to consent in the sex trade are contentious issues. From some perspectives, women's involvement in the sex trade is *always* coerced to some degree, in that in a patriarchal society any consent is always compromised by the gendered imbalances of power that inhere in sexual transactions between men and women. On this view, the sex trade itself is a function of patriarchy.[16] On others, it is possible for women to find work in the sex industry personally and politically empowering, and is a valid expression of their freedom to work in the ways that they find most fulfilling and/or lucrative.[17] For example, as Hamilton has argued, prostitution is 'a livelihood; the profession of a wife and mother is not. A woman

---

12 The lack of consensus here is not, I would argue, a weakness. Indeed, the multiplicity of views encompassed by feminist work may be seen as a key aspect of its strength. With their commitment to reflexivity and plurality, feminists are concerned not to reproduce patterns of oppression by claiming to speak universally. (I thank Dr Madeleine Jowett for discussion on this point.)

13 See further Cook, R (ed), *Human Rights of Women*, 1994, Philadelphia: University of Pennsylvania Press; MacKinnon, C, 'Rape, genocide, and women's human rights' (1994) 17 *Harv Women's LJ* 5; Fraser, A, 'Becoming human: the origins and development of women's human rights' (1999) 3–4 *Human Rights Quarterly* 853.

14 CoE 2003, *op cit* fn 6, p 4.

15 Hughes, 2002, 1999, *op cit* fn 4; Ryan and Hall, *op cit* fn 7; Kohm and Selwood in Oppermann, *op cit* fn 7, pp 123–31.

16 See, eg, Pateman, *op cit* fn 11; Edwards, S, *Sex and Gender in the Legal Process*, 1996, London: Blackstone.

17 See further Bell, *op cit* fn 9; Kempadoo and Doezema, *op cit* fn 9.

can support her children by prostitution; she cannot do so by performing the duties ordinarily associated with motherhood'.[18] Indeed, as I have argued elsewhere, women's position in the cyber-sex trade is, at the very least, ambiguous.[19] However, I am wary of suggesting that women who work in the cyber-sex industry (or sex industry generally) are all coerced as, whilst I think that strong arguments can be made out as to the patriarchal nature of the majority of the sex trade, to suggest that women's willing engagement in sex work is solely a function of false consciousness can, I believe, disempower sex workers, and also serve to maintain moral distinctions between 'good' and 'bad' professions, ie feminist academic as morally superior to sex worker.[20] I am also aware, though, that difficult economic conditions or cultural differences may serve to pressure women's choices, and must concede that 'coercion' can be more than physical, sexual or psychological violence.[21] To use the word 'trade' to signal coerced sex work is, for me at least, an unsatisfactory term, but hopefully one that recognises the fact of some women's coercion, whilst acknowledging that not all women who work in the sex trade are unwilling, or victims. It is important to state that some women *are* used as sexual slaves, but this assertion needs to be made with care. In her work on prostitution and choice, Doezema argues that the dual categories of 'forced' and 'voluntary' prostitution can in themselves be oppressive, in that they serve to underscore what is known as the 'Madonna/whore' dichotomy, where women are either 'innocent' and 'pure', or 'fallen' women worthy of censure. 'Forced' becomes allied with 'innocent', whereas 'voluntary' takes on associations of 'guilt', a judgment that would not be made about other forms of chosen work.[22] Also, the discourse of 'force' can hide racist undertones, as Doezema explains:

> The 'voluntary' prostitute is a Western sex worker, seen as capable of making independent decisions about whether or not to sell sexual services, while the sex worker from a developing country is deemed unable to make this same choice; she is passive, naïve, and ready prey for traffickers.[23]

Although 'prostitute' is the preferred legal term, in this chapter I have chosen to use the term 'sex worker' as opposed to 'prostitute'[24] wherever possible in order to emphasise that such sex work is *a form of labour* as opposed to an 'identity'. I have taken this suggestion from Kempadoo and Doezema, who observe that:

> Identity, rights, working conditions, decriminalisation and legitimacy have been central issues collectively addressed by prostitutes for many years. Through these struggles the

---

18 Hamilton in Kramarae and Treichler, *op cit* fn 3, p 363.

19 Chatterjee, B, 'Last of the rainmacs: thinking about pornography in cyberspace', in Wall, D (ed), *Crime and the Internet*, 2001, London: Routledge.

20 This is an argument that emerges strongly in Bell, *op cit* fn 9.

21 See further Skrobanek *et al*, *op cit* fn 11.

22 Doezema in Kempadoo and Doezema, *op cit* fn 9, pp 34–51.

23 Doezema in Kempadoo and Doezema, *op cit* fn 9, p 42.

24 It is worth mentioning that the term 'whore' has, to an extent, been reclaimed by sex workers, who are proud to use it as a term of self-identification. However, this term is, arguably, commonly understood to be derogatory outside the sex workers' movements. See further Kempadoo and Doezema, *op cit* fn 9, p 3. I have chosen not to change 'prostitute' as it appears in quotes.

notion of the sex worker has emerged as a counterpoint to traditionally derogatory names ... 'sex worker' ... reflect[s] the current use of the word throughout the world ... a term that suggests we view prostitution not as an identity – a social or a psychological characteristic of women, often indicated by 'whore' – but as an income-generating activity or form of labour for women and men.[25]

Changes in the sex trade: a digital difference?

Arguably, the introduction of new technologies can be empowering for women, in that they can use new technologies to engage in the sex trade on terms more favourable to them. For example, it may be safer, and perhaps more lucrative, for a woman to sell sex 'virtually' and remotely via a website, where she is more in control of the transaction and not reliant on a pimp or other third party, rather than in person in 'real' space.[26] This may sound similar to a peep show, where customers are permitted only to look and not touch (in theory, at least), but such shows may not be on the sex workers' own terms, unlike a self-owned and produced website. Also, with the distance that virtuality gives, customers can be screened or vetted in a way that cannot be done with customers who are physically there in person. Without wishing to perpetuate the myth that the 'home' is always a 'safe' place for women, it is arguable that a woman charging for a home sex show broadcast over the Internet, where the viewer does not (and cannot) touch her, does not run the same risk of immediate physical violence from customers that the woman selling sex 'traditionally' encounters. This is not to say that such websites are entirely without risk, or that physical violence is the 'only' sort of violence that may occur. Indeed, several feminist commentators have noted the rise of 'cyber-stalking',[27] whereby stalkers inflict psychological violence on their objects of fixation via email, text or other means of communication, a risk which could be increased by selling sex via the Internet.[28]

From Hughes' perspective, although ICTs have indeed transformed the sex trade, these changes are not positive at all. 'Technology,' she states:

has given the sex industry new means of exploiting, marketing and delivering women and children as commodities to male buyers. Usually when a new technology is

---

25 Kempadoo and Doezema, *op cit* fn 9, p 3.

26 Contrast the view of Hughes, 2000, *op cit* fn 4, who argues that the ISPs are themselves effectively acting as 'virtual' pimps in their support of the sex industry online.

27 Eg, Mershman, J, 'The dark side of the web: cyberstalking and the need for contemporary legislation' (2001) 24 *Harv Women's LJ* 255; Brail, S, 'The price of admission: harassment and free speech in the wild, wild west', in Cherny, L and Wise, E (eds), *Wired Women*, 1996, Washington, DC: Seal; Ellison, L, 'Tackling harassment on the Internet', in Wall, D (ed), *Crime and the Internet*, 2001, London: Routledge.

28 On this point it is interesting to note the decision in *R v Ireland* [1998] AC 147 where it was held that psychological intimidation from silent telephone calls could be counted as an assault. Arguably, this decision could be extended to threatening emails and text messages. The Protection from Harassment Act 1997 goes some way towards recognising the impact of psychological violence, and the recently proposed Additional Protocol (2003) to the Convention on Cybercrime requires Parties to the Protocol to introduce legislation to prevent cyber-mediated xenophobic and racist material *as a matter of protecting human rights*, but one is left wondering why this is not taken further to specifically include gender- and sexuality-based material.

introduced into a system of exploitation it enables those with power to intensify the harm and expand the exploitation.[29]

In her most recent work on this subject, Hughes identifies three broad instances in which ICTs affect the sex trade in novel ways: first, the use of a combination of old and new technologies; secondly, the use of new technologies *per se*; and thirdly, the use by abusers and exploiters of new technologies for anonymity and disguise. She concludes that all these changes are detrimental, and simply facilitate abuse in new forms. Regarding the use of old and new technologies, Hughes argues that combining the two simply compounds and proliferates the sex trade's abuse of women. She cites the use of scanners and digital cameras in turning old photographic or film images into electronic and uploadable formats for the Internet. The rapidity of conversion, along with the smaller risk of detection (as digital formats do not need professional processing) means that more people are exploiting more images. Hughes argues that, due to the rapid growth of sexually explicit images though digital media, the market is increasingly turning to those that are 'rougher, more violent, more degrading'[30] in order to increase trade. She also remarks that the increase in competition has meant the sex industry's relocation to various key sites in Eastern and Central Europe, which have lower production costs. 'Budapest', she notes, 'is now the biggest center for pornography production in Europe, eclipsing rivals such as Amsterdam and Copenhagen'.[31]

With regard to the use of new digital technologies *per se*, Hughes points to the deployment of the Digital Versatile Disk (DVD), newsgroups, websites and chatrooms in the sex trade. DVDs, for example, give the viewer a great degree of editorial control. She explains that, with DVDs, scenes can be shot from different angles, and from all points of view. The viewer can select the angles and sequences of the images or, if more than one person is depicted, select images from another's point of view.[32] Whilst acknowledging that such technology has wider uses beyond the sex trade, and can enable creativity and interactivity, Hughes questions whether this is necessarily a good thing in the context of pornographic films. Such technology, she argues, may:

> raise the question of the impact on people, their relationships, and expectations about relationships. A portion of men who use pornography and seek out women in prostitution do so either because of their lack of social skills or their misogynistic attitudes prevent them from establishing relationships with their peers. Technology such as this may further distance some men from meaningful and realistic relationships.[33]

Whilst I do not entirely agree with Hughes' arguments about the nature of customers' relationships with prostitutes (as 'meaningful' and 'realistic' could easily be equated with heteronormative), I do think that there is some strength behind her suggestion that the increase in editorial control that DVDs bring may mean that the

---

29 Hughes, 2000, *op cit* fn 4; cf Hughes, 1999, 2002, *op cit* fn 4.
30 Hughes, 2002, *op cit* fn 4, p 131.
31 Hughes, 2002, *op cit* fn 4, p 131.
32 Hughes, 2002, *op cit* fn 4, p 133. A further issue is that digital images can be stored, copied and repeatedly transferred without degradation in quality.
33 Hughes, 2002, *op cit* fn 4, p 134.

stereotype that women must/should passively submit to every sexual request can be reinforced here. Such editorial control can in this way simply increase women's objectification. Although I do not mean to suggest that it is (or should be) the sole job of the sex industry to combat negative images of women, it is arguably naïve to think that it has no impact upon them at all.

Hughes suggests that other digital media are being used to found new abuses of women. She is particularly critical of the opportunities that digital media offer pimps and traffickers for abuse, and describes how newsgroups, websites and chatrooms can all be used for exploitation. She identifies how such cyberspaces can be used by pimps and traffickers for posting 'reviews' of prostitutes, or advertising their services. Hughes comments that these websites can be harmful – not all the pictures that are posted on prostitution websites were originally intended for that purpose, and the woman in them may not have consented,[34] or even known that their images were being used in this way.[35] She also argues that whereas in a pre-Internet era few people would have had the opportunity to obtain extreme material, the advent of websites makes violent sites – including those depicting actual rape – globally available, and only serves to increase their demand.[36]

However, those who traffic in images and women, she argues, are not concerned by the escalation in quantity and violence, as they are using ICTs for evading the law. Using mobile phones makes it harder to trace calls, and using different forms of anonymised or encrypted communication over several jurisdictions also compounds the difficulty in tracking information. Similarly, the transience of cyber-communications makes them harder to trace, and Hughes cites the example of web TV, which, unlike some ICTs, does not have a file cache, so that illegal material is not 'accidentally' stored and thus open to police recovery.

Changing legal attitudes: recognising rights?

I have sought to show above how ICTs have impacted upon the sex trade, yet are these changes reflected in current legal measures – are the harms to women redressed in any way, or identified as human rights issues?

As long ago as 1917, in an essay on the traffic in women, Emma Goldman observed that it seemed as though the sex trade had been miraculously 'uncovered', when in reality it had been around for centuries, only to be flagged up and

---

34 A recent case touched on these issues: in *O'Shea v MGN Ltd and Another* [2001] EMLR 20, the claimant pursued a claim in defamation on the basis that a picture on a pornographic website that was the 'spit and image' of her. The picture itself was of a 'Miss E', a 'well known glamour model', taken and used with her permission. It is interesting to observe that the claimant was described as 'a *respectable* young woman of 24' (emphasis added). In the event, the claim failed, but *dicta* in the case suggest that the defamation case would have succeeded had the image actually been of the claimant. However, in using defamation to prevent unauthorised pictures, it would seem that one has to deploy the language of respectability and the image of the sex worker as deviant in order to make the claim. See further Coad, J, '"Pressing social need" and strict liability in libel' (2001) 12(7) *Entertainment Law Review* 199; Hamilton, A, 'Live sex streamed videos' (1993) *Computers and Law* 29.

35 Hughes, 2002, *op cit* fn 4, pp 136–37.

36 Hughes, 2002, *op cit* fn 4, p 139.

deployed as a matter of convenience to detract attention from other social ills.[37] Goldman was critical of legal and political attempts to address the sex trade and the traffic in women – attempts that she perceived as futile:

> Whether our reformers admit it or not, the economic and social inferiority of woman [sic] is responsible for prostitution ... there is not a single modern writer on the subject who does not refer to the utter futility of legislative methods in coping with the issue.[38]

Goldman's words seem prophetic in that there is currently a renewed emphasis on sexual exploitation, with a particular focus on the use of ICTs and cyberspace. There are also some real questions over whether legal measures will still be inefficient in dealing with the problem. Indeed, evidence of this renewed scrutiny of the sex trade can be seen at several levels – from recent Home Office documents referring to prostitution and related legislation to newly introduced measures in International Law. However, upon examination it will be seen that these recent measures arguably fall short of recognising and protecting the human rights of workers in the sex trade, particularly those working in cyberspace.

At domestic level, several legal measures have highlighted the need for more robust laws to deal with the sex trade. Intended to address the pressures on the UK asylum and immigration system, the White Paper *Secure Borders, Safe Haven* included amongst its proposals that 'immigration crimes' such as facilitating illicit entry (ie trafficking) of persons into the UK for purposes of sexual exploitation should be made a serious and punishable crime.[39] The trafficking offences proposed in *Secure Borders* were instituted in the Nationality, Immigration and Asylum Act (NIAA) 2002, which explicitly stated for the first time in UK law that trafficking or the facilitation of trafficking would be punishable by a maximum penalty of 14 years' imprisonment. This new statutory measure went some way towards acknowledging the seriousness of the offence, bringing the sentence for trafficking people in line with sentences for trafficking drugs. It was an improvement on the previous law, whereby traffickers could only be prosecuted under the Sex Offenders Act 1956, which did not specifically *name* trafficking as a crime, and which carried much shorter sentences.

The proposals of *Secure Borders* were echoed later that year in *Protecting the Public*, a White Paper[40] on reforming and reinforcing the law on sexual offences. *Protecting the Public* stated in a rare moment of frankness that 'the law on sexual offences as it stands is archaic and incoherent – it is also discriminatory'. Accordingly, it proposed the new offence of commercial exploitation of adults, which would include inciting or procuring prostitution, and the control of prostitution. Additionally, trafficking people for the purposes of commercial exploitation, including 'recruiting,

---

37 Goldman, *op cit* fn 11; cf Rosen, R, *The Lost Sisterhood*, 1982, Baltimore: Johns Hopkins UP.

38 Goldman, *op cit* fn 11, pp 20, 31–32.

39 Cm 5387, February 2002, s 5, pp 83–85.

40 Cm 5668, November 2002. See also *Setting the Boundaries – Reforming the Law on Sex Offences*, 2000. *Setting the Boundaries* focuses on sex offences, whereas *Protecting the Public* centres more on sex offenders. Both papers inform the Sexual Offences Act 2003. The Act was at the Bill stage at the time of writing the majority of this chapter, and received Royal Assent on 20 November 2003.

harbouring and facilitating the movement' of another person for the purposes of commercial exploitation, would also be an indictable offence. It was recognised in *Protecting the Public* that the measures enacted by the NIAA were 'stop-gap' measures, and would need to be updated. The Sexual Offences Act 2003, which is intended to enact the proposals of *Protecting the Public*, therefore contains measures on prostitution and trafficking, whereby causing or inciting prostitution for gain will be an offence carrying a maximum of seven years' imprisonment, and intentionally arranging or facilitating trafficking (entry into or departure from the UK) for the purposes of sexual exploitation will be an offence with a maximum sentence of 14 years.[41] The Act also aims to create gender-neutral prostitution offences, with the term 'prostitute' itself being defined in the statute as 'a person (A) who, on at least one occasion and whether or not compelled to do so, offers or provides sexual services to another person in return for payment or a promise of payment to A or a third person'.[42]

These domestic provisions can be seen, in part, as the culmination of European and International efforts to recognise and protect the human rights of women. The proposals in the NIAA 2002 and Sexual Offences Act 2003 were foreshadowed by the Council of Europe's Proposal for a Council Framework Decision on Combating Trafficking in Human Beings (2000), which stated that trafficking in human beings for labour and sexual exploitation was an increasing concern, exacerbated by globalisation and modern technologies. The Proposal recognised that measures were needed to address the problem at each stage of the chain of exploitation, and that any comprehensive policy needed to recognise and combat the gendered, structural causes of trafficking, such as the feminisation of poverty, discrimination against women, and lack of access to resources.

An awareness of gender specificity and a concern to protect as well as punish can also be seen in the recent United Nations Protocol to Prevent, Suppress and Punish Trafficking in Persons, especially Women and Children (2003), which was introduced as a supplement to the United Nations Convention against Transnational Organised Crime (2000).[43] The Trafficking Protocol specifically states in its preamble that a 'comprehensive international approach' is required in order to punish traffickers, and also to protect those trafficked through the protection of their human rights. States Parties are required[44] to criminalise trafficking, which is understood by Article 3 of the Protocol as, *inter alia*:

> the recruitment, transportation, transfer, harbouring or receipt of persons, by means of the threat or use of force or other forms of coercion ... abuse of power or of a position of vulnerability ... for the purpose of exploitation.

---

41 Sections 51–60.

42 Section 51(2).

43 See further Gallagher, A, 'Human rights and the new UN Protocols on trafficking and migrant smuggling: a preliminary analysis' (2001) 23(3–4) *Human Rights Quarterly* 975; Obokata, T, 'Human trafficking, human rights and the Nationality, Immigration and Asylum Act 2002' (2003) 4 *EHRLR* 410.

44 Article 5.

States Parties are required to protect the privacy and identity of trafficking victims, and asked to consider implementing measures to provide for the victim's recovery and wellbeing, through measures such as appropriate housing and counselling.[45] Regarding the status of those trafficked, States Parties are required to consider adopting legal measures permitting them to remain either temporarily or permanently in the receiving state, in appropriate cases.[46] Giving recognition to the structural factors implicit in trafficking, Article 9 of the Protocol states that States Parties shall take (or strengthen) measures to alleviate the social and economic factors that make women and children vulnerable to trafficking, and adopt (or strengthen) measures to discourage 'the demand that fosters all forms of exploitation of persons, especially women and children, that leads to trafficking'. These recent measures echo the previous sentiments of the 1949 Convention for the Suppression of the Traffic in Persons and of the Exploitation of the Prostitution of Others, and the 1979 United Nations Convention on the Elimination of All Forms of Discrimination Against Women, both of which explicitly condemn prostitution and trafficking.[47]

From examining the above international and European provisions, it would seem that there is a clear recognition of human rights issues, and an acknowledgment that sexual exploitation is a complex, structural issue that can only be dealt with by a combination of legal and socio-economic solutions. The concern for victims' rights is strongly reiterated in Anti-Slavery International's influential report on trafficking, where they argue for legal measures to focus on protecting the human rights of the victim as much as recognising and punishing the crimes committed against them.[48] However, do these rights correspond to, or reflect in any way, the singular issues that Hughes has suggested are posed by the use of digital media? How accessible are they, and will they be effective?

It is worth pausing at this stage to consider whether it even makes sense to speak about 'rights' in this context, given that, as Hughes has asserted, the experiences of women in the sex trade may not conform or clearly map on to the idea of human rights as they are understood in law.[49] It should be noted that there is some debate amongst feminist legal theorists over the efficacy of the law in helping women, in that women's oppression and inequality are usually rooted in *structural* injustices, which are beyond the scope of any court judgment, and rarely articulated in law. There is a substantial feminist critique of the international human rights framework and, as these feminist commentators point out, there are problems with human rights discourse at several levels. Human rights instruments usually reflect civil and

---

45 Article 6.
46 Article 7.
47 See further Fitzpatrick in Cook, *op cit* fn 13, pp 532–71; Gallagher, *op cit* fn 43.
48 Anti-Slavery International/Pearson, E (eds), *Human Traffic, Human Rights: Redefining Victim Protection*, 2002, report available from www.antislavery.org. Anti-Slavery International is the world's oldest international human rights organisation and a registered charity. It campaigns against slavery, and was founded in 1839. Its 2002 report, based on research reports in ten countries, contains a useful synopsis of global legal provisions on trafficking, including those of the UK. However, since the enactment of the Sexual Offences Act 2003, readers should be aware that the report's section on the UK will now be outdated.
49 Hughes, 2002, *op cit* fn 4, pp 129–30.

political rights, as these are seen as universal and inherent. However, on the other hand, social and economic rights are seen as a question of social policy rather than human rights issues, and are left as a matter of state policy to evolve over time. This approach is fatally flawed, as it fails to recognise that civil and political rights are usually gendered (ie male) prerogatives, and that the majority of inequality that women face is caused by social and economic factors.[50] A further problem lies in the enforcement of human rights. As the existing human rights framework is structured around the relationship of the state and citizen (ie the state undertakes to protect the rights of its citizens), the enforcement of rights by women is made more difficult. This conceptualisation of human rights as belonging solely to the public sphere serves to underscore the public/private dichotomy that works to the disadvantage of women. For example, women's rights may frequently be infringed by non-state actors, but such infringements are not usually claimable as human rights abuses under the current legal framework.[51] However, when their human rights are infringed by the state, problems of access to redress and justice arise, in that women's relationship with the state 'remains mediated by men, be they husbands, fathers, brothers, or sons who at the same time acquire their authority over women from the state or traditional political community'.[52]

Given these difficulties, the rubric of human rights may be *doubly* ill-fitting here, given that human rights were not originally drafted with women's oppressions or experiences in mind,[53] nor for a cyber context, where, as Hughes argues, new abuses arise. However, I take the position that the pursuit of human rights in this context is apposite for a number of reasons. As Charlesworth has cogently argued, the legal discourse of human rights can be an effective way to articulate gender difference and inequality, because it is *recognised by those in power*.[54] Moreover, if it is noted that there are problems with the existing framework of human rights in recognising and validating women's experiences, there is nothing to stop us actively and critically engaging with that framework, and shaping it to reflect different perspectives more closely. It is true that the discourse of cyber-rights is a new feature in the field of human rights law generally, but that very novelty means that this is an ideal time to set the agenda, and put feminist concerns to the fore.

To recall Hughes' arguments, women in the cyber-sex trade in particular face a number of unique difficulties that may or may not translate into legal human rights

---

50 Kerr, J (ed), *Ours by Right*, 1993, London/New Jersey: Zed, pp 3–7.

51 Eg, the argument put forward by Copelon that domestic violence should properly be recognised as torture: see Copelon, R, 'Intimate terror: understanding domestic violence as torture', in Cook, *op cit* fn 13.

52 Kerr, *op cit* fn 50, quoting Ashworth, G, *Changing the Discourse: A Guide to Women and Human Rights*, 1993, London: Change. The view that human rights abuses should be enforced against non-state actors is beginning to gain ground: see, eg, Clapham, A, *Human Rights in the Private Sphere*, 1993, Oxford: Clarendon; Hunt, M 'The "horizontal effect" of the Human Rights Act: moving beyond the public-private distinction', in Jowell, J and Cooper, J (eds), *Understanding Human Rights Principles*, 2001, Oxford: Hart. I am particularly grateful to my colleagues Georgina Firth, Steven Riley and Sigrun Skogly for discussion on this point.

53 Cook, *op cit* fn 13; Kerr, *op cit* fn 50; MacKinnon, *op cit* fn 13; see also Tomaševski, K, *Women and Human Rights*,1993, London/New Jersey: Zed.

54 In Cook, *op cit* fn 13, pp 4 ff.

claims as we currently understand them; the increasing instances of violence in digital images, the issue of whether the woman consented to have her image used in advertising prostitution or pornography and the difficulty of identifying images, the creation and reinforcement of dangerous and negative stereotypes of women, and, perhaps most difficult of all, the jurisdictional issues that are inherent where websites are concerned, in that images and sex shows may be accessible from every jurisdiction, whilst not being easily traceable to any one. Whereas the images of the women may move across national borders, the women themselves may not.

When considering the issues of consent, violence and stereotypes, it is not easy to fit these into existing categories of recognised human rights. Whereas in principle it is easy to argue that the right to personal and bodily integrity should be a legally protected human right, it may be difficult to see how this maps on to actual existing rights guaranteed by human rights instruments – such rights may be too conceptually diffuse to be legally recognisable. When considering the issue of consent and anonymity in the reproduction of photographs and other images on websites, we could link this in to the recognised human right of privacy as guaranteed by Article 8 of the European Convention on Human Rights, but there does not appear to be a right in that Convention that clearly corresponds to that of 'sexual' or 'bodily integrity' as it relates to damaging and negative stereotypes. By not explicitly and specifically acknowledging such violations as contrary to human rights, the efficacy of the human rights provisions are arguably weakened. As Fitzpatrick, quoting the Australian jurist Justice Elizabeth Evatt, asserts, 'there is a need to lift the issue of violence out of the sphere of discrimination and private rights and to put it squarely on the mainstream human rights agenda'.[55]

Regarding violence against women as depicted on 'real' rape websites, this is, I would argue, instinctively an affront to human rights, yet how this translates into a legally recognised violation against human rights is less clear. As Fitzpatrick has argued, whereas rape undoubtedly affects the quality of women's lives, human rights treaties largely fail to call for governments to take specific action to prevent this.[56] The Convention on the Elimination of All Forms of Discrimination Against Women (CEDAW) can be read as prohibiting rape as a form of discrimination that affects women's enjoyment of the right to life[57] and, further, that the CEDAW can be taken to imply a state duty, according to Articles 2.f, 5 and 10.c, 'to seek to eradicate

---

55 Fitzpatrick in Cook, *op cit* fn 13, p 560 n 18. Cf Clapham, *op cit* fn 52.

56 Fitzpatrick in Cook, *op cit* fn 13, p 534. It is worth pointing out that since Fitzpatrick's comments, Article 7 of the 1998 Statute of the International Criminal Court lists, *inter alia*, rape and forced prostitution as crimes against humanity. However, to be thus acknowledged, they have to be committed as part of a widespread and systematic attack against a civilian population. Given this context, it would not seem that Article 7 could be used horizontally in situations where states permit prostitution to occur; however, it does bring the issue of prostitution (and rape) squarely within the remit of a strong International human rights agenda. I am most grateful to my colleagues Sigrun Skogly for bringing this to my attention and Steven Riley for discussion on this point.

57 Fitzpatrick in Cook, *op cit* fn 13, p 534.

attitudes towards women as limited to stereotyped roles, attitudes that justify the use of gender-based violence to perpetuate the structures of subordination'.[58] However, as Kerr reminds us, the Convention has not received much active support, and its monitoring committee lacks the funds and human resources required to monitor adherence and investigate violations.[59]

To reproduce the image of rape via a website arguably compounds the violation, but it is difficult to see how such an act can be conceived of as a violation of rights under the current rights framework, unless brought under the heading of the right to respect for one's private life or possibly freedom from torture.[60] However, as argued above, legal rights are seen as co-extensive with the public sphere, and it may perhaps be that women are unlikely to see themselves as legal agents, with legally protected rights.[61] Even if a claim is considered, if a 'private' individual (ie a non-state actor) has committed the violation, the claim may not be recognised as involving a breach of human rights, bearing in mind the relationship of accountability between human rights and the state. Of more concern is the problem of tracing the image to its 'owner' and bringing the claim. Although there is an increasing effort to trace the images of children in digital images, this initiative would appear to be limited to children alone. Hughes reminds us that although the rise of international co-operation to combat child pornography is a laudable effort, this can be at the cost of focusing on the violation of adults as well.[62] Bearing in mind the global and trans-jurisdictional nature of the Internet and current emphasis on channelling resources into combating child pornography, the woman violated on the rape website may never be located. Even if she is, for the reasons outlined above, it may be difficult to bring a claim.[63]

The most challenging issue, perhaps, is the issue of trafficking as it relates to the cyber-sex trade. Trafficking is clearly seen as a violation of human rights – as a violation of the right of freedom from enslavement, and as an issue of discrimination.[64] As seen above, there is a concerted domestic, European and

---

58 Fitzpatrick in Cook, *op cit* fn 13, p 535.

59 Kerr, *op cit* fn 50, pp 4–6. Since Kerr's research, an 'Optional Protocol' to the CEDAW has been established (in force 2000), which provides a right for women to file individual complaints with the CEDAW 9th Committee where their states have ratified the Convention. This may provide a potential avenue for complaints for women who feel their rights have been violated through digital images, but there is little experience with procedure as yet. I am most grateful to my colleague Sigrun Skogly for bringing this to my attention.

60 But cf Copelon, *op cit* fn 51.

61 But cf Clapham, *op cit* fn 52. The courts appear to recognise that in some situations the state may have an obligation to defend individual rights against non-state actors, as seen, eg, in *Hatton and Others v UK* (2002) 34 EHRR 1, ECtHR, where noise pollution near Heathrow Airport was considered to be a breach of Article 8 of the ECHR. Perhaps such judicial willingness to read beyond the public/private dichotomy could be used to advantage in the fight for legal redress in the context of the women's human rights violations.

62 Hughes, 2002, *op cit* fn 4, p 139.

63 Bringing a case for the unauthorised use of images in pornography or prostitution websites as a violation of one's right to privacy arguably runs into the same difficulties.

64 See, eg, CEDAW, Articles 2 and 3; International Covenant on Civil and Political Rights 1966, Article 8; European Convention for the Protection of Human Rights and Fundamental Freedoms 1950, Article 4.

international effort to stop trafficking. Trafficking for the purposes of prostitution may relate to the cyber-sex trade in that women may be coerced into appearing on websites as prostitutes or selling sex in some other way across the Internet, but may not *physically* cross any borders to do so. This point of movement, or lack thereof, is key, as movement would appear to be crucial to the offences of trafficking. In the Council of Europe Proposal, it was stated that to make the criminal offence of trafficking reliant on movement would be undermining. The Proposal explains:

> the key elements of the offence of trafficking should focus on the exploitative purpose, rather than on the 'movement' across a border. If the requirement of the cross-border element would be maintained, there would be a paradox that a European citizen forced into prostitution and trafficked within its own country, would be less protected than citizens from third world countries.[65]

However, upon examining the principle domestic measures on trafficking – the Sexual Offences Act 2003 – movement and travel appear to be key, which contradicts the logic of the Council of Europe's Proposal. The Sexual Offences Act states that where the relevant offence is trafficking, then:

57(1) A person commits an offence if he intentionally *arranges or facilitates the arrival* in the United Kingdom of another person (B) ...

58(1) A person commits an offence if he intentionally *arranges or facilitates travel* within the United Kingdom by another person (B) ...

59(1) A person commits an offence if he intentionally *arranges or facilitates the departure* from the United Kingdom of another person (B) ...[66]

The travel aspect is problematic, in that even though the Act recognises that people may be trafficked within the country, the emphasis on movement makes this difficult to apply to 'virtual' trafficking, where the actual person may remain static, but is effectively *virtually* trafficked/prostituted across borders in cyberspace. The provisions on prostitution are slightly more useful, in that under ss 52 and 53:

52(1) A person commits an offence if –

    (a) he intentionally causes or incites another person to become a prostitute in any part of the world, and

    (b) he does so for or in the expectation of gain for himself or a third person.

53(1) A person commits an offence if –

    (a) he intentionally controls any of the activities of another person relating to that person's prostitution in any part of the world, and

    (b) he does so for or in the expectation of gain for himself or a third person.

These provisions would not appear to hinge on movement, and would seem to apply globally, thus arguably including prostitution websites; however, the definition of prostitute as stated by the Act does not draw any distinction between

---

65 Communication from the Commission to the Council and the European Parliament, 'Combatting trafficking in human beings and combating the sexual exploitation of children and child pornography', COM(2000) 854 (final), p 9.

66 Emphasis added. The element of intent is not present in the former 'stop-gap' measures of the NIAA 2002, and arguably make the offence weaker, in that traffickers will simply argue that they did not have the requisite *mens rea*.

those coerced into prostitution and those who have entered into it without compulsion. As we can see from the interpretative s 51:

> 'prostitute' means a person (A) who, on at least one occasion and whether or not compelled to do so, offers or provides sexual services to another person in return for payment or a promise of payment to A or a third person; and 'prostitution' is to be interpreted accordingly.

As argued in the introductory part of this chapter, such lack of distinction can be problematic.[67]

Even if digitally mediated prostitution and trafficking could be brought under any of the legal provisions available, there is arguably a lack of emphasis on positively recognising and implementing the victim's human rights. At an international level, reference is made to human rights, as can be seen, for example, in the Trafficking Protocol, where Article 6 requests that States Parties shall 'in appropriate cases' protect victims' identities and privacy, and shall 'consider' implementing measures to look after them. Arguably this is not the same as requiring states to adhere to a positive human rights obligation, and this failure compromises the protection of human rights. The Council of Europe Proposal, although also making reference to protecting the human rights of trafficking victims, does not appear to place any positive obligation on Member States to enforce these rights. Likewise, the NIAA and Sexual Offences Act, whilst establishing that trafficking and prostitution are to be criminal offences, arguably do little to promote the human rights of the victims, such as including a positive right to information and protection. It is also arguable that these instruments do little to address the causes of trafficking and prostitution, although these are clearly recognised and enumerated in their preparatory consultation documents, and in the international measures. Indeed, similar criticisms have already been levelled against the proposals suggested by the Council of Europe and the United Nations Trafficking Protocol by the European Women Lawyers Association (EWLA). The EWLA point out that whereas the attempts to prevent trafficking are positive, attendant protection for the victims and a concerted focus on their rights is also necessary. They argue that, in particular, the lack of human rights or protection for women victims simply increases their vulnerability to trafficking, whereas recognising and protecting their human rights will be an incentive to those trafficked to co-operate with the state in prosecutions against traffickers.[68]

From the above analysis, it would appear that although legal efforts are clearly moving towards protecting women, particularly those in the sex industry, these efforts fall short of their aims, especially when it comes to protecting human rights. As I have argued, women are already facing considerable difficulty, in that their

---

67 A similar (but not identical) provision can also be seen in the United Nations Trafficking Protocol 2003, where Article 3(b) states that 'The consent of a victim trafficking in persons to the intended exploitation ... shall be irrelevant where any of the means set forth in subparagraph (a) [ie threat or use of force or other forms of coercion] are established'.

68 Resolution of the EWLA on Trafficking in Human Beings regarding a future European Convention on Trafficking in Human Beings, General Assembly of EWLA, Helsinki, Finland, 8 June 2003; see also Anti-Slavery International/Pearson, *op cit* fn 48.

rights are infrequently acknowledged and, when they are, they are rarely enforced. The particular problems posed by cyberspace do not appear to have been considered in the provisions of the recent domestic legislation, nor do they appear to be foremost in the minds of those who draft the wider international measures. Arguably, as long as human rights remain issues in the public sphere, and fail to reflect the experiences of women, it would seem that Hughes' criticism that women 'fall into gray areas' still, regrettably, holds good.

Chapter 3

The New Face of Child Pornography
Marie Eneman[1]

Introduction

Sexual abuse is one of the most heinous acts to which a child can be subjected. Child pornography, which is the documentation of such an act, is an extension of this abuse, causing continuing harm to the victim. Even in cases where the perpetrator is caught, the victim identified and the criminal case successfully prosecuted, the harm to the child involved continues as the documentary material remains accessible and distributable. This chapter takes as its foundation that child pornography is always an infringement of the rights of the child.[2] Even though sexual exploitation of children and child pornography are considered serious social and legal issues in almost every state, the international community's efforts to protect the rights of children in relation to this problem have not moved ahead in the manner that is needed. In particular, their efforts in relation to information and communications technology (ICT) have been particularly weak. ICT is today the most common medium for dissemination and consumption of child pornography.[3] The advent of ICT has allowed the consumption of child pornography to evolve from a concealed and often expensive activity into something that can be accessed easily, rapidly, anonymously and in many cases at no cost. However, the use of ICT as a medium for the distribution and consumption of child pornography should not simply be seen as an additional channel of communication: the harnessing of digital technologies in relation to child pornography has changed the traditional problem, creating a new, more serious, situation. It will be argued in this chapter that this is due, in part, to the creation of new paedophile communities which have harnessed the power of the technology to give them anonymity, security and community enforcement,[4] but further, this chapter argues that states are failing to prioritise the rights of the child. By focusing on more media-friendly issues such as freedom of

1 PhD Student, Göteborg University. I would like to thank Alisdair A Gillespie, Annethe Ahlenius, Elisabeth Kwarnmark and Per-Erik Åström for sharing their extensive knowledge; all errors remain my own. This work is part of a project funded by *The Crime Victim Compensation and Support Authority (Brottsoffermyndigheten)*.
2 Article 34 of the United Nations Convention on the Rights of the Child requires 'States Parties [to] undertake to protect the child from all forms of sexual exploitation and sexual abuse. For these purposes, States Parties shall in particular take all appropriate national, bilateral and multilateral measures to prevent:
   (a) The inducement or coercion of a child to engage in any unlawful sexual activity;
   (b) The exploitative use of children in prostitution or other unlawful sexual practices;
   (c) The exploitative use of children in pornographic performances and materials'.
3 Defining 'child pornography' is extremely complex. The term is used in this chapter as the focus for discussion as it is presently the most widely accepted nomenclature. See below for a further discussion regarding the definition and use of the term.
4 For a discussion of the self-enforcing effects of closed communities on personal values, see Sunstein, C, *Republic.com*, 2001, Princeton: Princeton UP.

expression and privacy, states are failing to fulfil their moral and legal obligations to protect children.

Child pornography violates children's rights

In order to understand why something must be done about the distribution of child pornography over the Internet, one must understand the content of these materials.[5]

The term 'child pornography', which is commonly used to describe the violation of the rights of the child, is unfortunate. The term has been labelled an 'oxymoron' by Edwards, as it reduces the gravity of what the material portrays. Child pornography is the documentation of 'systematic rape, abuse and torture of children'.[6] The term is also misleading as it invites comparisons with pornography. Gillespie argues that the term should not be used in legislation: instead he argues the terms 'indecent' or 'abusive' images should be used since these terms more clearly describe the material.[7] The debate on pornography often focuses on issues such as obscenity or whether it degrades, subordinates or silences women.[8] These can be seen as questions of degree and opinion. It is, however, important to understand that child pornography should in no way be compared to adult pornography: the two are fundamentally different. Where adult pornography may involve levels of consent and awareness among those participating in its production, child pornography is based upon the degradation, assault and sexual violation of children by adults – there can be no question of voluntary participation.

Sexual abuse of children is a complex social problem with a long history; it is, however, a relatively new field of academic research.[9] As noted by Taylor and Quayle, child pornography is not a new phenomenon: over its long history it has been produced in different forms, using whatever technological media were available at the time.[10] Unfortunately, child pornography historically has not been recognised as a serious social problem. Jenkins justifies the importance of recognising child pornography as such: 'what is not recognised as a problem is not studied, and the less we know about the phenomenon, the less incentive there is for research or invention. If we don't see a menace, we are not even trying to fight it.'[11] Despite the late recognition of child pornography as a social problem, it is today recognised and established on the political agenda in most states, and in many cases the debates are concerned with the relationship of child pornography and ICT. While both the legal definitions and controls of child pornography can differ greatly between jurisdictions, it is possible to discern a generally accepted definition of the

---

5   Esposito, LC, 'Regulating the Internet: the new battle against child pornography', *Case Western Reserve Journal of International Law*, 1998, 30, no 2/3 (spring/summer), 541.

6   Edwards, SSM, 'Prosecuting "child pornography"' (2000) 22 *Journal of Social Welfare and Family Law* 1.

7   Gillespie, AA, 'The Sexual Offences Act 2003: (3) Tinkering with "child pornography"' [2004] *Crim LR* 361.

8   Saul, JM, *Feminism: Issues and Arguments*, 2003, Oxford: OUP.

9   Svedin, C and Back, C, *Varför berättar de inte?*, 2003, Stockholm: Save the Children Sweden.

10 Taylor, M and Quayle, E, *Child Pornography: An Internet Crime*, 2003, Hove: Brunner-Routledge.

11 Jenkins, P, *Beyond Tolerance*, 2003, New York: New York UP.

term. According to this general opinion, it can be defined as any representation where children[12] are engaged, or appear to be engaged, in some kind of sexual act or situation: this is the definition which will be applied in this chapter.

Child pornography is illegal in most Western countries. Its production, distribution and possession are considered to be serious crimes. Even though the legislation concerning child pornography may vary between countries, it is important to be aware of the fact that child pornography is always a violation of children's rights, no matter what shape or form it takes. Child pornography consists of a record portraying child abuse and harm of children and this harm is ongoing for as long as the material is accessible.

Child pornography and ICT

Since it was so easy and convenient to access child pornography from my home computer and I felt that I had seen all there was to see of adult pornography I started to access more and more child pornography. If it hadn't been so easy and anonymous I don't think I would have done it.[13]

Child pornography has changed radically since the mid-1990s. The underlying reasons for this change can be explained partly by the effects of the dissemination of ICT and partly by the effects of changes in child pornography laws. Historically, the dissemination of child pornography was achieved through costly magazines, photographs and videos,[14] and therefore child pornography was limited by economic, physical and logistical boundaries. With the development and use of ICT, the nature of child pornography has changed significantly.

Due to the criminality of their actions and society's attitudes towards them, paedophiles take a great deal of trouble to ensure that they can safeguard their identities and protect their anonymity.[15] Prior to the wide dissemination of ICT, obtaining child pornography involved a degree of physical exposure, which increased the risk of being identified. The risks lay in the requirement of either visiting certain suppliers in person, or an exposure of the paedophile's name and address so that the material could be delivered. By comparison, modern ICT offers a high degree of security. It is possible to be almost completely anonymous. Paedophiles usually use pseudonyms and do not reveal their real identity, even to each other: this increases their level of personal security and reduces the risk of getting caught. The material distributed is often both encrypted and password protected. A side effect of the technology is that digital copies do not deteriorate

---

12 The definition of 'child' is not uniform. In this chapter a child is defined in accordance with Article 1 of the United Nations Convention on the Rights of the Child: 'a child means every human being below the age of eighteen years unless, under the law applicable to the child, majority is attained earlier.'

13 Anonymous paedophile, interview, 2004.

14 Carr, J, *Theme Paper on Child Pornography for the 2nd World Congress on Commercial Sexual Exploitation of Children*, 2001. Available at www.ecpat.net/eng/ecpat_inter/projects/ monitoring/wc2/yokohama_theme_child_pornography.pdf.

15 Armstrong, HL and Forde, PJ, 'Internet anonymity practices in computer crime', *Information Management & Computer Security* 11/5 [2003].

from the original and can be reproduced endlessly without loss of definition or any other qualities. This section of the chapter will look at how the production, distribution, access to and networking of child pornography have changed due to the use of ICT. In addition, it will briefly examine how ICT has altered the way paedophiles make contact and communicate with children.

First, ICT makes it easy to produce child pornography at a low cost. By using digital technology, images and films can easily and quickly be produced and stored. The development of ICT has enabled non-technically skilled users to record, store and manipulate images in a way that was previously only available to people with the requisite technical skills and costly equipment. Therefore, today even amateurs can record their abuse of children and thereafter easily distribute the material through ICT. Secondly, ICT offers software tools that can easily be used to produce so-called morphed images, also called pseudo-photographs.[16] Similarly, ICTs have affected the volume of material which it is now possible to distribute across networks like the Internet. The technology offers features to manage large amounts of data easily, rapidly, at low cost and is readily available without a high level of technical knowledge. Responses from a study carried out by the COPINE project show that the collections of paedophiles who use ICT as a medium for accessing child pornography have increased. The ease of downloading via ICT led, for many of the paedophiles, to huge collections of child pornography.[17]

Computer networks also allow paedophiles to create online communities. These communities allow them to meet other paedophiles, and together in the community they can legitimise their interests.[18] Paedophiles often use communities where some kind of internal control of the users takes place through passwords.[19] The communities also function as places where paedophiles share and trade information and material, especially pornographic images and videos. Paedophiles also establish important contacts within these communities. Results from a study have shown that members can, besides gratifying themselves, obtain status within the community by supplying other participants with child pornography (especially material that is difficult to obtain) and by producing new material.[20] This means that pornographic images are used to both justify and legitimise paedophile behaviour within these communities. Social contact and interaction with other

---

16 Using digital graphics software, it is now possible to combine two images into one, or distort pictures to create a totally new image: a process called morphing. Using this process, non-pornographic images of real children can be made to appear as pornography, and pornographic images of 'virtual' children can be generated. For a discussion of morphing, see Beier, T and Neely, S, *Feature-Based Image Metamorphosis*, Proceedings of the 19th Annual Conference on Computer Graphics and Interactive Techniques (SIGGRAPH 92), Chicago, IL, available at www.hammerhead.com/thad/morph.html.

17 Taylor and Quayle, 2003, *op cit* fn 10.

18 Interview with Kwarnmark, E, psychologist and psychotherapist in the Swedish Prison and Probation Service, May 2004. For a discussion of the self-enforcing effects of closed communities on personal values, see Sunstein, 2001, *op cit* fn 4.

19 Kronqvist, S, *Brott Och Digitala Bevis*, 2003, Stockholm: Norstedts Juridik AB.

20 Durkin, K, 'Misuse of the Internet by pedophiles: implications for law enforcement and probation practice' (1997) 61(3) *Federal Probation* 14.

paedophiles is considered to be valuable and important among paedophiles.[21] This can be explained by the fact that it is important for paedophiles to feel that their sexual interests for children are accepted by people around them, and that they feel they obtain social status and support within these environments. Further, ICTs have created new ways and conditions for people to establish contacts and to interact with other people, including children. According to Durkin, paedophiles use ICT in different ways to contact children to prepare for later physical meetings and/or communicate with children to attain sexual gratification (with no intention of arranging physical meetings).[22] As the old Internet adage states, 'On the Internet nobody knows you are a dog':[23] ICT offers features for users to portray themselves to better fit their purpose and, of course, they can retain their anonymity by using pseudonyms. The ability to contact children through ICT also increases the number of children available compared to real life, where geographical limitations and social exposure decrease this availability. Another aspect that facilitates paedophiles in contacting, communicating and interacting with children through ICT is the lack of parental knowledge. Parents often do not know what their children are actually doing when spending time online.[24]

An illustrative example of how ICT can be used as a medium for exploiting children is the Orchid Club,[25] a paedophile ring exposed in California in May 1996. The Orchid Club is not the largest such ring to have been exposed, but it is a significant example of how these rings can operate. It is also considered to be the first case of online broadcasting of live child abuse through a video conferencing system. Members of the club used the ring to share and exchange photos and videos of girls aged five to ten. The majority of the material exchanged was produced by the participants themselves. While members of the ring were logged on to the video conferencing system, a child was sexually abused and the abuse was broadcast to those logged onto the system. At least 11 men, situated in different countries, watched this child being sexually abused in real-time. These men were able to take part in the abuse of the child by using functions in the video conferencing software that enabled them to communicate by typing messages requesting different poses and abusive acts to be carried out. As this example shows, ICT has in certain respects paved the way for paedophiles to develop new methods of exploiting children. The technology made it possible for the members, regardless of their physical location, to participate in the abuse of the child in real-time. The main features which ICT offers and that facilitate the existence of child pornography rings are the technical capacity (rapid transfer of material) and the high level of security and anonymity involved (which reduces the risk of getting caught). The Orchid

---

21 Kwarnmark, 2004 *op cit* fn 18.
22 Durkin, 1997, *op cit* fn 20.
23 Originally from a cartoon by Peter Steiner in *The New Yorker* (Vol 69 (LXIX) no 20) 5 July 1993, p 61.
24 EU SAFT project, www.sou.gov.se.
25 ECPAT, www.ecpat.net/eng/ecpat_inter/publication/other/english/html_page/ ecpat_prot_child_online/files/internet8.htm.

Club case illuminates clearly that ICT has created a new paradigm regarding child pornography.

Legal position

The threat to the rights of the child posed by child pornography has led to legal developments both at international and national levels. On an international level, the United Nations created, in 1989, the Convention on the Rights of the Child, which is a significant tool in the development of a co-ordinated approach to controlling and combating child pornography. Among other things, the Convention provides that 'States Parties shall take all appropriate legislative, administrative, social and educational measures to protect the child from all forms of physical or mental violence, injury or abuse, neglect or negligent treatment, maltreatment or exploitation, including sexual abuse, while in the care of parent(s), legal guardian(s) or any other person who has the care of the child',[26] and 'States Parties undertake to protect the child from all forms of sexual exploitation and sexual abuse. For these purposes, States Parties shall in particular take all appropriate national, bilateral and multilateral measures to prevent ... (c) The exploitative use of children in pornographic performances and materials'.[27] As can be seen, Article 19 attempts to prevent all types of abusive treatment and to create a secure environment in which children can develop. This is complemented by Article 34(c), which requires signatory states to enact legislation to protect children from the specific abuse caused by child pornography. This latter provision also strives to create an environment conducive to international co-operation within this area. The Optional Protocol to the Convention on the Rights of the Child on the sale of children, child prostitution and child pornography,[28] which has recently been added to the Convention, furthers these attempts to control and combat child pornography.

While this Convention, with the Optional Protocol, is an important tool for the protection of children's rights, the developing use of ICT in this area has led to a need for further regulation, leading to attempts to develop a more comprehensive set of rules designed specifically for the purpose of controlling and combating child pornography carried out through ICT. One such provision is the Council of Europe's Convention on Cybercrime.[29] This is based on the understanding that co-operation between nations considerably increases the effectiveness of policing all crimes carried out in cyberspace, including the production and distribution of child pornography. Article 9 of the Convention deals specifically with some of the

---

26 Article 19.
27 Article 34.
28 The Protocol came into force on 18 January 2002: see www.unhchr.ch/html/menu2/6/crc/treaties/opsc.htm.
29 http://conventions.coe.int/Treaty/en/Treaties/html/185.htm.

problems of child pornography and ICT.[30] This provision was the result of much discussion of the Heads of State and Government of the Council of Europe,[31] and was set out in their Action Plan.[32] It can be seen as part of the Council of Europe's commitment to the combating of child pornography, and forms part of the wider international effort, including the Optional Protocol to the UN Convention on the Rights of the Child on the sale of children, child prostitution and child pornography and the recent European Commission initiative on combating sexual exploitation of children and child pornography.[33] Article 9 criminalises various aspects of the electronic production, possession and distribution of child pornography. While it was recognised that most states already had adequate provisions criminalising the production, possession and distribution of traditional child pornography, the use of ICT was such that to have any effect the legal efforts to control digital content must take place on an international level using a fully co-ordinated approach. The explanatory report stated the need for further action against ICT-based child pornography: 'It is widely believed that such material and on-line practices, such as the exchange of ideas, fantasies and advice among paedophiles, play a role in supporting, encouraging or facilitating sexual offences against children.'[34] It should be noted in particular that, according to Article 9(2)(c), realistic images should be included in the paragraph 'child pornography'. This means that morphed images and pseudo-photographs should be seen as child pornography.

At a national level, many states have recently strengthened their positions against such content. Recent changes have taken place in both Swedish and UK legislation in the aim of combating child pornography. These changes, however, are not innovative legislative changes but rather represent a series of modifications to existing legislation. Gillespie has referred to this legislative approach as 'tinkering with the law'.[35] Such tinkering on a national level is further complicated by the fact that states, while attempting to update their laws in pursuit of further harmonisation, focus on different issues. This leaves the international protection of

---

30 Article 9 states that: '(1) Each Party shall adopt such legislative and other measures as may be necessary to establish as criminal offences under its domestic law, when committed intentionally and without right, the following conduct: (a) producing child pornography for the purpose of its distribution through a computer system; (b) offering or making available child pornography through a computer system; (c) distributing or transmitting child pornography through a computer system; (d) procuring child pornography through a computer system for oneself or for another; (e) possessing child pornography in a computer system or on a computer-data storage medium. (2) For the purpose of paragraph 1 above "child pornography" shall include pornographic material that visually depicts: (a) a minor engaged in sexually explicit conduct; (b) a person appearing to be a minor engaged in sexually explicit conduct; (c) realistic images representing a minor engaged in sexually explicit conduct. (3) For the purpose of paragraph 2 above, the term "minor" shall include all persons under 18 years of age. A Party may, however, require a lower age-limit, which shall be not less than 16 years.'
31 At the second summit, Strasbourg, 10–11 October 1997.
32 Item III.4.
33 COM2000/854.
34 Explanatory Report, Convention on Cybercrime (2001, ETS No 185).
35 Gillespie, 2004, *op cit* fn 7.

the rights of children a patchwork of protections rather than a coherent approach to the use of ICT in child pornography. To better understand what this means we shall look at the key problems of child pornography, age and possession, and briefly see how these problems are approached.

One of the first stumbling blocks is establishing the age of majority. The UN Convention on the Rights of the Child states: '… a child means every human being below the age of eighteen years unless under the law applicable to the child, majority is attained earlier.'[36] In England and Wales the age of consent is 16;[37] however, the definition of a child for the purposes of the production and possession of pornography is defined as those under the age of 18.[38] This means that one may commit a sexual act at age 16 but recording or documenting such an act is illegal unless one is over 18.[39] Equally confusingly, while the Sexual Offences Act 2003 has raised the age of a child, for the purposes of pornographic imagery, to 18 within England and Wales, the age of majority in such cases within Scotland remains at 16.[40] In fact, while the Sexual Offences Bill was progressing through Westminster, the Holyrood Parliament was considering the Criminal Justice (Scotland) Bill. Here the Scottish Parliament made specific changes to the law in Scotland governing child pornography, but left the age of majority unaltered.[41] This means that possession of an image depicting a 17 year old involved in a sexual act is illegal in Bowness-on-Solway, but currently legal in Annan, two towns physically around three miles apart. If the Scottish and English Parliaments cannot achieve harmonisation in this area, what chance is there for greater international harmonisation and co-operation?

The Swedish legislators have attempted to avoid this type of problem completely. There a child is defined as 'a person whose puberty development is incomplete, or when it can be discerned from the image or from the circumstances around it, is under 18 years old'.[42] Therefore, the primary rule for deciding whether a person is a child is the development of puberty, not their chronological age. This was intended to provide a greater level of protection for children. However, in a recent case[43] problems with this inexact definition have arisen. In this case, the defendant paid two 16 year old girls to take part in pornographic films. The girls informed him of their age before filming took place. The courts interpreted the law to mean that if

---

36 Article 1.

37 This is true of both homosexual and heterosexual acts following equalisation in the Sexual Offences (Amendment) Act 2000.

38 As defined by s 7(6) of the Protection of Children Act 1978, as amended by s 45(2) of the Sexual Offences Act 2003.

39 There is a rather curious defence provided by s 1A of the Protection of Children Act 1978 (added by s 45(3) of the Sexual Offences Act 2003) for persons who, at the time the offence was charged, were married to the 'child' or were living together with the child as partners in an enduring family relationship. This means that images produced within a couple, where one party was aged 16–17, remain legal so long as the couple remain together. On separation/divorce they become potentially criminal.

40 Section 52 of the Civic Government (Scotland) Act 1982.

41 By s 19 of the Criminal Justice (Scotland) Act 2003, the maximum penalty for possession of child pornography was increased from three years' imprisonment to ten years.

42 Swedish Criminal Code Chapter 16, para 10a (author's translation).

43 Stockholm District Court Case nr B 7047-01.

the age of the girls could not be discerned by the images, the man could not be guilty of producing or distributing child pornography despite the fact that he was aware of their age. The court found that the girls had passed through puberty and therefore it was not possible to understand from the images that they were underage. This case went on to the Court of Appeal which confirmed the lower court's position, and has now been appealed to the Supreme Court. Therefore, the present position of Swedish law is that if the child appears to be 18 or older it is, despite knowledge to the contrary, not possible to gain a conviction on the basis of production or distribution of images involving children.

Further evidence of a failure to achieve international consensus in the fight against child pornography may be seen from recent cross-border police actions. Possession of child pornography is illegal both in Sweden and in the United Kingdom. In May 2004 a co-ordinated police action in Sweden, Finland, Denmark and Norway led to the finding that many of the Swedish suspects had paid for access to child pornography sites via their credit cards and had then viewed the material via their computers. Despite technical evidence, proof of economic transactions, and even some confessions, these actions were not found to be illegal under Swedish law. According to Swedish law, possession of child pornography (barnpornografibrott) requires possession of a physical copy.[44] It is not enough that a copy may have been saved in the computer's cache memory: to be illegal the copy has to be made intentionally on a storage medium under one's control. The Swedish National Criminal Investigation Department consider this to be a major problem for the police in their work.[45] Under the equivalent UK law,[46] downloading child pornography has been held to amount to making child pornography,[47] while in the recent case of *R v Westgarth Smith and Jayson*,[48] the interpretation of 'making' was extended further to include deliberate downloading of an indecent image so that it is displayed on screen. Following this case, it is no longer necessary for the offender to go further and save the image, although the prosecution does have to prove that the accused knew what sort of image he was calling for. In Jayson's case, this proof arose from the simultaneous presence of both thumbnails and the full-size pictures.

Incentives and implications

Disturbingly, recent research has shown that people who have no prior history of paedophilia or as consumers of child pornography are both accessing and distributing child pornography through ICT.[49] This indicates that the medium attracts new consumers of such materials, which can be explained by the fact that the ICT environment offers certain characteristics which facilitate the paedophile.

---

44 Swedish Criminal Code Chapter 16, para 10a.
45 Interview with Ahlenius, A, Child Pornography Group at the Swedish National Criminal Investigation Department, 2004.
46 Section 1(1) of the Protection of Children Act 1978.
47 *R v Bowden* [2000] 1 Cr App R(S) 26.
48 *R v Westgarth Smith and Jayson* [2003] 1 Cr App R 13.
49 Quayle *et al*, 'The Internet and offending behaviour: a case study' (2000) 6 *Journal of Sexual Aggression* 78.

When Taylor and Quayle[50] discuss the problem of child pornography they differentiate between production and viewing. It is easier for the legal system to focus their limited resources on the production element, as it is at this point that the abuse of the victim occurs. However, it is of vital importance to consider viewing as a serious criminal activity. A prerequisite for the viewing of child pornography is that child abuse has occurred and has been documented. This therefore means that the viewer is guilty of creating a demand for these kinds of images, meaning that those who produce and those who view are both guilty of the abuse.

A recent study[51] of the consumption habits of those convicted of child pornography possession was carried out by the Swedish National Council for Crime Prevention. This study showed that the perpetrators often started with a curiosity and a desire to test limits and explore taboos. They experienced excitement in the search for, and downloading of, child pornography. In some cases, what began on a relatively small scale led to the collection of very large amounts of images and film sequences. The results of this study are comparable to studies carried out in other countries.[52] Today, paedophiles can download child pornography, often at no cost, in large quantities and in the privacy of their own homes. This represents a reduced risk to the individual when acquiring material, allows for the size of collections to grow, and creates a constant demand for novel and more varied material. Meeting this increased demand for new material inevitably means that more children are involved in the production of child pornography. Recent research shows that three to four new children become victims of child pornographers every week. Additionally, evidence indicates that the children involved in child pornography are getting younger.[53]

In addition to the abovementioned connection between child pornography and child abuse, there is also a debate on whether viewing child pornography increases the viewer's propensity to commit abuse. It is impossible to say whether a person who views child pornography will abuse children; however, there is evidence that points to a strong connection between the crimes.[54] In current research there are four main hypotheses on the paedophile's use of child pornography:[55] (1) to develop sexual motivation; (2) lowering the level of sexual impulse control; (3) as a substitute for sexual contact with a child; and (4) to break down the child's resistance while attempting to seduce the child. A study presented in 2003 showed that two-thirds of perpetrators arrested for Internet sex crimes against children also possessed images and film sequences containing child pornography.[56] For many

---

50 Taylor and Quayle, 2003, *op cit* fn 10.
51 Nilsson, L, *Sexuell exploatering av barn – vad döljer sig bakom sexualbrottsstatistiken?*, Brottsförebygganderådet (BRÅ) S 2003:05.
52 SOU 2004:71 Sexuell exploatering av barn i Sverige, June 2004.
53 Taylor and Quayle, 2003, *op cit* fn 10.
54 SOU 2004:71, *op cit* fn 52.
55 Martens, PL, *Pedofili – Barnpornografi och sexuella övergrepp mot barn*, 1998, BRÅ.
56 Wolak, J, Mitchell, K and Finkelhor, D, *Internet Sex Crimes Against Minors: The Response of Law Enforcement*, Crimes against Children Research Center, November 2003, University of New Hampshire.

paedophiles the consumption of child pornography is a primary stage before committing actual child abuse.[57] The introduction and wide use of ICT in child pornography has helped in establishing a market for child pornography. Prior to the dissemination of ICT there was little economic incentive to carry out extensive production and distribution of child pornography.[58] However, there are a growing number of examples that these circumstances have changed. In August 2001 a paedophile ring was uncovered, which included an American company, Landslide Promotions. This company managed credit card billing and password access services for one Russian and two Indonesian child pornography sites. The ring had 250,000 subscribers and made a gross profit of $1.4 million each month by providing child pornography to its paying customers.[59] Therefore, when looking at the economics of ICT-based child pornography we can see two parallel trends. On the one hand, the consumption of child pornography has moved from an underground, costly and complex process to become a widely available, inexpensive and simple process. On the other hand, we can see a growth in commercialisation of child pornography. Examples of this growing commercialisation extend from the extreme, including the selling of children for live abuse online,[60] to more simple sites offering images. The anonymity offered by the medium has, however, significantly lowered the social costs of the buyers, which in turn has increased the demand for the material. This increase in demand for the material ensures that there is a continuing profitability in the supply of child pornography. The result of these two trends is that the total amount of child pornography available is steadily increasing. Together they create a market and an economic base for the continued exploitation of children.

Balancing rights

To date, in discussions of rights and technology, most attention has been focused upon the popular rights of freedom of expression and privacy. The attention paid to these two important civil rights has, arguably, led to the result that other rights seem to have been overshadowed. Other values, including some important rights of the child, have not been allowed to develop as fully as they have needed to.

An example of the conflict between freedom of expression and the rights of the child can be seen in the US approach to attempts to limit freedom of expression within cyberspace. The American position on free expression is very strong.[61] The First Amendment states that no law shall be made which limits this right. Recognising the need to act forcefully to combat child pornography, the US enacted the Child Pornography Prevention Act (CPPA) in 1996. This legislation employed broad definitions, and included computer generated images and morphed

---

57 Lanning, K, Presentation at The Fifth COPINE Conference, Cork, Ireland, May 2004.
58 Interview with Åström, P-E, Save the Children Sweden, 2004.
59 Anonymous, 'US breaks child cyber-porn ring', BBC News, 8 August 2001: http://news.bbc.co.uk/2/hi/americas/1481253.stm.
60 Palmer, T, 'Just one click: sexual abuse of children and young people through the Internet and mobile telephone technology', Barnardo's 2004.
61 See Vick, Chapter 4.

photographs in its definition of what could be considered to be child pornography. The question posed in the subsequent legal challenge to the Act in the case of *Ashcroft v The Free Speech Coalition*[62] was whether or not the CPPA was too broad and unnecessarily encroached upon the right to free expression. The Supreme Court found that it did. The CPPA was found to be unconstitutional since it defined even digitally created images of children to be child pornography. The court noted that, unlike traditional images, digitally created images depicting child pornography lacked a real-life victim. The court chose to simplify the issue by discussing the case in terms of imagination and computer code. This means that the creation of digital child pornography cannot be considered to be anything other than bytes, code and imagination and the criminalisation of this would be akin to creating a thought crime. Therefore, the court ruled digital child pornography to be an information exchange which is protected by freedom of expression.

In his paper, Levy discusses the potential harms of digitally created child pornography and presents some of the arguments set forth by Attorney-General Ashcroft. These include: '(1) Child pornography causes child abuse; (2) Virtual child pornography will be used to seduce actual children; (3) Allowing virtual child pornography makes laws banning real child pornography unenforceable; (4) Child pornography, actual or virtual, on the Internet allows isolated paedophiles and potential paedophiles to contact each other and reinforce each other's desires. It thus increases the probability of offences.'[63] These arguments mirror some of the arguments presented earlier in this chapter. By failing to act positively in this case, the Supreme Court may be charged with failing to protect the weakest members of society. In any society, the primary duty with which we are charged is protection of those who cannot protect themselves; primary among this group are children. Privacy, although an important civil liberty, has been in the focus of the civil liberties and technology debate for more than a century.[64] The importance of privacy has been set out in several international conventions, European directives and national laws and constitutions. This focus has ensured that any attempts to limit privacy are met with great scepticism and protest from the powerful privacy lobby. However, as this chapter has shown, privacy is one of the cornerstones of the recent and extensive growth in online child pornography. Without the ability to maintain their anonymity, many of those consuming child pornography would choose not to run the risk of exposure and the market for child pornography would decrease, as would the economic incentive to produce and distribute it.

The increase in child pornography poses a serious setback to children's rights. If states are to fulfil their moral and legal obligations to protect children, this trend in the growth of child pornography must be stopped. To enable this, we must accept limitations in other civil liberties that have been used to protect child

---

62 535 US 234 (2002); 198 F 3d 1083. It may also be noted that the Canadian Supreme Court made a similar ruling in the case of *R v Sharpe* [2001] 1 SCR 45. In England and Wales though, under s 1 of the Protection of Children Act 1978, pseudo-images are dealt with in a similar manner to 'real' images.

63 Levy, N, 'Virtual child pornography: the eroticization of inequality' (2002) 4 *Ethics and Information Technology* 319.

64 See Wong, Chapter 12.

pornographers. Privacy and freedom of expression have received a great deal of attention in the discussions of the individual's rights in digital environments. However, while privacy and freedom of expression are important rights, which deserve to be protected, they must not take precedence over all other rights such as the right of the child not to be abused. The rights of privacy and freedom of expression should continue to be defended, but it is time that we also discuss the price that is paid for these rights.

Chapter 4
Regulating Hatred
Douglas W Vick

Some see the Internet as an instrument of cultural imperialism, through which American values are exported with little concern for the sensitivities, cultural integrity, or sovereign prerogatives of receiving countries.[1] The reluctance of the United States to enter into international agreements on a number of important Internet-related issues in particular has engendered resentment. Nowhere is this more apparent than in connection with the United States' refusal to co-operate with international efforts to control the global dissemination of hate speech – a somewhat indeterminate category that arguably includes any message that promotes hatred on the basis of race, religion, gender, sexuality, ethnicity, or national origin.[2]

While it is recognised that hate speech laws implicate the principle of freedom of expression, no society in the world has concluded that free speech is an absolute barrier to state regulation of harmful expression. Different countries have tried different legal strategies for stemming the propagation of hate messages, and where the line is drawn between unlawful hate speech and permissible expression has varied widely from country to country. There is a particularly wide gap between the approaches of the United States and other Western democracies, so much so that many countries have accused the United States of creating a haven for bigots who disseminate their messages of intolerance in a global medium. European dissatisfaction with the permissiveness of US law came to a head in *LICRA v Yahoo! Inc*, a case characterised as 'a backlash response to the cultural and technological hegemony of the United States in the on-line world'.[3]

Yahoo! Inc, a US-based Internet service provider, maintained auction sites via which third parties offered, among other items, Nazi memorabilia for sale. In 2000, anti-hate campaigners based in France commenced legal proceedings against Yahoo!, alleging violation of French penal laws prohibiting the public display of Nazi 'uniforms, insignia or emblems' within French borders. The Superior Court of Paris asserted jurisdiction over Yahoo! because its auction sites could be accessed in France; the court ruled that the US company must 'take such measures as will dissuade and render impossible' access to auction sites selling Nazi paraphernalia

---

1 See, eg, Perritt, H, 'Cyberspace and state sovereignty' (1997) 3 *J Int Leg Stud* 155; Note, 'Cyberspace regulation and the discourse of state sovereignty' (1999) 112 *Harv L Rev* 1680, pp 1686–87; Wu, T, 'Cyberspace sovereignty? The Internet and the international system' (1997) 10 *Harv J L & Tech* 647.

2 See generally Boyle, K, 'Hate speech – the United States versus the rest of the world?' (2001) 53 *Maine L Rev* 487; Tsesis, A, 'Hate in cyberspace: regulating hate speech on the Internet' (2001) 38 *San Diego L Rev* 817.

3 Fagin, M, 'Regulating speech across borders: technology vs values' (2003) 9 *Michigan Telecommunications and Technology L Rev* 395, p 421, at www.mttlr.org/volnine/Fagin.pdf. The *Yahoo!* case is discussed in Lapres, D, 'Of Yahoos and dilemmas' (2002) 3 *Chicago J Int L* 409, and Murphy, C, 'International law and the Internet: an ill-suited match' (2002) 25 *Hastings Int & Comp L Rev* 405.

and any other sites containing pro-Nazi propaganda, and awarded civil damages to the organisations that instigated the action.[4] After receiving a report from a panel of experts concerning the feasibility of blocking the offending content, the Superior Court also ordered Yahoo! to employ filtering and other strategies to prevent French Internet users from accessing Nazi-related material and threatened the company with a daily fine if it did not do so.[5]

The United States did not acquiesce to this assertion of power to control communicative activities originating within its borders. Although Yahoo! Inc revised its internal policies so as to prevent dissemination of Nazi-related material over its services anywhere in the world, it also raised an action in a US federal court seeking a declaration that the French decisions were unenforceable in the US because they violated the free speech clause of the First Amendment to the US Constitution.[6] The US, like most countries, will recognise the civil aspects of a foreign judgment unless it offends fundamental public policy. Following previous cases,[7] the US court found that the French judgments had indeed violated basic precepts of US law: 'Although France has the sovereign right to regulate what speech is permissible in France, this court may not enforce a foreign order that ... chill[s] protected speech [occurring] simultaneously within our borders.'[8]

These cases, which attracted considerable international attention, only served to reinforce a perception of US perversity in refusing to recognise the growing global consensus about the need for strong measures in response to the ready availability of racist, sexist, homophobic and xenophobic material on the Internet. However, closer examination reveals that the constitutional predicament of the US is more difficult than is often realised outside the US, and the discretion of policy-makers to co-operate with international measures taken against hate speech is strictly circumscribed. Nor is it transparently obvious that the American position, however lonely, is wrong. To fully appreciate the international stand-off between the US and other Western democracies in this area, this chapter will first consider the consensus concerning the regulation of hate speech outside the US; review the position taken by the United States Supreme Court on the permissibility of hate speech laws under the First Amendment; and critically assess the Supreme Court's position in light of a growing chorus of criticism both inside and outside the US.

---

4 *LICRA et UEJF v Yahoo! Inc*, TGI Paris, 22 May 2000, at www.lapres.net/yahen.html.

5 *LICRA et UEJF v Yahoo! Inc*, Ordonnance Refere, TGI Paris, 20 November 2000, at www.lapres.net/yahen11.html.

6 The First Amendment provides that the state 'shall make no law ... abridging the freedom of speech'.

7 See *Telnikoff v Matusevitch*, 702 A2d 230 (Md 1997); *Bachchan v India Abroad Publications Inc*, 585 NYS 2d 661 (NY 1992).

8 *Yahoo! Inc v La Ligue Contre le Racisme et L'Antisemitisme*, 169 F Supp 2d 1181, p 1192 (ND Cal 2001).

The consensus outside the US

Most national and international laws targeting hate speech have been adopted in the past 50 years.[9] These rules seek to alleviate a variety of psychological, sociological and political harms attributed to 'words that wound'.[10] Hate speech can inflict immediate emotional distress as well as cause longer-term psychological harm by intensifying an individual's previous experience of degradation or humiliation.[11] Its victims may come to question their self-worth and identity, particularly if their 'daily experience tells them that almost nowhere in society are they respected and granted the ordinary dignity and courtesy accorded to others'.[12] Hateful statements not only dishonour those to whom they are directed: they can buttress deeply ingrained discriminatory attitudes in society at large.[13] Members of stigmatised groups may suffer mental illness and psychosomatic disease as a result of societal attitudes perpetuated by hate speech.[14] In an environment in which hate speech is tolerated, the targets of such speech may feel disempowered and come to doubt their acceptance in 'mainstream' society.[15] Effectively, they may be silenced, as they withdraw from participation in broader public discussions and debates. And it is not just the targets of hate propaganda that are harmed: if states do not redress the harms of hate speech, they are vulnerable to the charge that they lack commitment to the ideals of egalitarianism and respect for individual dignity.[16]

Legal strategies for combating hate speech differ from country to country. Virtually all countries, including the US, punish speech that incites imminent violence.[17] Most countries go much further, though, prohibiting expression that promotes discrimination or hatred, or even causes anger and resentment, without requiring evidence that it will lead to a breach of the peace. For example, there are German laws intended to protect individuals and groups against defamation, insult and verbal assault; prevent expression that disparages the memory of the dead; prohibit incitement to hatred, including attacks on human dignity directed against individuals or groups because of their race, religion, nationality or ethnic origin; and punish Holocaust denial.[18] Although Article 5 of Germany's Basic Law guarantees freedom of expression, the balance struck between free speech and the (sometimes) conflicting value of respect for human dignity is informed by the

---

9 See generally Kubler, F, 'How much freedom for racist speech? Transnational aspects of a conflict of human rights' (1998) 27 *Hofstra L Rev* 335.

10 See Delgado, R, 'Words that wound: a tort action for racial insults, epithets, and name-calling' (1982) 17 *Harv Civil Rights-Civil Liberties L Rev* 133. See also Matsuda, M *et al*, *Words That Wound*, 1994, Boulder, CO: Westview.

11 Delgado, R and Stefancic, J, *Must We Defend Nazis?* 1997, New York: New York UP, p 9 (quoting Clarke, K, *Dark Ghetto*, 1965, New York: Gollancz, pp 63–64).

12 *Ibid*, p 5.

13 *Ibid*, pp 4–5.

14 *Ibid*, pp 5–6.

15 See *R v Keegstra* [1990] 3 SCR 697, p 746.

16 See Delgado and Stefancic, *op cit* fn 11, p 7.

17 See Rosenfeld, M, 'Hate speech in constitutional jurisprudence: a comparative analysis' (2003) 24 *Cardozo L Rev* 1523, p 1529.

18 See Kubler, *op cit* fn 9, pp 340–47. These laws have been enforced with particular vigour in cases involving anti-Semitic propaganda. See Rosenfeld, *op cit* fn 17, p 1551.

country's experiences under the Third Reich, which underscored the corrosive effects of racist propaganda.[19] Thus, the German Constitutional Court has upheld the validity of laws punishing or suppressing hate speech in the face of legal challenges under Article 5, provided they are applied against statements of fact and not statements of opinion,[20] with little concern that such laws undermine the principle of freedom of expression. Germany's hate speech laws have been applied to online content and to non-Germans who post hate propaganda on the Internet from outside the country.[21]

While hate speech laws in Germany and some other continental European countries were partly a response to the horrors of the Holocaust, in other Western societies they were an answer to years of violence against immigrants and racial minorities. In the UK, for instance, racial unrest in the 1960s led to the banning of 'threatening, abusive, or insulting' public statements made with the intent to incite racial hatred.[22] It is also a crime in the UK to possess with the intent to publish material or recordings which are likely to stir up racial hatred.[23] In addition, whenever the commission of crimes such as assault, harassment or criminal damage is motivated by racial or religious animus, the punishment for those crimes is enhanced.[24] British courts have not entertained a claim that the UK's hate speech laws violate the principle of freedom of expression, but the Canadian Supreme Court has upheld similar legislation challenged under the Canadian Charter of Rights.[25] In that case, a high school teacher made anti-Semitic statements to his

---

19 For discussions of German law, see Kommers, D, *The Constitutional Jurisprudence of the Federal Republic of Germany*, 2nd edn, 1997, Durham, NC: Duke UP; Stein, E, 'History against free speech: the new german law against the "Auschwitz" – and other – "Lies"' (1986) 85 *Michigan L Rev* 277; Witman, J, 'Enforcing civility and respect: three societies' (2000) 109 *Yale LJ* 1279; Rosenfeld, *op cit* fn 17, pp 1548–55.

20 This distinction is not always easy to make. In the *Holocaust Denial Case*, 90 BVerfGE 241 (1994), the court held that denying the Holocaust constituted statements of demonstrably false facts and could be punished under criminal laws against insult, agitation, and the denigration of the memory of the dead. On the other hand, in the *Historical Fabrication Case*, 90 BVerfGE 1 (1994), the court held that a claim that Germany was not to blame for the outbreak of World War II, while unwarranted, was a statement of opinion and thus speech protected by the Basic Law. See Rosenfeld, *op cit* fn 17, pp 1552–53.

21 Case BGH NJW 2001, p 624, discussed by Sieber, U, 'The fight against hate on the Internet', at www.jura.uni-muenchen.de/einrichtungen/ls/sieber/article/zrp/hass-zrp_en.pdf.

22 Race Relations Act 1965, s 6(1). See generally Robertson, G and Nicol, A, *Media Law*, 4th edn, 2002, London: Sweet & Maxwell, pp 217–21. This law, now found in the Public Order Act 1986, defines 'racial hatred' as hatred against a group based on their 'colour, race, nationality (including citizenship) or ethnic or national origins'; see s 17. This definition only inconsistently covers hatred based on religion. In *Mandla v Dowell Lee* [1983] 1 All ER 1062, the House of Lords stated that an ethnic group is 'a segment of the population distinguished from others by a sufficient combination of shared customs, beliefs, traditions and characteristics derived from a common or presumed common past'. Under this test, courts have found that hatred against Jews and Sikhs is covered by the Act, but hatred against Muslims and other groups is not. A proposal for an offence of incitement of religious hatred was put forward by the government in the Anti-Terrorism, Crime and Security Bill in 2001 but was removed following opposition in the House of Lords. A similar attempt was made in the Religious Offences (Private Member) Bill in 2002, but this proposal has not been enacted.

23 Public Order Act 1986, s 23.

24 See Crime and Disorder Act 1998, ss 28–33, 96; Criminal Justice (Scotland) Act 2003, s 74.

25 *R v Keegstra* [1990] 3 SCR 697. See generally Mahoney, K, 'The Canadian constitutional approach to freedom of expression in hate propaganda and pornography' (1992) 55 *Law and Contemporary Problems* 77.

students, in violation of a criminal statute prohibiting the intentional promotion of hatred against identifiable racial, religious or ethnic groups. The Court noted that the harms associated with hate speech went well beyond any immediate threat of violence that might flow from it, as it offends and stigmatises its targets and in the longer term may desensitise others to messages imputing racial or religious inferiority.[26] These harms, the Court found, outweighed the value of such expression to any of the purposes served by protecting freedom of speech.

The juridical attitudes of these countries toward hate speech reflect the consensus view in the West outside of the US. Moreover, hate speech is condemned in numerous international human rights covenants adopted since World War II. Although these covenants recognise the fundamental nature of the right to free expression, they refuse to concede that this right should immunise statements intended to incite hatred and discrimination. For example, the International Covenant on Civil and Political Rights calls for national laws against 'advocacy of national, racial, or religious hatred that constitutes incitement to discrimination, hostility or violence'.[27] Similarly, the International Convention on the Elimination of All Forms of Racial Discrimination requires its signatories to outlaw 'dissemination of ideas based on racial superiority or hatred'.[28] The First Additional Protocol to the Council of Europe's Convention on Cybercrime, stressing that 'all human beings are born free and equal in dignity and rights', requires the adoption of measures prohibiting the transmission of racist or xenophobic messages through computer systems.[29] When hate speech laws adopted by national governments have been challenged on free speech grounds in international tribunals, these challenges have usually failed.[30]

The US has signed these international accords, but subject to reservations relieving it of any obligation to adopt legislation that would conflict with the First Amendment to the US Constitution.[31] The US's refusal to adopt anti-hate speech laws is not simply the manifestation of some notion of American 'exceptualism'. As is detailed below, most of the laws adopted in other countries to control hate speech would violate the First Amendment. In the hierarchy of American law, the Constitution is paramount and treaties are inferior to it. A treaty would be unenforceable within US borders if it failed to conform to the requirements of the First Amendment, and US officials lack the power to enter into international agreements that do not comport with the US Supreme Court's interpretation of the First Amendment.[32] In other words, under its Constitution the US *cannot* agree to

---

26 [1990] 3 SCR 697, p 747.

27 999 UNTS 171 (opened for signature 16 December 1966), Article 20(2).

28 660 UNTS 195 (opened for signature 21 December 1965), Article 4.

29 See Convention on Cybercrime, ETS No 185 (opened for signature 23 November 2001); First Additional Protocol to the Convention on Cybercrime (opened for signature 28 January 2003).

30 See, eg, *Jersild v Denmark* (1995) 19 ECHRR 1; *Faurisson v France*, Communication No 550/1993, UN Doc CCPR/C/58/D/550/1993 (1996).

31 See, eg, 138 *Congressional Record* 8070 (1992) (reservation with respect to Article 20 of the International Covenant on Civil and Political Rights); 140 *Congressional Record* 12185 (1994) (reservation with respect to Article 4 of the International Convention on the Elimination of All Forms of Racial Discrimination). While the US has signed (but not ratified) the Convention on Cybercrime, it has not signed the First Additional Protocol.

32 See, eg, *Reid v Covert*, 354 US 1 (1957), p 17.

any treaty provision that would offend the First Amendment rights of its citizens. This does not foreclose altogether the negotiation of international agreements concerning the regulation of the Internet, as some areas of the law – those governing intellectual property rights, fraud, misleading advertising, and child pornography for instance – do not implicate free speech values deemed important in the American legal culture. However, regulation of a wide range of communications that are permissible in other Western democracies are prohibited in the US, debarring the US from entering international agreements that would require it to adopt similar regulations. Laws governing hate speech fall in this latter category.

Hate speech and the First Amendment

Although it may not be immediately apparent to outsiders, the objectives of US policy toward hate speech are the same as those pursued elsewhere: promoting tolerance and discrediting ideas and theories that devalue people because of their sex, race, religion or nationality.[33] The US, however, employs very different means for achieving these ends – a *laissez-faire* approach that emphasises the autonomy of the individual and is highly suspicious of any action of the state that might impinge upon that autonomy. The favourite metaphor of US free speech law is the 'marketplace of ideas',[34] and the presumption is that the state must refrain from regulating the content of speech of any kind and instead rely on the common sense of the people to discover the truth through unrestricted discussion and debate. The US Supreme Court has insisted that the 'bedrock principle underlying the First Amendment' is that the state 'may not prohibit the expression of an idea simply because society finds the idea itself offensive or disagreeable'.[35]

To a large extent, this approach is rooted in the centrality of freedom of expression to the American national identity. A sense of this is given by the famous concurring opinion of Justice Brandeis in *Whitney v California*, which attributed a libertarian conception of freedom of expression to the nation's 'Founding Fathers':

> Those who won our independence ... believed that freedom to think as you will and to speak as you think are means indispensable to the discovery and spread of political truth; that without free speech and assembly discussion would be futile; that with them, discussion affords ordinarily adequate protection against the dissemination of noxious doctrine; [and] that the greatest menace to freedom is an inert people. ... [T]hey knew that order cannot be secured merely through fear of punishment for its infraction; that it is hazardous to discourage thought, hope and imagination; that fear breeds repression; that repression breeds hate; that hate menaces stable government; that the path to safety lies in the opportunity to discuss freely supposed grievances and proposed remedies; and that the fitting remedy for evil counsels is good ones. Believing in the power of reason as applied through public discussion, they eschewed silence coerced by law – the argument of force in its worst form.[36]

---

33 See Boyle, *op cit* fn 2, pp 489–90.
34 Originating from Justice Holmes' dissent in *Abrams v United States*, 250 US 616 (1919).
35 *Texas v Johnson*, 491 US 397 (1989), p 414.
36 274 US 357 (1927), pp 375–76.

This passage marshals several distinct arguments for protecting expression from state interference. The justification with particular rhetorical resonance in the United States is that a 'free trade in ideas' will advance the search for truth.[37] When false ideas are expressed by some citizens, the best response is not sanction by the state but vigorous rebuttal by other citizens. Reliance on state regulation makes for an 'inert people', the 'greatest menace to freedom', but unimpeded public discussion allows the 'power of reason' to triumph in the end. By applying this argument to political discourse, a second rationale emerges which maintains that free expression is a necessary condition for democratic self-government, and that curtailing speech through state regulation might deny citizens the information and open debate necessary for making intelligent decisions affecting public policy.[38] Further, suppression of unpopular opinion will impede the development of new ideas and hinder society's adaptation to changing circumstances. It will also threaten the stability of a polity by cultivating resentment, social unrest, and even political violence. Suppression of pernicious ideas may even inadvertently boost their appeal. On the other hand, by allowing the unfettered expression of opinions despicable to the majority of citizens, the fundamental liberal value of tolerance may be promoted.[39]

These arguments stress the benefits of free expression for society at large. Others focus more directly on the interests of individuals within society, emphasising that free speech is a necessary precondition for individual autonomy, self-realisation and self-fulfilment.[40] A state cannot legitimately interfere with this autonomy by 'protecting' individuals from ideas or arguments.[41] Moreover, individuals not only have the right to receive information uncensored by the state: they have the right to form their own beliefs and express them to others. The state cannot legitimately prevent some people from expressing themselves 'on the ground that their convictions make them unworthy participants' in public discussion; when official suppression of speech has the effect of favouring certain viewpoints over others, the state fails to treat its citizens equally.[42] State suppression of speech therefore violates the 'sanctity of individual choice' and is an affront to the dignity of the individual.[43]

The US Supreme Court's First Amendment jurisprudence has been informed, albeit inconsistently, by these arguments. Nonetheless, it has not foreclosed regulation of harmful communications altogether. Some forms of expression are not seen to be relevant to the free speech principle: the state can require disclosure of a wide range of financial information relevant to securities trading or tax collection;

---

37 See Schauer, F, *Free Speech*, 1982, Cambridge: CUP, pp 15–34; Marshall, W, 'In defense of the search for truth as a First Amendment justification' (1995) 30 *Georgia L Rev* 1.

38 See, eg, Meiklejohn, A, *Free Speech and its Relation to Self-Government*, 1948, New York: Harper; Meiklejohn, A, 'The First Amendment is an absolute' (1961) *Sup Ct Rev* 245.

39 See Bollinger, L, *The Tolerant Society*, 1986, New York: OUP.

40 See, eg, Wells, C, 'Reinvigorating autonomy: freedom and responsibility in the Supreme Court's First Amendment jurisprudence' (1997) 32 *Harv Civil Rights-Civil Liberties L Rev* 159.

41 *Ibid*, p 162; Dworkin, R, *Freedom's Law*, 1996, Oxford: OUP, p 200.

42 See Dworkin, *ibid*; Schauer, *op cit* fn 37, p 62.

43 Schauer, *op cit* fn 37, pp 62, 68.

punish perjury, conspiracy, solicitation or misrepresentation; impose liability based on the language used on package labels; and regulate communications that further misleading or deceptive practices.[44] Such communications do not fall within the hypothetical scenarios defining freedom of expression in American culture. It is not unusual for nations to define the specific applications of general constitutional principles – principles broadly shared with other nations – by reference to their own peculiar historical and cultural experiences. This is why there is such wide variation in the interpretation of the free speech principle throughout the world, even though the general principle is identified in most of the world's constitutions in broadly similar language.[45] Most Western countries do not regard hate speech as falling within the hypothetical scenarios defining the ambit of freedom of expression; the US does.

The Supreme Court has not always blocked efforts to punish hate-mongers: in a case decided when the Holocaust was a fresh memory, the Court upheld the conviction of a white supremacist who had distributed racist leaflets, concluding that they contained statements amounting to 'group defamation' unprotected by the First Amendment.[46] This decision is aberrational, however; more frequently, the Court has held that the First Amendment requires forbearance of ideas that the overwhelming majority of people find distasteful or discomforting. Thus, restrictions on the propaganda of extremist groups have been disallowed because the history of such laws in the United States shows that they are often used against socialists, pacifists and peaceful (though perhaps eccentric) protesters against the status quo. Suppressing expression by the Ku Klux Klan, it is feared, could be the thin edge of the wedge leading to the suppression of all dissenting voices.[47]

Accordingly, the First Amendment has been interpreted to protect those who disseminate hate speech, subject to a few narrow exceptions. One exception is that the state may punish 'fighting words' – insults directed at another that are so offensive as to prompt an immediate violent reaction.[48] In addition, the state may punish 'true threats' – statements communicating a serious intention to commit acts of violence which are intended to engender fear.[49] Finally, the state can proscribe incitements to 'imminent lawless action'. This exception is interpreted strictly. Thus, in *Brandenburg v Ohio*,[50] the Supreme Court overturned the conviction of a KKK leader for statements made at a rally staged for television, because while the defendant had advocated racial violence, he had not incited it. The line drawn

---

44 See Greenawalt, K, *Speech, Crime, and the Uses of Language*, 1990, Oxford: OUP, pp 132, 239–80, 315–21; Schauer, F, 'Free speech and the cultural contingency of constitutional categories' (1993) 14 *Cardozo L Rev* 865, p 872; Vick, D, 'Exporting the First Amendment to cyberspace: the Internet and state sovereignty', in Morris, N and Waisbord, S (eds), *Media and Globalization*, 2001, Boulder, CO: Rowman & Littlefield, pp 12–13.

45 See Vick, *ibid*, pp 13–14.

46 *Beauharnais v Illinois*, 343 US 250 (1952).

47 Schauer, *op cit* fn 44, pp 878–79.

48 See *Chaplinsky v New Hampshire*, 315 US 568 (1942).

49 See *Watts v United States*, 394 US 705 (1969). Intent to cause hurt feelings, disgust, anger or outrage will not suffice.

50 395 US 444 (1969).

between advocacy and incitement echoed the distinction applied in criminal cases in which communists had been charged with advocating the forcible overthrow of the US government.[51] In effect, hate speech was equated with the politically-motivated expression of extremist views.

The rights of bigots have been vindicated in numerous controversial cases. For example, when the Village of Skokie refused to permit neo-Nazis to march through a neighbourhood with a large Jewish population (including Holocaust survivors), the courts ruled that the Village acted unlawfully: although the proposed march was intended to provoke intense feelings, it did not constitute an incitement to violence.[52] In *RAV v City of St Paul*,[53] the Supreme Court struck down a local ordinance that prohibited persons from placing burning crosses or Nazi swastikas on public or private property with the knowledge that this would arouse 'anger, alarm or resentment in others on the basis of race, colour, creed, religion or gender'. The Court found that the ordinance targeted 'expressive conduct', which did not necessarily amount to an incitement to violence; to the extent that a burning cross constitutes 'fighting words', the ordinance discriminated on the basis of the viewpoint expressed since it criminalised some messages constituting 'fighting words' but not others.[54] In 2003, the Court revisited the issue of cross burning in *Virginia v Black*,[55] holding that under the 'true threat' exception it was permissible for the state to punish such conduct if it was intended to intimidate a specific individual or group. However, the state could not treat the act of cross burning as *prima facie* evidence of an intention to intimidate, because the act equally could be an expression of one's solidarity with the KKK, or one's adherence to a particular political ideology, neither of which can be prohibited. The fact that the ideology in question is an ideology of hate is irrelevant, as far as the limits imposed by the First Amendment are concerned.[56]

The US attitude toward the regulation of hate speech was perhaps best encapsulated by constitutional scholar Gerald Gunther: 'The lesson I have drawn from my childhood in Nazi Germany and my happier adult life [in the US] is the need to walk the sometimes difficult path of denouncing the bigot's hateful ideas with all my power, yet at the same time challenging a community's attempt to suppress hateful ideas by force of law.'[57] The US Supreme Court has made clear that this approach will govern cases involving Internet communications.[58] Indeed, the

---

51 See *Yates v United States*, 354 US 298 (1957).

52 See *National Socialist Party of America v Village of Skokie*, 432 US 43 (1977); *Village of Skokie v National Socialist Party of America*, 373 NE 2d 21 (1978) (Illinois Sup Ct).

53 505 US 377 (1992).

54 *Ibid*, p 391.

55 538 US 343 (2003); 123 S Ct 1536.

56 The contention of leading critics of the US position that 'the prevailing First Amendment paradigm' will be gradually replaced by a new era of 'First Amendment realism' more receptive to hate speech laws (see, eg, Delgado, R, 'First Amendment formalism is giving way to First Amendment legal realism' (1994) 29 *Harv Civil Rights-Civil Liberties L Rev* 169, p 170) has been put to rest for now by *Virginia v Black*.

57 Quoted in Kasper, G, 'Tribute to Professor Gerald Gunther' (2002) 55 *Stanford L Rev* 647, p 649.

58 See *Reno v ACLU*, 521 US 844 (1997).

recognised exceptions to the general rule against content regulation probably have less relevance to the Internet than other media of communication. The 'fighting words' and 'incitement to imminent lawless action' exceptions will rarely apply, since the creator of an electronic message will rarely be in the physical presence of someone who might be provoked. Legislation directed at harassment through emails or message boards might fall within the 'true threat' exception, but beyond that First Amendment law appears to forbid the regulation of Internet hate speech (and prevents US officials from agreeing to abide by international standards prohibiting it).

Battle lines drawn

US law has been widely criticised for ignoring the more subtle harms associated with expression that incites hatred and discrimination. It is viewed by many as being overly concerned with the rights of speakers at the expense of those who are targets of hate speech, and of society's interest in avoiding the social harms attributed to extremist expression. Critics remain unconvinced that privileging hate speech achieves any of the purposes of freedom of expression. For example, they question whether protecting politically extremist and often anti-democratic messages serves any useful purpose in preserving and promoting democracy.[59] While libertarians might argue that tolerance of extremist speech strengthens a polity's commitment to democracy by inspiring vigorous rebuttal by democracy's defenders, critics maintain that these benefits are lost if targeted groups feel threatened and withdraw from political participation. Richard Delgado and Jean Stefancic have argued that racial insults 'contribute to a stratified society in which political power is possessed by some and denied to others', undermining the democratic aspiration that all members of society are equally free to contribute to discussions of matters of public concern.[60] They also challenge the contention that respect for individual autonomy requires unqualified support for the right of speakers to freely express themselves, as 'a racial insult is only in small part an expression of self: it is primarily an attempt to injure through the use of words'.[61] To these critics, the interests of the speaker are more than offset by the right of autonomy and the respect owed others.

The most sustained attack on the US approach, however, has been directed against the central metaphor of First Amendment law. The notion that truth will emerge from a 'free trade of ideas' has been assailed for presupposing that truth has a determinable meaning that can be 'discovered', and that humans are essentially rational and thus capable of perceiving that a particular proposition is true.[62] The Canadian Supreme Court, for instance, showed little faith that truth will prevail in an open competition with falsehood: 'We know that under the strain and pressure

---

59 See, eg, Rosenfeld, *op cit* fn 17, p 1533.
60 Delgado and Stefancic, *op cit* fn 11, p 24.
61 Delgado and Stefancic, *op cit* fn 11, p 23.
62 See, eg, Gibbons, T, *Regulating the Media*, 2nd edn, 1998, London: Sweet & Maxwell, pp 22–23; Keane, J, *The Media and Democracy*, 1991, Cambridge: Polity, pp 37–38.

in times of irritation and frustration, the individual is swayed and even swept away by hysterical, emotional appeals, [and we] act irresponsibly if we ignore the way in which emotion can drive reason from the field.'[63] It may be more likely that hate propaganda will result in harmful action than reasoned rebuttal, particularly when systemic social problems like racism, sexism and homophobia are involved. Some argue that when such problems 'are imbedded in ... the set of meanings and conventions by which we construct and interpret reality', those who speak out against them will be 'seen as extreme, political, or incoherent'.[64] In these circumstances, freedom of expression becomes 'a tool for legitimating the status quo', as 'the dominant paradigm renders certain ideas unsayable or incomprehensible'.[65]

However, while critics have chipped away at the philosophical underpinnings of US law, they have been less successful in defending the practical efficacy of hate speech laws themselves, either in protecting vulnerable groups or in changing attitudes. It is far from certain that sexism, racism, homophobia or religious intolerance are greater problems in the US than in countries with well-developed anti-hate legislation. In the UK, for example, prosecutions under hate speech laws are infrequent.[66] Moreover, those whom such laws are intended to protect often find themselves being prosecuted. The first person convicted under the UK's modern hate speech laws was a black man who directed a racial slur against a white policeman, and in the 1960s a disproportionate number of cases involved the utterances of members of disadvantaged groups against those they perceived to be their oppressors.[67]

Such cases illustrate a broader phenomenon: hate speech laws invariably are enforced against those marginalised members of society who are most likely to be attracted to extremist ideologies. In such circumstances, driving expressions of hatred 'underground' may only serve to intensify feelings of resentment and provide a cloak of martyrdom for those expressing pernicious views. Some critics of US law have maintained that more than the views of the marginalised are actually at issue, because hate speech often is but a 'pathological extension of majority feelings or beliefs'.[68] One reason why the 'marketplace of ideas' theory has been dismissed is that many manifestations of intolerance may be so deeply imbedded in a society's culture they will not be perceived as wrong by those in the marketplace.[69] However, this begs the question: if this is true, why would the majority (whose views theoretically would prevail in democratically-elected legislatures) choose to criminalise ideas not far removed from their own, or condone prosecution of those who express them? Only those pressing ideas considered well beyond the boundaries of social acceptability will find themselves in breach of hate speech laws.

---

63 *R v Keegstra* [1990] 3 SCR 697, p 747.
64 Delgado, *op cit* fn 56, p 171.
65 Delgado, *op cit* fn 56, p 171.
66 Robertson and Nicol, *op cit* fn 22, p 218.
67 See Robertson and Nicol, *op cit* fn 22, p 220; Rosenfeld, *op cit* fn 17, pp 1525, 1546–47.
68 Rosenfeld, *op cit* fn 17, p 1561.
69 See, eg, Delgado and Stefancic, *op cit* fn 11.

Perhaps the biggest challenge to those who advocate hate speech laws is the problem of drawing the line between the tolerable expression of controversial ideas and the intolerable expression of hatred. 'Hate' is an emotion inevitably bound up with the subjective feelings of those who experience it, and it is not easily reduced to the objectifying definitions of the law. Some have characterised this concern about line drawing as a slippery slope argument: neat lines between the acceptable and unacceptable are elusive, and therefore regulation of offensive speech will gradually expand toward censorship of all forms of controversial expression. Such arguments could be made about state regulation in most areas of human endeavour, but while line-drawing problems are not unknown to other areas of law, they manifest themselves constantly in connection with proposals for regulating hate speech. For example, at what point does criticism of American foreign policy bleed into anti-Americanism? Should a distinction be made, as Delgado and Stefancic suggest, between racial insults and espousing the view that race discrimination is justified?[70] Should arguments that immigration ought to be curtailed because it will cause job losses be suppressed simply because they encourage discrimination against immigrants? Does the answer to this question change if one advocates immigration limits in order to preserve 'national identity' or 'cultural identity'? Does the answer depend on whether the advocate uses crude or sophisticated language?

These dilemmas are especially acute when statements regarding religion are at issue, because religion is not only the basis of group identity but an ideology, the support or opposition of which lies at the historic heart of freedom of belief and expression. Can criticism of a religion for its position on homosexuality or attitudes toward women constitute hate speech? Would characterising the Pope's opposition to contraception as indifference to human suffering caused by overpopulation be an impermissible expression of anti-Catholicism?[71] Moreover, problems of definition become particularly vexing when Internet communications are at issue, because what constitutes hate speech can be culturally specific, tied to a society's history, the status of groups as majorities or minorities in that society, and the 'customs, common linguistic practices, and the relative power or powerlessness of speakers and their targets within the society involved'.[72] This makes line-drawing in international agreements governing the Internet particularly difficult.

Conclusion

Whether hate speech laws undermine the purposes served by the principle of free expression remains a hotly disputed question, but this question cannot be divorced from scrutiny of the efficacy of hate speech laws themselves. By choosing to draw lines – by condemning some messages but not others – a state may inadvertently legitimate expression that is insidious but just on this side of being illegal in a way that an absence of regulation would not have done. More fundamentally, hate

---

70 Delgado and Stefancic, *op cit* fn 11, p 24.
71 See Rosenfeld, *op cit* fn 17, pp 1564–65.
72 Rosenfeld, *op cit* fn 17, p 1565.

speech laws ultimately do not address the real problem hate speech exposes: the conditions that allow for the festering of intolerance and discrimination in society. As has been noted, it is the marginalised and disaffected who are prosecuted for violations of hate speech laws. It is unlikely that such prosecutions will make the hatred of the alienated abate. Hate speech laws – and the *laissez-faire* approach of the US, for that matter – do not address the problems of poverty, social isolation and ignorance that lie at the heart of group hatred.

Chapter 5
Free Expression and Defamation
Diane Rowland

Speech is essential to self-realisation, social life, politics, economic activity, art and knowledge. But speech can inflict serious harm ... How should we deal with this tension?[1]

Introduction

The debate surrounding the conflicting interests in protection of reputation and freedom of expression is obviously not one which is unique to the Internet, but it has certainly been reinvigorated and exacerbated by the potential for mass communication brought about by global computer networks. Accepting that a balance needs to be drawn between the right to speak freely and the right not to be falsely impugned, the focus of the debate is where to draw the line. For the purposes of this discussion, this also includes a consideration of whether the line should be drawn in the same place with respect to the Internet as with other media. Given the domination of the US in the development and use of the Internet and World Wide Web (WWW), this will be discussed with particular reference to the determination of that balance in the US, with its strong constitutional commitment to free speech expressed in the First Amendment,[2] and also in the UK, often referred to as the libel capital[3] of the world because of its apparent bias towards the alleged victims of defamation.[4] Although freedom of expression is protected under both the First Amendment to the US Constitution and Article 10 of the European Convention on Human Rights, the latter is more specific about the need to balance this against other interests protected by law, and Article 10(2) makes explicit reference to the protection of reputation as a potential fetter on the right of free expression. This chapter will consider certain facets of the application of the law of defamation to publication on the Internet and WWW together with some of the salient aspects of the conflict and balance between free expression and defamation as demonstrated in the context of that medium of communication.

The medium and the message

Global computer networks, typically exemplified by the Internet and WWW, have the capacity to make material available to a much wider audience at a much greater speed, and with much less opportunity for scrutiny and quality control than has

---

1   Abel, R, *Speech and Respect*, 1994, London: Sweet & Maxwell, p 29.
2   See Vick, Chapter 4.
3   See, eg, Robertson, G and Nicol, A, *Media Law*, 4th edn, 2002, London: Sweet & Maxwell, p 71.
4   See, eg, the comments of Lord Hoffmann in *Berezovsky v Michaels* [2000] 2 All ER 956, p 1005 that the case had been brought in the UK because it was thought unlikely to succeed in the US.

been the case with both conventional hardcopy publication or broadcast media. The Internet has enabled many voices to be heard that would have been denied an audience in the traditional media either because of cost, opportunity or substance. This vast increase in participation in the dissemination of information has eroded the traditional distinctions between creators and consumers of news and information. The Internet facilitates not only dissemination akin to traditional publication, where there is a clear division between the publisher and the reader, but also allows participants to slip easily from one role to another, 'blurring the distinction between "speakers" and "listeners" ... the receiver can and does become the content provider'.[5] Many, if not most, participants on the Internet simultaneously assume both of these roles with a consequent enhancement of dialogue and discussion. In addition, those who have embraced this medium of publication have potential access to a wide, perhaps even global, audience. Further, whether the consequent debate, diatribe and dialogue is of a humdrum and routine, or an erudite and visionary, nature is immaterial to its capacity to be brought to the attention of a wide audience ranging across all sectors of society. Never before has the average citizen had such potentially easy access to contemporary movers and shakers. 'Through the use of Chatrooms, any person with a phone line can become a town crier with a voice that resonates farther than it could from any soapbox. Through the use of web pages, mail exploders, and newsgroups, the same individual can become a pamphleteer.'[6] Much has been written about this democratising effect of the Internet and WWW on speech and communication and whether or not it has the ability to approach the idealistic vision of the 'marketplace of ideas'.[7] On the other hand, there have been criticisms that the 'everlasting world-wide conversation', far from pushing back the frontiers of discourse in a quest for truth, has descended to the level of the inane, with a consequent devaluation of its worth as speech. In this vein, Lidsky comments that the 'participatory nature of Internet discourse threatens to engulf its value as discourse'.[8] Others have been much more welcoming of the increased potential for communication and debate. 'Given the unique nature of the Internet for fostering open and honest debate, the value of hearing the new speakers far outweighs any damage, dignitary or otherwise, that simply letting them speak without fear could do.'[9]

The ingredients of defamation

The precise nature of an action for defamation varies with the jurisdiction but there are some commonalities that can be discerned. The statement must be injurious to the reputation or dignity of the person allegedly defamed and it must be published

---

5 *ACLU v Reno*, 929 F Supp 824 (1996), p 844.

6 *Reno v ACLU*, 521 US 844 (1997), p 870.

7 A concept referred to by Holmes J (dissenting) in *Abrams v United States*, 250 US 616, p 630; L Ed 1173 (1919), p 1180 and traceable to John Stuart Mill's treatise *On Liberty*; see, eg, discussion in Baker, CE, *Human Liberty and Freedom of Speech*, 1992, New York: OUP, especially Chapters 1–2.

8 Lidsky, L, 'Silencing John Doe: defamation and discourse in cyberspace' (2000) 49 *Duke LJ* 855, p 903.

9 Furman, J, 'Cybersmear or Cyber-SLAPP' (2001) 25 *Seattle U L Rev* 213, p 244.

or communicated to another who must understand its connection with the person allegedly defamed. There are a number of common defences – including truth or justification, which is often, although not always, a complete defence – and a number of privileged positions for traditional media defendants. In civil law jurisdictions the action is frequently an aspect of the criminal law which may or may not be supported by civil damages. In the common law world, on the other hand, although criminal libel remains a possibility, an action for defamation is usually discussed in terms of tortious injury to reputation. There are some significant differences between the law of defamation in the US, particularly with regard to public figures, and that in the UK. In the former jurisdiction, the Supreme Court held the common law of defamation to be incompatible with First Amendment rights in *New York Times v Sullivan*[10] and, as a consequence, public figures cannot sue for defamation in the US in the absence of actual malice (meaning, in this context, knowledge of falsity or reckless disregard for the truth rather than the usual sense of ill will, hatred or a purpose to injure).[11]

Defamation and chilling

There are a number of theoretical bases that are used to justify what is seen by many as the moral imperative of free speech. Arguments based on personal autonomy and the achievement of individual fulfilment relate primarily to individual interests, although it could be argued that it is for the wider good of society for individuals to be able to develop ideas and thoughts in the way that is fostered by free speech and expression. More overtly collective justifications are based on both the need for free speech to ensure effective participation in a democratic society and the widely held belief that truth can only emerge from free and uninhibited discussion.[12] However, the latter implies a causal relationship between discussion and truth which has never been, and indeed is not, susceptible to verification.[13]

Within many human rights discourses, freedom of expression is often examined in the context of state actions which inhibit and infringe that right and so, to coin the well-accepted phrase, have a 'chilling effect' on speech. In many jurisdictions, the effect of an action for defamation, being a uniquely private wrong, is more often considered in relation to privacy[14] than to free expression. However, just as the right to privacy of one individual can restrict the ability of another to comment about their activities, so an action for defamation (or the threat of one) may have the same

---

10 376 US 254; 11 L Ed 2d 686 (1964).

11 For further discussion see 50 Am Jur 2d § 4.

12 See Vick, Chapter 4.

13 *Ibid.*

14 Nevertheless, these are quite distinct legal concepts. See, eg, 50 *Am Jur* 2d § 13 pointing out that although defamation and privacy actions might be closely allied, they are 'separate and distinct claims serving different objectives and protecting different interests. Privacy actions involve injuries to emotions and mental suffering, while defamation actions involve injury to reputation'. This view is reflected in the Report of the Younger Committee, Cmnd 5012 (1972), para 71: 'We believe that the concepts of defamation and intrusion into privacy should be kept distinct from one another.'

propensity to exert a chilling effect on free expression as more obviously public restrictions. Recognising this fact, most jurisdictions would expect to include some checks and balances within their law of defamation to enable the interests in free expression and the protection of reputation to be appropriately reconciled. This led the Faulks Committee to note that 'the law of defamation has two basic purposes: to enable the individual to protect his reputation and to preserve the right of free speech. These two purposes necessarily conflict. The law of defamation is sound if it preserves a proper balance between them'.[15] However, there is room for considerable disagreement over where that 'proper balance' should lie and for quite different standards and approaches to be taken in different societies and environments.[16]

In an empirical study, Barendt *et al* considered the use of an action in defamation or the threat of one as a method of censorship.[17] Their study surveyed the views of a representative section of those publishing in different traditional, commercial media and concluded overall that 'uncertainty in both the principles of defamation law and the practical application induce great caution on the part of the media'[18] and that, in consequence, the decision of traditional media as to whether to publish was certainly influenced by a fear of libel proceedings. Overall 'the impact of defamation law on various media has demonstrated clearly that the chilling effect in this area does genuinely exist and significantly restrict what the public is able to read and hear'.[19] Chilling can occur as a result of editing or because certain subjects or individuals come to be considered off-limits.[20] Similarly, in a comprehensive review of the law of libel in the US, Anderson suggests that 'the most relevant source of the chilling effect is not the danger of losing a judgment but the prospect of having to pay the costs of the defendant'.[21] There have also been a number of judicial pronouncements referring to the potentially chilling effect of defamation actions. Butler Sloss LJ in *Derbyshire County Council v Times Newspapers* remarked that 'the threat of libel proceedings is seen as a deterrent both by the individual and

---

15 Report of the Committee on Defamation, Cmnd 5909, para 19 (1975).

16 See, eg, *Dow Jones v Gutnick* [2002] HCA 56, para 23; *Bachchan v India Abroad Publications Inc*, 585 NYS 2d 661, p 665; and *Telnikoff v Matusevitch*, 702 A 2d 230, p 248: 'Maryland defamation law is totally different from English defamation law in virtually every significant respect.'

17 Barendt, E *et al*, *Libel and the Media*, 1997, Oxford: Clarendon.

18 *Ibid*, p 186.

19 *Ibid*, p 191, and compare the views of Anderson, D, 'Is libel law worth reforming?' (1991) 140 *U Pa L Rev* 487 and Lidsky, *op cit* fn 8, p 890: 'Media defendants identify litigation costs as a primary source of the chilling effect.'

20 There have been a number of instances where celebrities and others in the public eye have acted promptly to try to have information about them, which they do not wish to be in circulation for a variety of reasons, removed from the Internet, whether or not there was any legal basis for its removal. See, eg, Hendrie-Liaño, J, 'Playing Canute with defamation law' (2003) 14 *Computers and Law* 34; Greenslade, R, 'What do these people have in common?' *Guardian (Media)*, 17 November 2003, p 6. In 2000, Edwards ('Defamation on the Internet', in Edwards, L and Waelde, C (eds), *Law and the Internet: A Framework for Electronic Commerce*, 2nd edn, 2000, Oxford: Hart) suggested that a change had become apparent in relation to the Internet in the previous three years, with threats of libel actions beginning to be used as a mechanism for ensuring the take-down of unwanted material.

21 See Anderson, *op cit* fn 19, p 516.

also by larger organisations, even the press'.[22] When the same case reached the House of Lords, Lord Keith of Kinkel made explicit reference to the potential chilling effect produced by the threat of civil actions for libel which could 'prevent the publication of matters which it is very desirable to make public'.[23] Despite this academic and judicial comment on chilling, the Law Commission concluded,[24] as a result of a survey of practitioners (albeit a fairly small sample), that there was no evidence that libel actions were initiated as a means of 'stifling unwanted exposure' and that no further study was required.

In the US, strong protection given by the First Amendment has tended to give the impression of a hierarchy of rights and this idea has, to a degree, been perpetuated in Europe, especially in relation to the importance given to free political speech. However, as pointed out in *Reynolds v Times Newspapers*, 'even in the US the opinions of jurists differ in the extent to which the collectively cherished right of free speech is to be preferred to the individually cherished right to personal reputation'.[25] There have been a number of cases in which it has been suggested that the protection of expression under the European Convention on Human Rights (ECHR), and now under the Human Rights Act 1998 (HRA), should be accorded some privileged status over other rights. Further, one construction of s 12(3) of the HRA, which provides that publication before trial should not be prevented unless 'the court is satisfied that the applicant is likely to establish that publication should not be allowed', could reinforce this view. These issues were discussed in *Cream Holdings v Banerjee*,[26] in which the existence of such a hierarchy of rights was rejected on the basis that although freedom of expression may well take precedence over the 'societal' rights or interests referred to in Article 10(2), these should be more properly regarded as justifications for restricting rights and that there was no implied precedence over other protected rights under the ECHR and HRA. 'It is one thing to say ... that the media's right to freedom of expression, particularly in the field of political discussion "is of a higher order" than the "right of an individual to his good reputation"; it is however, another thing to rank it higher than competing basic rights.'[27]

Although there may not be a hierarchy of competing rights and interests, within freedom of expression there is undoubtedly a hierarchy of speech, some of which is accorded more protection than others. The importance of ensuring full participation in a democratic society has caused courts in both Europe and the US to give pre-eminence to political speech. Thus, the European Court of Human Rights has affirmed that 'freedom of political debate is at the very core of the concept of a

---

22 [1992] 3 All ER 65, p 96.

23 [1993] AC 534, p 548 (HL).

24 Law Commission, *Aspects of Defamation Procedure: A Scoping Study*, May 2002, at www.lawcom.gov.uk/files/defamation.pdf.

25 Lord Cooke in *Reynolds v Times Newspapers* [1999] 4 All ER 609, p 639.

26 [2003] 2 All ER 318 and see discussion in Rogers, H and Tomlinson, H, 'Privacy and expression' (2003) EHRLR (special issue).

27 [2003] 2 All ER 318, p 335, *per* Simon Brown LJ, referring to *Loutchansky No 2* [2002] 1 All ER 652, para 22 and Sedley LJ in *Douglas v Hello!* [2001] 2 All ER 289, p 323.

democratic society'[28] and the right of freedom of expression has been described as having a 'higher normative force'.[29] A hierarchy of speech was underlined in *X and Church of Scientology v Sweden*, where it was accepted that commercial speech was entitled to protection but that this 'must be less than that accorded to the expression of "political ideas"'.[30] As a result, judicial pronouncements concerning the balance between the right of free expression and the necessary protection of reputation are most clearly evident in actions that might have some inhibiting effect on political comment. This is particularly evident in the US, where, as already noted, the Supreme Court in *New York Times v Sullivan*[31] found the common law of defamation to be antithetical to the First Amendment. In the UK, Butler Sloss LJ has noted the 'profound national commitment to the principle that debate on public issues should be uninhibited, robust and wide open and that it may well include vehement, caustic and sometimes unpleasantly sharp attacks on government and public officers'.[32]

At the other end of the scale, 'the moral right to freedom of expression gives virtually no protection to communicators of false information'[33] and 'a discourse that has no necessary anchor in truth has no value to anyone but the speaker';[34] courts and academic commentators seem to be generally agreed that there is no constitutional or other legal protection available for the dissemination of untrue statements. Thus, in *Reynolds*, Lord Hobhouse suggested that the case, being concerned with factual statements which were not correct, did not relate to freedom of speech. 'There is no human right to disseminate information that is not true. ... The workings of a democratic society depend on members of that society being informed, not misinformed.'[35]

The intractable question is where Internet speech lies on this spectrum and the value which cybercommunities place on the ability to speak freely.

The argot of the Internet and the reasonable reader

Speech on the Internet is far more varied than that in most traditional outlets. 'Modern day Luthers still post their theses, but to electronic bulletin boards rather than the door of the Wittenberg Schlosskirche. More mundane (but from a constitutional perspective, equally important) dialogue occurs between aspiring artists, or French cooks, or dog lovers, or fly fishermen.'[36] The Internet can be used

---

28 *Lingens v Austria* (1986) 8 EHRR 407, para 42. See also *Oberschlick v Austria* (1991) 19 EHRR 389, and *deHaes and Gijsels v Belgium* (1998) 25 EHRR 1.

29 Lord Steyn in *Reynolds v Times Newspapers* [1999] 4 All ER 609, p 628.

30 *X and Church of Scientology v Sweden* (1979) XXII Yearbook of the European Convention on Human Rights 244, p 252.

31 376 US 254; 11 L Ed 2d 686 (1964).

32 *Derbyshire County Council v Times Newspapers* [1992] 3 All ER 65, p 94 (CA) and citing with approval Brennan J in *New York Times v Sullivan*.

33 Gardner, J, 'Freedom of expression', in McCrudden, C and Chambers, G (eds), *Individual Rights and the Law in Britain*, 1995, Oxford: Clarendon, p 219.

34 See Lidsky, *op cit* fn 8, p 903.

35 [1999] 4 All ER 609, p 657.

36 Dalzell J in *ACLU v Reno*, 929 F Supp 824, p 881.

simultaneously for passive information retrieval and active discussion, which can be cultured, utilitarian or scurrilous. Although manifesting itself in apparently written form, the argot of the Internet is more akin to the spoken word with its spontaneity and lack of editing and corroboration prior to utterance. Many bulletin boards and newsgroups are used by a closed group (or cybercommunity) for whom immoderate and vituperative language is the norm. While this may not be appreciated by outsiders, it is well established that 'group members can use language that would be intolerable from outsiders'[37] and 'environment may affect emotional tone ... group dynamics can reinforce or undermine the message'.[38] There may be no freedom to speak false information but this does not extend to misguided opinion, and comment cannot be denied protection merely because it is criticised for being cryptic, uninformed and inane. What effect does the nature and tenor of the discussion have on its capacity for damage? How does the reader view the information gleaned from the Internet? As gossip or tittle tattle? As authoritative? As reliable as that from traditional media? Whether a participant in a chatroom or bulletin board is aware of the nature of the *lingua franca*, or completely innocent of the prevailing idiom, may be relevant to whether comments are genuinely disparaging and injurious to reputation. In relation to certain intemperate exchanges on a bulletin board, the court in *Global Telemedia International Inc v Does* found that the fact that the views expressed lacked formality and polish, used exaggeration, figurative speech and broad generalities together with a great deal of linguistic informality all served to alert 'a reasonable reader to the fact that these observations are probably not written by someone with authority or firm factual foundation for his beliefs'.[39] The very existence of such informal, unpolished interchange may be an encouragement to participate and an enhancement of speech. If individual cybercommunities can be identified, should the standard of speech be judged by reference to the 'reasonable reader' in an analogous way to the community standard in relation to obscenity? If so, should that standard of reasonableness be judged according to the community in question or in relation to the wider audience for the Internet?

Publication and liability

Where does publication occur?

Publication is an essential ingredient of defamation. However defamatory a person's thoughts may be, they will cause no damage to anyone's reputation unless communicated to another. In deciding where something is published there is a distinction to be made between the act of publication and the fact of communication to a third party, but 'even that distinction may not suffice to reveal all the

---

37 Abel, *op cit* fn 1, p 139.
38 Abel, *op cit* fn 1, p 141.
39 132 F Supp 2d 1261 (2001), p 1269.

consideration relevant to locating the place of the tort of defamation'.[40] Whether or not a case can be brought in a particular jurisdiction will depend, *inter alia*, on where the damage occurs and also whether there has been publication in that state.[41] Publication via the Internet potentially makes that information available to a global audience. Does this mean that the defamation can give rise to an action in all the places in which it can be accessed? What are the limits, if any, placed on place of publication in this situation? In *Macquirie Bank Ltd and Another v Berg*,[42] an injunction was refused in relation to Internet publication on the basis that this would be a restraint on publication anywhere in the world. This rather simplistic view[43] would equate Internet publication with publication to all jurisdictions whether or not there had been any access. On the other hand, support for the view that publication should be equated with actual access can be found in *Godfrey v Demon Internet*.[44]

Place of publication was crucial to the decision in *Dow Jones & Co v Gutnick*,[45] in which an Australian resident brought an action for defamation in a court in Victoria on the basis of an article published in the Internet version of a New York-based magazine. In its lengthy judgment,[46] the High Court of Australia found that the Victorian court had jurisdiction, despite the fact that there was no particular intention to publish the libel in Victoria, on the basis that Gutnick both resided in Victoria and enjoyed a reputation there, since 'it is only when the material is in comprehensible form that the damage to reputation is done and it is damage to reputation which is the principal focus of defamation, not any quality of the defendant's conduct. ... It is where that person downloads the material that the damage to reputation may be done'.[47] The corollary of this is that damage will only be done if the person in question actually enjoys a reputation in the latter place. This fact, of itself, will limit the number of actions which can succeed regardless of any legal technicalities surrounding the definition of publication. Further, the court suggested that 'the spectre of global liability should not be exaggerated'[48] as in reality no damages would be forthcoming if there was no reputation to protect.

The thrust of the decision in *Dow Jones* was very much to concentrate on the fact of damage, the place in which the damage occurred and the connection with that state. In contrast, a rather different approach to where 'publication' occurs considers whether the information has, in fact, been targeted at the receiving state. In *ALS Scan Inc v Digital Service Consultants*,[49] a copyright case, the US Court of Appeals for the Fourth Circuit considered that an argument that 'the Internet's electronic signals

---

40 *Dow Jones & Co v Gutnick* [2002] HCA 56, para 11.

41 In this connection see, eg, Article 5(3) of the Convention on Jurisdiction and the Enforcement of Judgments in Civil and Commercial Matters 1968 (the Brussels Convention) and its interpretation in respect of libel in *Shevill and Others v Presse Alliance SA* [1995] All ER (EC) 289.

42 [1999] NSWSC 526, available at www.austlii.org.

43 See discussion in Kohl, U, 'Defamation on the Internet – a duty free zone after all' (2002) 22 *Sydney L Rev* 119.

44 [1999] 4 All ER 342, p 347.

45 [2002] HCA 56.

46 Parts of which are also referred to below.

47 [2002] HCA 56, para 44.

48 *Ibid*, para 165.

49 293 F 3d 707 (2002).

are surrogates for the person and that Internet users conceptually enter a State to the extent that they send their electronic signals'[50] was far too broad and more would be needed to establish such a personal connection. This decision was built upon in *Young v New Haven Advocate*,[51] where the issue was whether an action for defamation could be pursued in Virginia, where the claimant had a reputation to protect, on the basis of publication in newspapers in Connecticut when the only method of making that information available in Virginia was via the Internet. Rather than consider any damage, the court looked for an intention to direct the publication at Virginia demonstrated by something more than mere accessibility or passive availability of the information. On the facts, it appeared to the court, by consideration of the local articles, information and advertisements offered, none of which was relevant to an audience in Virginia, that the websites were maintained to 'expand the reach of their papers in local markets' and there was no manifest intent to target readers in Virginia.[52] On this basis, personal jurisdiction was denied, producing a completely different outcome from that in *Dow Jones*.

In a different context, the European Court of Justice (ECJ) has held that the mere placing of data on the Internet does not amount to transfer of that data to all the third countries where there are the technical means needed to access the Internet.[53] Although this may be a convenient policy decision in terms of the provisions of the Data Protection Directive, the reasoning seems to be drawing a distinction between what could be termed active and passive publication. The reasoning employed by the ECJ was that although the data in question was placed on the Internet in Sweden, it was not thereby transferred to any other jurisdiction as 'an Internet user would not only have to connect to the Internet but also personally carry out the necessary actions to consult those pages … [the] Internet pages did not contain the technical means to send that information automatically to people who did not intentionally seek access to those pages'.[54] This fact is at the heart of all Internet use – that information has to be sought out[55] rather than arriving on the user's screen unbidden. A distinction between such passive and active publication which would depend on the effort made to bring the matter to the attention of the publishee, arguably does not assist the victim whose reputation is damaged or whose personal data is made available over the Internet. Nevertheless, it may have the merit of limiting the global reach of publication, if that is seen to be problematic.

These cases highlight not only some of the difficulties in the interpretation of publication, but also the tension between the approach in the US and that in the UK and Australia in particular.[56] This tension is further illustrated by the refusal of American courts to give effect to judgments of English courts in libel cases on the

---

50 *Ibid*, p 712.
51 315 F 3d 256 (2002).
52 *Ibid*, pp 263–64.
53 Case C-101/01 *Lindqvist*, judgment of 6 November 2003, available at http://curia.eu.int.
54 *Ibid*, para 60.
55 See, eg, discussion in *ACLU v Reno*, 929 F Supp 824, p 844.
56 See also the judgment in *Dow Jones* generally ([2002] HCA 56) and specifically paras 181–99.

basis that they have an adverse effect on the right of free expression.[57] Given the US domination of the Internet, certainly in its earlier stages of development, its influence on the developing Internet jurisprudence may not, of itself, be surprising, but is not susceptible to easy resolution.

Republication

In principle, liability for defamation arises with every new publication. It is now common for newspapers and other publications to provide an online archive – does each new 'hit' on this archive amount to a republication? Even before the advent of the Internet it had been recognised by the Faulks Committee that such a rule was capable of causing iniquity and the committee recommended no right of action on republication without leave of the court,[58] although this has never been acted upon. The issue has been dealt with in the US by the 'single publication rule'.[59] This rule has two important consequences: the first is that only one action can be brought no matter where the defamation has been distributed; the second is that the limitation period begins to run from the initial (ie the 'single') publication. This avoids one of the problems in *Loutchansky v Times Newspapers*,[60] in which (having discussed the single publication rule) each access to an online archive was deemed to amount to a new publication and the start of a new limitation period. Neither did the Court of Appeal in this case accept that this could have a disproportionate effect on freedom of expression – maintenance of an archive had a 'social utility' but was a 'comparatively insignificant aspect of freedom of expression'.[61] The defects of the usual multiple publication rule and the question of whether a single publication rule was more appropriate for Internet publication was discussed and rejected in *Dow Jones v Gutnick*[62] on a number of bases, including the need for technology-neutral rules and for not exceeding the permissible limits of judicial innovation.

Liability of ISPs

Liability may also fall, not just on the original author, but also on those who assist in the propagation of a libel.[63] This could include not only first originators and publishers of the libel but also those who form part of the distribution chain. Internet service providers (ISPs) may not necessarily employ, or be able to employ, the same scrutiny as can occur during the primary publishing process. Even though the act of distribution has contributed to the dissemination of the libel, this may be

---

57 See, eg, *Bachchan v India Abroad Publications Inc*, 585 NYS 2d 661 and *Telnikoff v Matusevitch*, 702 A 2d 230.

58 Cmnd 5909, para 291.

59 Applied explicitly to a website publication in *Firth v State of New York*, 775 NE 2d 463 (2002), discussed in *Defamation and the Internet: A Preliminary Investigation*, Scoping Study No 2, Law Commission, December 2002, para 3.19; see www.lawcom.gov.uk/files/defamation2.pdf. *Firth* and the single publication rule are also discussed in *Dow Jones v Gutnick* [2002] HCA 56, paras 29–37.

60 [2001] EWCA Civ 1805; [2002] 1 All ER 652.

61 *Ibid*, p 676.

62 [2002] HCA 56, paras 118–38.

63 For a more detailed discussion of such liability see Sutter, Chapter 6.

done in innocence and with no knowledge of the potentially defamatory nature of the publication.[64] The effect of different levels of distributor knowledge can be seen in two early and now familiar cases of defamation on the Internet, namely *Cubby Inc v Compuserve Inc*[65] and *Stratton Oakmont Inc v Prodigy Services.*[66] In the former, the ISP provided access to a bulletin board but exerted no scrutiny or editorial control, while in the latter the ISP did perform a screening function with respect to the bulletin board at issue. In *Cubby*, the ISP was found to be a distributor and not liable for the dissemination whereas the court in *Stratton* found Prodigy to be a publisher, rather than a distributor, and therefore liable. Although the decision in the *Stratton* case can be rationalised in terms of the editorial functions undertaken, it still caused considerable controversy and disquiet over the extent to which ISPs could, or should, be liable for the content of allegedly defamatory material to which they were instrumental in providing access, especially in the light of the increasing volume of traffic on the Internet and the infeasibility of screening all content. In addition, these decisions gave rise to a real prospect that ISPs, fearing potential liability for defamation, would react by removing content which could be problematic, with the consequent possibility of chilling of genuine expression of opinion.[67] These factors led to the US Congress including a provision within the Communications Decency Act (CDA) which exempted ISPs from liability in such cases by providing that 'no provider or user of an interactive computer service shall be treated as the publisher or speaker of any information provided by another content provider'.[68] This provision was silent on whether or not there should be liability in the face of actual knowledge that defamatory content was in fact being distributed. In *Zeran v America Online*,[69] it was contended that, although the ISP could no longer be regarded as a publisher, it was not immune from incurring distributor liability if there was evidence of actual knowledge of the defamatory content, suggesting that the ISP should still be liable if it had failed to act on being given notice. This argument failed to persuade the US Court of Appeals for the Fourth Circuit, which held that this provision barred completely any action being taken against the ISP and that 'liability on notice would defeat the dual purposes advanced by § 230 CDA'.[70] Although followed in a number of cases, this approach has been the subject of some trenchant academic criticism and judicial concern over the issue of notice and the actual behaviour of ISPs,[71] and a recent decision declined to follow the same line of reasoning. The Californian Court of Appeal in *Barrett v Rosenthal*[72] reversed a decision of the trial court which had found, relying on *Zeran*,

---

64 For a more detailed discussion of such liability, see Sutter, Chapter 6.
65 776 F Supp 135 (SDNY 1991).
66 1995 NY Misc Lexis 229.
67 See Sutter, Chapter 6.
68 47 USC 230(1)(c) (1996).
69 129 F 3d 327 (1997).
70 *Ibid*, p 333.
71 See, eg, *Doe v AOL Inc*, 718 So 2d 385 (1998); *Blumenthal and Blumenthal v Drudge and AOL Inc*, 992 F Supp 44 (1998). See also *Lunney v Prodigy Services*, 94 NY 2d 242, in which the trial court found the ISP not liable using common law principles and the subsequent appeal was dismissed without specific consideration of the statutory rules.
72 9 Cal Rprtr 3d 142 (2004).

that the CDA gave Internet content providers immunity from actions stemming from republication. A considerable part of the appeal judgment was devoted to a critique of *Zeran*, holding that 'the court ascribed to Congress an intent to create a far broader immunity than that body actually had in mind or is necessary to achieve its purposes' and rejected the argument that 'section 230 reflects a superseding congressional desire to promote unfettered speech on the Internet'. Reference was made to the legislative history of the immunity provision and also to the burgeoning body of scholarly criticism of *Zeran*, and a number of academic opinions were reviewed. Although the court was emphatic that it took 'no position on whether distributor liability would unduly chill online speech', it was of the view that complete immunity failed to take account of the rights of victims of defamation. Acknowledging that the courts in the US had 'struggled to define the proper accommodation between the common law of defamation and the constitutional freedom of speech', the decision expressed reluctance to extend different rules to intermediaries in cyberspace from those available in more traditional media and stated that 'survival of knowledge-based liability under the common law would not render section 230 nugatory'. The outcome of such reasoning allows liability to be imposed where there has been actual knowledge or notice of offending material.

If this interpretation of s 230 is followed,[73] it will result in a situation similar to that pertaining in the UK, where the relevant liability is governed by the Defamation Act 1996 which, rather than grant immunity from suit, provides a defence of innocent dissemination which can be relied on by those who are not the actual author, editor or publisher of the offending material provided they took reasonable care in relation to the publication and 'did not know' or 'had no reason to believe' that they had 'contributed to publication of a defamatory statement'.[74] The application of this section to ISPs was at issue in *Godfrey v Demon Internet*,[75] in which the ISP was unable to avail itself of the defence as there was evidence that it knew of the defamatory nature of the material but did not remove it from its servers. Since *Godfrey*, the provisions of the Electronic Commerce (EC Directive) Regulations 2002[76] limit ISP liability in certain areas including defamation. Regulation 19 grants immunity to ISPs, in relation to hosting services, unless they have 'actual knowledge of unlawful activity or information and, where a claim for damages is made, is not aware of facts or circumstances from which it would have been apparent to the service provider that the activity or information was unlawful'. This could still be interpreted as requiring 'take down on notice' and it will be interesting to see whether subsequent courts view the liability of ISPs in any different light in the future.

As the post-*Zeran* debate in the US has illustrated, where there is evidence that the ISP had actual knowledge of its part in the distribution of defamatory material

---

73 The California Supreme Court has since granted review of this decision and its narrow interpretation of s 230 of the CDA, so the case may not currently be relied on as precedent. See also *Perfect 10 v CC Bill* 71 USPQ 2d 1568 (2004) fn 28.

74 Defamation Act 1996, s 1.

75 [1999] 4 All ER 342.

76 SI 2002/2013, implementing the Directive on Electronic Commerce, Directive 2000/31/EC of 8 June 2000 [2000] OJ L178/1.

and had not acted to remove it, there is an argument for the imposition of liability, as was the actual case in *Godfrey*, above. However, in the absence of such evidence, the fact that there is a legal basis for such liability can itself exert a significant pressure on ISPs to remove allegedly defamatory postings, even when there is no verification that the material would be judged legally defamatory. This creates an obvious and significant clash with free expression of opinion, although as the extensive debate in *Barrett v Rosenthal* demonstrates, the extent to which this would actually exert a chilling effect on free expression is not easily quantifiable. On the other hand, the provision of total immunity, as illustrated by *Zeran*, is also capable of creating significant injustice. The problems in locating the appropriate balance have been discussed extensively by the Law Commission.[77] Although finding that the industry 'felt uncomfortable about censoring material that may not in fact be libellous',[78] it noted that the safest option for ISPs on notice was to remove allegedly defamatory material. The action of ISPs in such circumstances is obviously capable of exerting a 'chilling effect' but, equally, ISPs are unlikely to have the same commitment to defend an action as the actual publisher. Overall, the Law Commission concluded that because of the 'possible conflict between ... pressure to remove material, even if true, and the emphasis placed upon freedom of expression', together with the likely use of ISPs as 'tactical targets' for litigation, there was a 'strong case for reviewing the way that defamation law impacts on Internet service providers'.[79] This could be achieved by providing complete immunity but, as discussed above, this arguably moves the balance too far in the opposite direction. An alternative suggestion was to extend the innocent dissemination defence in s 1 of the Defamation Act which could include clearer guidance to ISPs on notice procedure by means of a statutorily supported Code of Practice.[80]

Anonymity and CyberSLAPPs

One reason that suit might be sought against an ISP, aside from their actual role in distributing the libel, is the fact that it is identifiable (and may also have assets which make it worth suing), in contrast to the originator of the allegedly defamatory material who will frequently have chosen to remain anonymous or pseudonymous. On a number of occasions, the Supreme Court has expressly supported the right of speakers to remain anonymous as constituting an integral part of the right of free expression guaranteed by the First Amendment.[81] Unless anonymity is treated as a necessary adjunct to this right, then individuals could be deterred from participation in democratic debate because of fear of reprisals or the

---

77 Scoping Study No 2, *op cit* fn 59.

78 Scoping Study No 2, *op cit* fn 59, para 2.32.

79 Scoping Study No 2, *op cit* fn 59, para 2.65. Interestingly, in the first Scoping Study (Law Commission, *op cit* fn 24, para 34) it had been found that 'tactical targeting was not a significant problem in practice', although it was acknowledged that the position of ISPs with respect to s 1 of the Defamation Act 1996 did need further consideration.

80 See Sutter, Chapter 6.

81 See, eg, *Talley v California*, 4 L Ed 2d (1960); *McIntyre v Ohio* 131 L Ed 2d (1996); and *Watchtower Bible v Stratton* 153 L Ed 2d (2002).

fear of being prejudged, for instance. Despite this judicial approval, there are many who have sought to unmask those who act anonymously by means of so-called SLAPP lawsuits.[82] On the other hand, the strongly held view that such actions are antithetical to First Amendment rights has led a number of states to pass anti-SLAPP statutes, of which the Californian example is perhaps the most wide-reaching. Although SLAPP lawsuits and anti-SLAPP statutes arose originally in the context of controversial political speech, courts have interpreted them to cover commercial speech too on the grounds that activities especially of large corporate players are a legitimate matter of public concern.

The use of anonymity and pseudonymity is arguably more widespread on the Internet than in real life, but that does not of itself mean that it is not equally worthy of protection.[83] In recent years, there has been a rapid rise in the numbers of so-called CyberSLAPP cases with the objective of lifting the veil of anonymity.[84] This may be because ISP immunity means that the only possible defendant is the actual author, but, despite the apparent coincidence of the removal of ISP immunity and the rise in CyberSLAPP lawsuits, it is evident that there are frequently motivations other than the recovery of damages. These include mere identification of the anonymous but may also include the intention to impose extrajudicial action such as dismissal in the case of employee defendants. Certainly those initiating CyberSLAPP are usually large corporate actors who seek to identify those who make disparaging comments about their affairs on the Internet, in a situation in which the balance of power between the large organisation and the individual may be reversed.

Some commentators have suggested that there has been too much concentration on the rights of John Doe at the expense of the rights of the corporations affected by vituperative and scurrilous cybersmears.[85] On the other hand, it could be argued that their reputations are not really at risk and that, far from suffering as a result of anonymous cybersmears (which may be understood as nothing more than colourfully expressed opinion), the ability to unmask the anonymous, if granted,

---

82 Strategic lawsuits against public participation.

83 For further discussion of some of these issues see Rowland, D, 'Privacy, freedom of expression and CyberSLAPPs: fostering anonymity on the Internet' (2003) 17 *Int Rev of Law, Computers and Technology* 303.

84 Cybersmear and CyberSLAPP cases have been the subject of extensive academic discussion in the US: see, eg, Smith, B, 'Cybersmearing and the problem of anonymous online speech' (2000) 18 *Comm Law* 3; Sobel, D, 'The process that John Doe is due: addressing the legal challenge to Internet anonymity' (2000) 5 *Va J L & Tech* 3; Furman, J, 'Cybersmear or CyberSLAPP: analyzing defamation suits against online John Does as strategic lawsuits against public participation' (2001) 25 *Seattle U L Rev* 213; Strickland, C, 'Applying *McIntyre v Ohio Elections Commission* to anonymous speech on the Internet and the discovery of John Doe's identity' (2001) 58 *Wash & Lee Rev* 1537; Spencer, S, 'CyberSLAPP suits and John Doe subpoenas: balancing anonymity and accountability in cyberspace' (2001) 19 *Marshall J Computer and Info L* 493; Reder, M and O'Brien, C, 'Corporate cybersmear: employers file John Doe defamation lawsuits seeking the identity of anonymous employee Internet posters' (2001) 8 *Mich Telecomm & Tech L Rev* 195; O'Brien, J, 'Putting a face to a (screen) name' (2002) 70 *Fordham L Rev* 2745; Scileppi, D, 'Anonymous corporate defamation plaintiffs: trampling the First Amendment or protecting the rights of litigants?' (2002) 54 *Fla L Rev* 333; Wilson, S, 'Corporate criticism on the Internet: the fine line between anonymous speech and cybersmear' (2002) 29 *Pepp L Rev* 533; Hines Jr, J, Cramer, M and Berk, P, 'Anonymity, immunity and online defamation' (2003) 4 *Sedona Conf J* 97.

85 See, eg, Wilson, *op cit* fn 84, p 574 and Lidsky, *op cit* fn 8, p 903.

would allow greater power over the individual and result in a significant chilling of speech.[86] Further, corporations also have access to the Internet, giving them an equal opportunity to counteract and respond to any putative reputational damage.

In the absence of a *prima facie* case of defamation, the courts' approach has been to safeguard anonymity to 'foster open communication and debate'.[87] In particular, the court in *Dendrite International v John Doe*[88] has formulated a four-stage test, based not only on the existence of a *prima facie* case, but also on the extent to which disclosure of identity is necessary to proceed, which tries to strike the balance between the freedom of speech and the rights of alleged victims of defamation.[89]

Conclusion

'Intuition suggests that the remarkable features of the Internet ... make it more than simply another medium of communication. It is indeed a revolutionary leap in the distribution of information including [information] about the reputation of individuals.'[90] Do these 'remarkable features', of themselves, affect where the balance should lie between the rights of reputation and those of free speech? Does the interchange of speech on the Internet come close to the marketplace of ideas or a never-ending world wide conversation? Does it matter if the opinions expressed in that conversation are inane or outrageous, or commercial, personal or political? Is the Internet a public or a private forum? In reality, not only is the Internet capable of acting as both private and public forum, as passive information provider and vehicle for interactive interchange, and as propagator of a spectrum of different types on information, but it also has global reach. It is 'not simply an extension of past communications technology. It is a new means of creating continuous relationships in a manner that could not previously have been contemplated'.[91] The use of common keystrokes can mean that an intended cosy chat can be heard by the whole world. Within this environment there may be a higher probability that potentially defamatory comments come to the attention of their target,[92] but whether there will be a remedy still depends on the application of existing legal rules and the pre-existing tension between rights of reputation and those of free speech. Some of the speech may be confined to cyberspace and be the interchange between confederates on bulletin boards acting anonymously or pseudonymously, but that such speech can have effects outside of its originating cybercommunity is evident in cybersmear cases. The Internet has been seen by certain civil liberties organisations as a forum for entirely free speech and these have resisted, often successfully, attempts by governments to regulate content.[93] These are primarily

---

86 See, eg, O'Brien, *op cit* fn 84.
87 140 F Supp 2d 1088, p 1092.
88 775 A 2d 756 (2001).
89 See also, eg, O'Brien, *op cit* fn 84.
90 *Dow Jones v Gutnick* [2002] HCA 56, para 164.
91 *Ibid*, para 118.
92 See, eg, Edwards, *op cit* fn 20, p 249.
93 The prime example being the litigation engaged in by the American Civil Liberties Union in *Reno v ACLU*, 521 US 844, p 870 (1997); *ACLU v Reno*, 929 F Supp 824 (1996); and *Ashcroft v ACLU*, 217 F 3d 162.

dominated by the US and reflect the prominence given to First Amendment rights. Although at one time the Internet was dominated by US use, this is increasingly less true and, as a result, it can be argued that this influence on speech is waning, to be replaced by an assessment of individual rights in which free speech is not accorded such a pre-eminent position. On the other hand, it could be argued that the argot of the Internet is, by now, well known and those who use its diverse fora as a medium of communication should be deemed to accept implicitly both the consequent benefits and dangers.

A comparison of recent judgments shows that, far from moving towards a common position, the divergences between local legal and cultural norms in the approach to cross-border defamation and the balance between free expression and the rights of reputation protected by the law of defamation have been emphasised. Despite arguments for new legal rules, as the Internet increases in ubiquity, these divergences appear likely to increase rather than diminish.

Chapter 6
Internet Service Providers and Liability
Gavin Sutter

Introduction

The arrival of the World Wide Web in the early to mid-1990s opened up Internet technology to the average individual. Internet access is now readily and cheaply available in the home from a wide range of commercial Internet service providers, or ISPs. These intermediaries provide access to the Internet either in exchange for a subscription fee usually payable as a monthly direct debit from the subscriber's bank account, or by claiming a proportion of the customer's call charges. Often, ISPs offer more sophisticated additional services alongside this basic access service, such as hosting facilities, access to a subscriber-network of bulletin boards, simultaneous chat facilities, and so on. As with any service industry, ISPs face potential legal liability in relation to the services they offer should these prove defective. For instance, it may be that in a given set of circumstances an ISP could prove liable for a failure in its communications service. Increasingly, the major area of development in relation to ISP liability is that of responsibility relating to material provided by a third party and which is passed across or stored on an ISP's servers for a greater or lesser period.

ISP liability for third party provided content

The question of the appropriate level of responsibility to be placed upon the ISP in relation to content provided by third parties is complex, and largely influenced by policy. In the online world, it is often very difficult, sometimes impossible, to track down the source of unlawful material, such as child pornography, or a defamatory posting made to an online bulletin board. It logically follows that the party to whom those seeking the removal or deletion of such material should turn is the ISP responsible for its transmission or hosting. It does not automatically follow that the ISP should be held liable as a 'co-conspirator', equally responsible for the material as the original content provider, yet there may be circumstances in which it might be appropriate to impose some level of liability upon the ISP. Recent years have seen the emergence of a global consensus that ISPs should not be subject to absolute liability for the actions of the content provider. Typically, a qualified liability standard will be applied, with liability arising only where the ISP is in possession of sufficient knowledge (which may, according to the specific regime, be actual or constructive) of the unlawful conduct. In some instances it may be a significant factor that an ISP stands to gain from copying, possessing or transmitting the material. For instance, under the UK Obscene Publications legislation, mere possession of obscene material (excepting child pornography) is not an offence, whereas publication for gain or possession with intent to do so is a criminal act.[1]

---

1 Obscene Publications Act 1959, s 2; Obscene Publications Act 1964, s 1; cf Protection of Children Act 1978, s 1.

European Directive 2000/31/EC directly addresses the issue of ISP liability in this context under s 4, entitled 'Liability of Internet Service Providers'. The provisions in this section deal separately with transmission, caching, and hosting activities, applying a sliding scale of liability, increased liability corresponding with increased control over information on an ISP's servers. For the purposes of the Directive, an ISP is 'any natural or legal person providing an information society service'.[2] Information society services 'are services within the meaning of Article 1(2) of Directive 98/34/EC as amended by Directive 98/48/EC'.[3] The amended Article 1(2) of Directive 98/34/EC – the Technical Standards and Regulations Directive – defines information society services so as to include 'any service normally provided for remuneration, at a distance, by electronic means and at the individual request of a recipient of services'. The article elaborates further:

For the purposes of this definition:

- 'at a distance': means that the service is provided without the parties being simultaneously present,
- 'by electronic means': means that the service is sent initially and received at its destination by means of electronic equipment for the processing (including digital compression) and storage of data, and entirely transmitted, conveyed and received by wire, by radio, by optical means or by other electromagnetic means,
- 'at the individual request of a recipient of services': means that the service is provided through the transmission of data on individual request.

The normal activities of an ISP clearly fall within these delineations.

Article 12 of the E-Commerce Directive is concerned with the situation in which the ISP is a 'mere conduit', or a pass-through provider which simply passes on information provided by a third party customer, exercises no control over the content of transmissions, makes no alterations whatever to these transmissions, and does not store them any longer than strictly necessary to facilitate transmission. Where these conditions are met, the ISP will not be held liable in respect of any third party information which it transmits. This is subject to the proviso that at national level an ISP may be required to terminate or prevent an infringement. This would, however, be carried out as the result of a court order and thus the ISP would have actual and official notice of specific unlawful material, a very different situation from the imposition of liability upon the ISP for transmission of a data stream, the contents of which it could not reasonably be expected to have been aware.

Article 13 deals with third party information which is cached on an ISP's servers. Caching is here defined so as to include '... automatic, intermediate and temporary storage ... performed for the sole purpose of making more efficient the information's onward transmission to other recipients of the service upon their request ...'. This definition is likely in practice to mean a different delineation between caching and hosting than commonly understood. Returns from a search engine, for instance, will often provide a link to a cached copy on the search engine's servers. This cached copy may be several months, or even a couple of

---

2 Directive 2000/31/EC, Article 2(b).
3 Directive 2000/31/EC, Article 2(a).

years, old, and would seem unlikely to qualify as being 'automatic, intermediate and temporary storage' of the information. The Article 13 immunity from liability for third party provided information is conditional upon the absence of actual knowledge of the unlawful information: as soon as an ISP is in receipt of actual notification of its presence on the ISP's servers, it must remove or delete the material in question or face liability in respect of the same. Again, as with information merely transmitted, a national court may order an ISP to co-operate in the termination or prevention of an infringement.

The Article 14 immunity in respect of third party information hosted by the ISP on its servers is the most qualified of the immunities provided by the E-Commerce Directive, and reflects the greater potential for control on the part of the ISP over the material. In order for the immunity to apply, the ISP must not be in receipt of actual notification of the unlawful nature of the material in question, but there must also be an absence of knowledge of any facts or circumstances that make the illegality apparent. 'Upon obtaining knowledge or awareness', the ISP must '[act] expeditiously to remove or to disable access to the information'. The importance of such a qualified immunity for ISPs is readily apparent: unlike a traditional publisher, an ISP cannot be expected to be aware of the content of all information that its subscribers upload to its servers. Knowledge of the unlawful nature of content is especially important in relation to defamation, for instance. Very often the knowledge that a posting is defamatory may require more than even awareness of a specific posting (which may be one of hundreds on only one of thousands of pages hosted): for example, in the UK case of *Godfrey v Demon*,[4] the only indication that the posting complained of was made by someone other than the plaintiff lay in the fact that the plaintiff's forename was spelt incorrectly.

Article 15 provides, in relation to all the services covered by Articles 12, 13 and 14 – transmission, caching and hosting – that there is to be no general obligation imposed to monitor information which passes through or is hosted on their systems. This prevention of the imposition of any duty to monitor does not, however, prevent Member States from imposing duties which require that some level of care be taken in relation to what is stored or transmitted. National governments may also impose a duty to promptly inform the appropriate authorities where notice is received of illegal activities or such are discovered. ISPs would also be expected to remove the information in question promptly in such a case. Further, the option is left open for Member States to oblige the handover of identification details in respect of an ISP's subscribers with whom they have an agreement to provide hosting services.

Further, Articles 2–4 of the Copyright in the Information Society Directive[5] provide a collection of exclusive rights for copyright holders in respect of reproduction, communication to the public and distribution of their works online. Clearly such exclusive rights pose problems for ISPs whose servers are used to communicate and store information. They are, however, mitigated in part by Article 5, which provides an exception in relation to 'temporary acts of reproduction':

---

4   [1999] EMLR 542; see discussion below.
5   Directive 2001/29/EC.

> Temporary acts of reproduction ... which are transient or incidental, which are an integral and essential part of a technological process whose sole purpose is to enable ... a transmission in a network between third parties by an intermediary ... shall be exempted from the reproduction right ...

In other words, an ISP which is involved merely in transmitting the information or providing access to it, for example by providing a subscriber with access to an artist's website where an authorised copy of an artwork is located, will have a valid defence to the reproduction right. It should also be noted that the qualified immunities in Articles 12–14 of the E-Commerce Directive apply equally to copyright as to other forms of third party provided Internet content.

In the UK, the issue of ISP liability for third party provided content first came before the courts in the case of *Godfrey v Demon*.[6] It is a general principle of English defamation law that the publisher of a libel faces strict liability.[7] The Defamation Act 1996 was passed at a time when the World Wide Web was still a relatively new development, the commercial exploitation of which the government was keen to encourage. Concerns were raised relating to the position of an ISP publishing material online by virtue of making hosting services available. It was considered inequitable to impose the same level of liability upon an ISP as a traditional print publisher. Whereas a print publisher has complete control, considering everything it publishes at length before printing, referring to the company lawyers as necessary, an ISP which provides hosting services has little or no control over what subscribers choose to upload to its servers. Section 1 of the 1996 Act, which effectively places the old common law defence of innocent dissemination on a statutory footing, was passed with ISPs particularly in mind. This section provides a defence where the party responsible for publishing the material, such as an ISP, is only responsible for publishing a libel insofar as it is made available via the ISP's servers, is not the 'author, editor or publisher' of the defamation,[8] can demonstrate that it did not know and had no reason to believe that the statement in question was defamatory,[9] and can show that it took reasonable care in relation to the publication of the statement.[10]

The first question that naturally arises is whether an ISP might be categorised as a publisher for the purposes of s 1. Under s 1(3), so far as is here relevant:

> A person shall not be considered the author, editor or publisher ... if he is only involved –
>
> ...
>
> (c) in processing, making copies of, distributing or selling any electronic medium in or on which the statement is recorded, or in operating or providing any equipment,

---

6   [1999] EMLR 542.
7   *Hulton & Co v Jones* [1910] AC 20.
8   Defamation Act 1996, s 1(1)(a).
9   *Ibid*, s 1(1)(b).
10 *Ibid*, s 1(1)(c).

system or service by means of which the statement is retrieved, copied, distributed or made available in electronic form;

...

(e) as the operator of or provider of access to a communications system by means of which the statement is transmitted, or made available, by a person over whom he has no effective control.

These provisions have been clearly drafted in order to prevent ISPs from being automatically classified as publishers. Significantly, however, there is something of a Catch 22 in these provisions, in that ISPs must be careful to comply fully with the s 1(1) requirements, including the duty to take reasonable care in relation to material which is placed online, and overstepping the mark by assuming editorial responsibility and thus falling without the s 1(3) parameters will occasion the same level of liability as a print publisher.

The application of s 1 to ISPs was at issue in *Godfrey v Demon*. This case was a preliminary hearing in order to establish whether the ISP could escape liability by relying on the s 1 defence. The material facts were that a third party posted a message to the soc.culture.thai Usenet newsgroup, which Demon hosted but did not actively monitor, stating that all Thai women were intellectually deficient and fit only for employment as prostitutes. The message, which claimed to be from the plaintiff, was apparently posted by someone else. The plaintiff contacted Demon and demanded that the posting be removed as it was of a defamatory nature; however, the ISP failed to remove the posting prior to its automatic expiry several days later. The plaintiff then proceeded to bring an action in defamation against Demon. The court found that while Demon was not classifiable as an author, editor or publisher, the ISP could not rely on the s 1 defence from the point that it had been in receipt of actual notice of the defamatory posting but failed to have it removed from the servers. Significantly, however, the court held on the facts that the defence would be valid prior to the receipt of such notice. In future cases absent actual knowledge, it may be presumed that when seeking to establish whether the ISP took reasonable care in relation to the publication and had no reason to believe that it was defamatory, the courts would look to the context of the posting. For instance, while Demon could not, prior to the receipt of actual knowledge, reasonably have been expected to have been aware of a single defamatory posting on a newsgroup dedicated to discussion of Thai culture, had the newsgroup instead been entitled something like 'Gossip Central', with a reputation for soliciting and propagating potentially defamatory postings, the court may have viewed the ISP's position differently. The *Godfrey v Demon* judgment has been confirmed in the later case of *Totalise plc v Motley Fool Ltd*,[11] in which the court further held that an ISP must, in order to fully escape liability, hand over any identifying details it holds relating to the source of a libel which are requested by the claimant.

Although *prima facie* a straightforward decision, with Demon clearly at fault for failure to remove while in receipt of actual knowledge, civil liberties interests in the UK feared that this posed a danger to freedom of expression, whereby the threat of a defamation suit could be used to suppress free information. For instance, an

---

11 2001 WL 1479825; [2002] EMLR 20.

undergraduate student uses free web space provided by his ISP to set up a website detailing various human rights abuses by multinational companies. A leading manufacturer of training shoes objects to the website as it exposes the company's use of child labour in the third world factories where its products are produced. All of these allegations are perfectly true. The company, however, contacts the ISP and threatens to sue if they are not removed. In theory, the ISP should consider whether the material is likely to be defamatory or if the complaint is vexatious. In practice, however, it seems much more likely that the ISP would not take the risk of incurring liability (and the associated high cost of damages) and would instead remove the information as requested by the company. It would be entirely understandable for the ISP to act in this way: the potential threat to free expression online is readily apparent.

Recent developments in ISP liability within Europe

Similarities may be seen in the approach taken to date by the UK courts in applying the defences found in s 1 of the Defamation Act and that provided more generally by Article 14 of the E-Commerce Directive. Effectively both envisage a form of notice and take-down procedure whereby as soon as the ISP is in receipt of sufficient knowledge of unlawful content, it is obliged to remove or delete the material with reasonable speed.

In the UK, the Department of Trade and Industry (DTI) launched a public consultation on the Directive and its enactment in August 2001. Several respondents argued that there needed to be a clarification of certain technical issues relating to, for example, the delineation of transmission and caching. Also criticised was the burden placed upon ISPs to decide whether material complained of was indeed unlawful and should be removed from their servers. A popular suggestion made by respondents to the consultation was the introduction of an industry code of practice, possibly with statutory backing, setting out clear notice and take-down procedures for ISPs to follow. A major problem which the respondents identified with the Directive was that while it uses the term 'actual knowledge', there is no set definition of this phrase. Various suggestions were made to rectify this along the lines of codes of practice upon which ISPs could rely.[12] The DTI issued a second consultation in early 2002, this time with a draft of the E-Commerce (EC Directive) Regulations attached. Regulations 17, 18 and 19 repeated the wording of the qualified immunities for ISPs in the Directive almost verbatim, although the Regulations do make clear that the immunities apply to both civil and criminal unlawful content.[13] A significant addition to the Directive's provisions may be found in reg 22. Reflecting the criticisms made of the Directive in the earlier DTI consultation, reg 22 goes some way to address the issue of what constitutes 'actual knowledge'. The regulation provides a non-exhaustive, illustrative list of factors which a court may consider in determining whether a service provider has received

---

12 For further information on the responses to this consultation, see *DTI Consultation on Implementation of the Directive on Electronic Commerce (2000/31/EC): Summary of Responses*, available at www.dti.gov.uk.
13 E-Commerce (EC Directive) Regulations 2002, SI 2002/2013, regs 17–19.

en if no such control over the use made by others of an ISP's system to create
ng copies were possible, this offered no defence; the view here was simply
a business cannot operate within the limits of the law, the question to be
hould be whether it should carry on that business at all.

confused reasoning and conflicting judgments were addressed by the
Millennium Copyright Act 1998 (DMCA). This legislation introduced a new
o the US Copyright Act, providing a series of qualified immunities for ISPs
ct of third party content. First, an immunity from copyright infringement is
to pass-through providers whose systems automatically transmit material
d by a third party. The material in question must be transmitted unmolested
rvice provider, and only as an automatic response to the commands of a
ty: the service provider must have no part in the selection of the recipients.
his material may only be stored in the system for as long as it is required to
the transmission. Broadly similar provisions are made in relation to
with the addition of a requirement that any associated storage of cached
rt of 'an automated technical process'. Additionally, duties to comply with
s which may be imposed by the content provider, such as limitation of
only those who have paid an associated fee, as well as to promptly remove
infringing material upon actual notice of the same, are placed upon the
ovider. The DMCA also provides in s 512 a qualified immunity from
liability for ISPs hosting third party content where material is put online
d party subscriber. This immunity is conditional upon the fact that the ISP
er actual knowledge of infringement nor any awareness of 'facts or
ces' from which the infringement is apparent. Once in receipt of actual
of an infringement, the ISP must see that it is promptly removed from
. Further, an ISP which retains the right and ability in its system to
activities of its subscribers in relation to material which they upload to
n the ISP's servers will not be able to benefit from the immunity where it
benefited financially from the infringement. Any infringement must be
blocked promptly upon notification of its existence.

isions of s 512 bear clear similarity to those in the E-Commerce Directive
ommerce Regulations. There is, however, one very significant provision
A which is not mirrored in the EU and UK legislation. Under s 512(g) of
ation, an ISP will face no liability towards any aggrieved party where it
good faith to remove claimed infringing material. There is, however, an
ovided to this general rule in relation to material which, at the direction
criber, is being hosted on an ISP's servers and which is removed
a notice claiming copyright infringement. In order to be able to take
the immunity in such a case, the ISP must take reasonable steps to
he subscriber is promptly notified that the material has been removed
ly fully with the provisions in the DMCA for reposting that content.
is offers the subscriber a right of appeal where the material has been
ved pursuant to a vexatious or false notice of infringement. It remains
w well this will operate in practice over time; however, some form of
lure for the reposting of material unfairly removed may offer a degree
or free expression, helping to mitigate against the perceived threat to
e wake of *Godfrey*.

notice through any means of contact that the service provider has made available in
compliance with reg 6(1)(c). Regulation 6(1) obliges an ISP to make certain
information available to the end user 'in a form ... which is easily, directly and
permanently accessible'. Regulation 6(1)(c) refers to the service provider's contact
details, including email addresses, which facilitate rapid and direct communication
with the ISP. This requirement may easily be met by the placement on an ISP's
homepage of an obvious 'contact us' link, pointing to email, telephone and other
contact details. A dedicated complaints department email address may be helpful,
providing that it is regularly checked for incoming mail. Other factors which reg 22
lists for the consideration of the courts are:

  (b)   the extent to which any notice includes –

        (i)   the full name and address of the sender of the notice;

        (ii)   details of the location of the information in question; and

        (iii) details of the unlawful nature of the activity or information in question.

While it offers some form of clarification, Internet industry commentators remain
critical of this regulation, arguing that it still leaves too much uncertainty, at least
prior to an interpretation by the courts – and, post-*Godfrey*, no one wants to be the
test case. ISPs also remain concerned that no accepted standard exists with respect
to the time frame in which they are expected to act. The Regulations repeat the
Directive's requirement that once aware of the content in question, the ISP must act
'expeditiously' to see that it is removed: the lengths to which this is to be taken are
not yet clear. For instance, is acting within 24 hours sufficient? What about
weekends? If the company offices are only open Monday to Friday, is 24 *working*
hours sufficient, or must the responsible company employee be keeping a check on
complaints communicated during the weekend? It may be that in the near future
industry codes of practice may offer some degree of safeguard, particularly if the
suggestion made by some respondents to the original DTI consultation on the
Directive that such a code should provide some form of 'safe harbour' whereby
ISPs who follow it in good faith would be excused any form of liability for third
party content.[14] In the meantime, however, it seems likely that ISPs will continue to
take the safe option of summarily removing material complained of with all due
haste.

A significant omission in both the Directive and the Regulations is that of linking.
Where an ISP hosts a link to an external page, either in the form of a simple
hypertext link or a frame, containing unlawful material, it is at present uncertain as
to what liability may arise on the part of the ISP. Where a link provided by a third
party connects to another page containing a defamatory statement, it is likely that
this is sufficient to constitute a publication for defamation purposes. The ISP may,
however, have a defence where it can satisfy the requirements of s 1 of the
Defamation Act 1996. If the link also contains sufficient information to diffuse the
defamatory nature of the material linked to, the two may be taken together as a
whole to constitute one publication, thus negating any liability which may arise.[15]

---

14 DTI, *op cit* fn 12.

15 Collins, M, *The Law of Defamation and the Internet*, 2001, Oxford: OUP, para 5.30.

Article 14/reg 19 may also provide a defence which should be relatively easy for the ISP to prove, as the defamatory publication would arise out of a single link on a single Internet page which may be only one of hundreds of thousands of such files hosted by the ISP. It would therefore, in the absence of actual knowledge, be highly unlikely that, post-*Godfrey*, a court would (save in the presence of actual knowledge) find that the ISP could be said to have had sufficient awareness for liability to arise. In relation to all types of content, the nature of the link, its context, and any notoriety that the page it is located on may have acquired might be factors which would influence a ruling on liability.[16] For instance, a page with links such as 'Live Russian Lolitas' or 'Beat the Labels: Free MP3s of latest releases', and which has a reputation for containing child pornography or sound files which infringe copyright, may be considered in context to give rise to sufficient constructive knowledge on the part of the host ISP to occasion some degree of liability relating to the distribution of such content.

The Copyright and Related Rights Regulations 2003[17] make various amendments to the Copyright, Designs and Patents Act 1988, essentially enacting the European Copyright in the Information Society Directive and updating the UK copyright legislation for the Internet age. Regulation 8(1) inserts a new s 28A into the 1988 Act. Section 28A adds to the list of permitted acts in relation to copyright the making of temporary copies ('other than a computer program or database') where such copying is:

> ... transient or incidental, [and] ... is an integral and essential part of a technological process ... the sole purpose of which is to enable –
>
> (a) a transmission of the work in a network between third parties by an intermediary; or
>
> (b) a lawful use of the work;
>
> and which has no independent economic significance.

This new section gives effect in UK law to the Directive's Article 5 exemption of transmission service providers from the ambit of the exclusive right of reproduction granted to copyright owners in respect of their works in the digital environment.

The provisions for injunctions to be made against service providers in certain circumstances set out in reg 27 (which inserts ss 97A and 191JA into the Copyright, Designs and Patents Act 1988) merits attention as it illustrates the link between the E-Commerce Regulations and copyright law. 'Service Provider' is given the same definition as in the E-Commerce Regulations.[18] These new sections grant the High Court (in Scotland, the Court of Session) a 'power to grant an injunction where that service provider has actual knowledge of another person using their services to infringe copyright'[19] '[or] to infringe a performer's property right'.[20] Both new sections carry an identical provision outlining certain factors that a court shall

16 See above for discussion of the potential impact of *Godfrey v Demon* [1999] EMLR 542.
17 SI 2003/2498.
18 See Copyright, Designs and Patents Act 1988, ss 97A(3) and 191JA(3).
19 *Ibid*, s 97A(1).
20 *Ibid*, s 191JA(1).

---

consider when determining whether the service provid[] knowledge':

> ... a court shall take into account all matters which app[] circumstances to be relevant and, amongst other things, shall[]
>
> (a) whether a service provider has received a notice throug[] available in accordance with Regulation 6(1)(c) of the []Regulations 2002 (SI 2002/2013); and
>
> (b) the extent to which any notice includes –
>
> (i) the full name and address of the sender of the noti[]
>
> (ii) details of the infringement in question.[21]

The similarity between these provisions and reg 22 of [] is readily apparent; indeed (save for the omission of []the location of the information in question'), the wo[] not the only similarity here: the new sections in the [] being to some degree welcome, unavoidably raise th[] with respect to there being no firm outlining of the b[] least prior to interpretation of these sections by the [] seems likely that s 97A, which relates to 'actual kno[] [the service provider's] service to infringe copyrigh[] for the embattled music industry in its attempt to[] networks perpetuating the trade in infringing dig[] recordings. Where sufficient actual knowledge car[] matter for the courts to grant an injunction requiri[] to whom they provide Internet access from using[] sound files; effectively this might mean the cancell[]

The US provides an interesting point of compa[] ISP liability in respect of third party content. W[] developed in the field of defamation, the earl[] arena. *Playboy v Frena*[22] concerned a bulletin[] subscribers to upload material in which the[] copyright. The court found the operator of the B[] due to the direct copying undertaken by the sy[] images. The difficulty here is that while it migh[] system doing the copying on a technical level,[] by a third party. In *Religious Technology Center*[] the defendant ISP liable on grounds that the IS[] clear intent to copy: this could not be so if anc[] to be made. The court in *Playboy v Webbworl*[]

21 *Ibid*, ss 97a(2) and 191JA(2).
22 839 F Supp 1552 (MD Fla, 1993).
23 907 F Supp 1361 (ND Cal, 1995).
24 968 F Supp 1167 (ND Ill, 1997).

---

that ev[]
infring[]
that if[]
asked s[]

Such[]
Digital[]
s 512 in[]
in respe[]
granted[]
Provide[]
by the s[]
third pa[]
Further,[]
facilitate[]
caching,[]
copy is p[]
condition[]
access to[]
copyright[]
service p[]
copyright[]
by the thi[]
has neith[]
circumsta[]
notificatio[]
the server[]
control the[]
be hosted[]
has directly[]
removed o[]

The prov[]
and UK E-C[]
in the DMC[]
the US legis[]
has acted in[]
exception pr[]
of the subs[]
pursuant to[]
advantage o[]
ensure that t[]
and/or com[]
Effectively, t[]
unfairly rem[]
to be seen ho[]
official proce[]
of protection[]
the same in th[]

Outside of the copyright arena, ISPs in the US are provided with a wide immunity against civil liability for third party content uploaded to their servers by the content provider.[25] The basis of this immunity lies in the remnants of the Communications Decency Act 1996. This legislation was much vilified at the time of its passage due to other provisions which created new offences in relation to online pornography and its being made available to minors, and which were eventually found unconstitutional and struck out by the US Supreme Court.[26] Section 230, which remains, provides:

> No provider or user of an interactive computer service shall be treated as the publisher or speaker of any information provided by another information content provider ...

The leading case in the interpretation of s 230 is *Zeran v America Online*, in which it was held that no liability for hosting allegedly defamatory material would attach to the defendant, despite the fact that the ISP was clearly in receipt of actual knowledge of the claimed defamation yet failed to remove it.[27] The judgment in *Zeran* made reference to the fact that a key intention of the immunity was to encourage ISPs to monitor content and to adopt blocking and filtering measures, without fear of setting themselves up for potential liability under the *Stratton Oakmont v Prodigy* ruling in which an ISP was found liable in respect of third party provided content due to its having held itself out as a 'family-friendly' ISP, and taking active steps to monitor content, thus assuming responsibility for all material made available on its servers.[28] Whether commercial ISPs in general will in practice take it upon themselves to function as the moral guardians of the online society is quite another matter.

Zeran has been followed in several later cases, including *Blumenthal v Drudge*, in which the court held that despite America Online's editorial control over Drudge, a gossip columnist, the ISP could not be held liable for any defamatory comments he might make on grounds of the s 230 immunity which applies even where the ISP plays an active, aggressive role in making the content available to the public.[29] In *Ben Ezra, Wenstein & Co v America Online*,[30] erroneous stock values attributed to the plaintiff were held not to give rise to any liability on behalf of the ISP as the information had been provided by a third party. '*Zeran*', the court ruled, 'plainly immunizes computer service providers like AOL from liability for information that originates with third parties'. *Schneider v Amazon.com*[31] applied the immunity to the operator of what is, in effect, a form of bulletin board system. This case arose in relation to various allegedly defamatory remarks which various individuals

---

25 Section 230 of the Communications Decency Act 1996 explicitly excludes from its ambit matters of criminal law (with specific mention being made of child pornography and other obscene material) and matters of intellectual property law; see respectively ss 230(e)(1) and 230(e)(2). Also exempted is communications privacy law (s 230(e)(4)).

26 *ACLU v Reno*, No 96-511 (1997) (USSC).

27 129 F 3d 327 (4th Cir 1997). For a more in-depth analysis of cyber-defamation, see Rowland, Chapter 5.

28 23 Med LR 1794 (SC Nassau County 1995).

29 992 F Supp 44, pp 51–52.

30 DNM 1999.

31 Case No 46791-3-I, 31 P 3d 37 (Washington Court of Appeal, 17 September 2001).

included in reviews of books authored by the claimant, which had been uploaded to the reviews section of the entries for those works on Amazon.com's website.[32]

During 2003, the s 230 immunity was applied by US courts to a non-commercial publisher for the first time. In *Batzel v Smith, Cremers & Museum Society Network,*[33] the facts were as follows. Smith, the first named defendant, claimed to have overheard a conversation in which the claimant said that she was related to Gestapo chief Heinrich Himmler. Smith therefore concluded that Batzel's collection of European paintings which he had seen on display in her house were in fact stolen works of art, looted by the Nazis and in her possession as a result of her descent. Smith sent an email outlining this to Cremers, the editor of the Museum Society Network, a non-commercial organisation which publishes information about stolen paintings. Cremers did not inform Smith that he would publish the email; however, he did so with minor edits, and sent it on to 1,000 Museum Society Network mailing list subscribers. Batzel became aware of this, and issued proceedings against Smith, Cremers and the Museum Society Network. The Ninth Circuit Appeals Court, overruling the lower court, decided that the minor amendments made by Cremers were not sufficient to render it a separate piece of expression, and so the email forwarded by Cremers remained content provided by Smith. The Appeal Court found that whether s 230 could be applied to Cremers and the Museum Society Network hinged upon whether Cremers had a reasonable belief that Smith's email was intended for publication, and the matter was referred back to the lower court for a decision on the facts.

So what active steps should an ISP take in order to limit its potential liability in respect of third party provided and uploaded content? As regards simple 'pass-through' providers and caching, it should be a fairly straightforward matter of following the E-Commerce Directive and Regulations, or the DMCA where appropriate, to the letter, simply passing on the information when requested, to the addressee, and without making any alteration to the content or retaining it for any longer than strictly necessary, all of which can be achieved by setting up the ISP's network in the appropriate way.

The situation becomes more complex in relation to ISPs who wish to provide hosting services. The first key step here is the adoption of a clear, acceptable use policy to regulate the relationship with the end user of the services on offer. These should make clear the kinds of material which are unacceptable and should not be uploaded. The policy should also incorporate a notice and takedown policy, which informs users of the contact details of a specific person or office to which they can report any violations, such as a defamatory posting to a BBS, or an infringing MP3 copy of a song, and who will then be able to take action on behalf of the company to remove the offending material. These contact details should be clearly linked to

---

32 Similar application was made by the Illinois Court of Appeal in *Barrett v Fonorow*, 343 Ill App 3d 1184; 799 NE 2d 916; 279 Ill Dec 113, in which the court held that an Internet website was indeed a 'provider or user of an interactive computer service' within the meaning of the Communications Decency Act definition of 'interactive computer service': 'any information service, system, or access software provider that provides or enables computer access by multiple users to a computer server, including specifically a service or system that provides access to the Internet' – see s 230(f)(2).

33 No 01-56380 DC, No CV-00-09590-SVW, 24 June 2003.

from the ISP's home page in order to satisfy the requirements of the UK E-Commerce legislation.[34]

The contract of service with the subscriber should also contain some form of liability clause, where possible addressing both the ISP's provision of services and conduct of the subscriber. The clause should provide that the subscriber agrees not to post certain types of material to the ISP's servers, and that should (s)he do so, (s)he will indemnify the ISP against liability in respect of the same. Where such a clause is enforceable (remembering that in respect of consumer contracts, which the vast majority of these are likely to be, there are the provisions of the Unfair Contract Terms Directive and associated UK legislation to be met, alongside other requirements of consumer protection law), it will not prevent the ISP from any legal liability that may arise; however, the ISP will be able to sue the subscriber in question for recovery of losses. The usefulness of this particular approach in practice may be doubted, given that there will be few subscribers who will have the economic resources to meet such costs;[35] nevertheless, it may at least provide some form of deterrent.

Another very simple but certainly effective measure for an ISP to take would be to refuse to host certain types of Internet site, such as peer-to-peer file swapping sites on the Napster model, or gossip sites and newsgroups designed specifically to attract salacious and potentially libellous content. Where sites already hosted cause legal problems for the ISP by carrying on such activities, it goes without saying that the company should consider removing them from the servers, and terminating the relevant subscriber accounts. At no stage, however, should an ISP adopt a policy of general monitoring of its servers, as while ISPs, even in the US as regards copyright infringement under the DMCA, are obliged to work to a minimum standard of care, by actively monitoring content on their servers they risk opening themselves up to liability on a very broad scale. Article 15 of the E-Commerce Directive, with which the UK Regulations are compliant, merely prevents Member States from imposing upon service providers a legal duty to monitor all content they make available: it does not prevent any such duty and associated liability from being voluntarily assumed by an ISP.

Conclusion

As the World Wide Web matures, there seems to be an ever increasing maze of novel legal problems requiring novel solutions – or at least new ways of applying old legal concepts. The issue of service provider liability for third party provided content is one such area which will require further development and clarification in coming years. The potential threat to freedom of expression raised by the application of the s 1 defence in *Godfrey* has not been addressed by either the E-Commerce Directive or the subsequent UK Regulations. The exact delineation of

---

34 See the UK E-Commerce (EC Directive) Regulations 2002, reg 6(1)(c) and above discussion thereof.
35 In *Godfrey v Demon* [1999] EMLR 542 the ISP ended up paying out a reported £500,000 between damages and costs for both sides.

'actual knowledge' under these provisions remains to be clarified, either by the courts or by industry codes of practice – or both. Regulation 22 is a step in the right direction for the UK; however, many service providers still feel that it is insufficiently certain, and are displeased at the notion of waiting for case law to interpret the application of this regulation: no one wants to be the test case. Also remaining to be clarified in practice are such concepts as acting 'expeditiously', and the exact distinction between such concepts as hosting and caching, particularly where the EU Directive and corresponding UK Regulations would appear to place a different interpretation upon the duration of caching activities than is commonly held in practice.

In the long term, it can be said with a fair degree of certainty that the EU and the UK will maintain a position of qualified immunities, and that there will be no introduction of any uber-liberal regime such as that which applies in respect of certain content in the US, under s 230 of the Communications Decency Act, as interpreted in *Zeran*. Indeed, it must be noted that the current US position post-*Zeran* is very far in effect from what Congress intended when it passed that legislation in 1996. The most likely next step in the UK will be the introduction of industry codes of conduct under the auspices of an organisation such as the Internet Service Providers Association over the next few years, particularly in response to future developments as reg 22 is applied by the courts. Whether any such codes of conduct are left to develop on an entirely voluntary basis or are given some form of statutory backing providing that an ISP which abides by the codes will not face liability remains to be seen.

Chapter 7
The Digital Divide: Why the 'The' is Misleading

Daniel Paré[1]

As the global economy proceeds headlong into the Information Age, greater attention is being given to the disparities between the information-rich and the information-poor. It is increasingly apparent that greater reliance on digital technologies may foster new, and widen existing, asymmetries among countries and population segments within countries. Central to this is the concept of the digital divide. This term is ordinarily used to denote disparities in access to the Internet and the Web. In this chapter I argue that the binary distinction between haves and have-nots conveyed by the term 'the digital divide' is inappropriate. The 'the' conveys a flawed view of what is, in fact, a compendium of interrelated social, economic and technological considerations that influence Internet access and use. It also presupposes the presence of uniform imperatives for using technology and the deriving of uniform benefits from that usage.

In developing this argument, the ways in which the digital divide manifests itself in the e-commerce activities of small and medium-sized enterprises (SMEs) in eight developing countries is examined. If the goal of fostering greater inclusion in the global economy is to be attained, much greater sensitivity needs to be given to how the Internet and the Web are being used in different national and sub-national business settings where these technologies already have a presence. Socio-economic and technological factors combined with the motivations for Internet and Web use have direct repercussions for the success and failure of strategies aimed at bridging digital disparities through the promotion of electronic trading. This highlights the need for policy interventions that are based on evidence rather than normative assertions about technological possibilities.

Technology access and the digital divide

Throughout the last decade, the Internet experienced phenomenal growth. The Internet Software Consortium estimates that the number of individual computers connected to the Internet grew from 1.3 million in January 1993 to more than 233 million in January 2004.[2] In terms of people connected to the Internet, the rate of growth has been equally impressive, expanding from approximately 16 million in 1995 to more than 600 million at the end of 2002.[3] Estimates of the global online population for 2004 are in the range of 850 million people.[4] Despite this dramatic

---

1 Thanks to Ingrid Schenk for her comments on earlier drafts of this chapter.
2 Internet Systems Consortium, *Internet Domain Survey*, January 2004, at www.isc.org/index.pl?/ops/ds.
3 NUA, *How Many Online?*, 2003, at www.nua.ie/surveys/how_many_online/world.html.
4 ClickZ Network, *Population Explosion!*, at www.clickz.com/stats/big_picture/geographics/print.php/5911_151151.

growth, large disparities in Internet access and usage persist. More than 80% of the global online population reside in industrialised countries and some 90% of the world's population still cannot access the Internet.[5]

Despite national and international disparities in the number of people online, it is often assumed that the rise in the number of people accessing the Internet over the last decade means that the digital divide is shrinking. According to this view, existing disparities in physical access are not particularly problematic. Instead, the digital divide can be seen as a temporary phenomenon that reflects a period of institutional mismatch commonly associated with the diffusion of innovations.[6] Over time, disparities in access between, and within, countries will be overcome as digital technologies and their related benefits trickle down throughout societies. This has led some to argue that the digital divide is not a crisis as such, and that no major policy interventions are required to ensure the achievement of more equitable participation in the knowledge-based economy.[7]

For others, however, national and international disparities in the diffusion of information and communication technologies (ICTs), and especially access to the Internet and the Web, are a source of great consternation. The essence of this apprehension was aptly summarised in the United Nations' 1999 Human Development Report:

> The network society is creating parallel communications systems: one for those with income, education and – literally – connections, giving plentiful information at low cost and high speed; the other for those without connections, blocked by high barriers of time, cost and uncertainty and dependent upon outdated information.[8]

This view is linked to a broader discourse emphasising the potential social, economic and political benefits to be reaped through the implementation of ICTs. According to enthusiasts, increasing Internet penetration rates and overcoming access-related obstacles should be high on international and national policy agendas because digital technologies are a *sine qua non* for reducing barriers to trade, enhancing access to information, and expanding social networks.[9]

---

5   *Annual Report of the Global Digital Divide Initiative*, 2002, Geneva, World Economic Forum, at www.weforum.org/pdf/initiatives/digital_divide_report_2001_2002.pdf.

6   Freeman, C and Soete, L, *The Economics of Industrial Innovation*, 3rd edn, 1997, London: Pinter; Freeman, C and Perez, C, 'Structural crises of adjustment, business cycles and investment behaviour', in Dosi, G *et al* (eds), *Technical Change and Economic Theory*, 1988, London: Pinter; Perez, C, 'Structural change and assimilation of new technologies in the economic and social systems' (1983) 15(4) *Futures* 357; Perez, C, *Technological Revolutions and Financial Capital: The Dynamics of Bubbles and Golden Ages*, 2002, Aldershot: Edward Elgar.

7   Compaine, B (ed), *The Digital Divide: Facing a Crisis or Creating a Myth?*, 2001, Cambridge, MA: MIT Press; Stone, A, 'The digital divide that wasn't', *BusinessWeek Online*, 19 August 2003, at www.businessweek.com/technology/content/aug2003/tc20030819_4285_tc126.htm.

8   United Nations Development Programme, *Human Development Report 1999*, New York: United Nations, p 63.

9   Goldstein, A and O'Connor, D, *E-Commerce for Development: Prospects and Policy Issues*, 2000, OECD Development Centre Technical Papers No 164, at www.oecd.org/dataoecd/37/61/1922730.pdf; Panagariya, A, 'E-commerce, WTO and developing countries' (2000) 23(8) *The World Economy* 959; UNCTAD, *Ecommerce and Development Report 2001*, New York: United Nations; UNCTAD, *E-commerce and Development Report 2002*, New York: United Nations.

For developed countries, the key issue is seen to reside in ensuring that access to the Internet diffuses in an equitable manner across population segments. Developing countries, on the other hand, are encouraged to implement policy initiatives oriented toward upgrading existing ICT infrastructures and increasing the rate of growth of telecommunications networks. Broadband technology, in particular, is seen as prerequisite for providing the technical capacity needed to ensure inclusion into some abstract model of how the knowledge-based economy manifests itself. In its most radical articulation this technologically deterministic vision implies that the Internet and the Web are magic bullets for social and economic development.[10]

This techno-centric understanding of the digital divide is rooted in the approach traditionally used to monitor telephone diffusion in industrialised countries and, in particular, to universal service obligations.[11] The latter have long served as a benchmark for measuring telephone access at the household level as well as differences in urban/rural and regional penetration rates.[12] When applied to the realm of inter-networking, however, a telephony-based understanding of access constrains the digital divide concept to whether potential users have the means to connect to the Internet.

As DiMaggio and Hargittai[13] point out, there is a need to question whether telephony is the proper analogy to use when considering the diffusion of Internet technologies. This association focuses attention on the 'digital' rather than on the many facets of the 'divide'. As such, it conflates the significant differences between the functionalities of the Internet and those provided by telephones.[14] The skills required to use and to fully reap the benefits of these two technologies also diverge in important ways. Logging on to the Internet and having the capability to use it in an informed manner is manifestly different from the ability to pick up a receiver and find a dial tone. Similarly, the experiences and activities that one may engage in online are strongly influenced by the type of connection one uses to log on to the Internet.

There are two additional shortcomings with a binary distinction between those who have physical access to the Internet and those who do not, each of which has major implications for policy-makers and practitioners. First, linking attempts to tackle the digital divide to the ability to access the Internet suggests that the latter is a specific artefact or appliance rather than complex processes of inter-networking made possible by a series of inter-linked computer networks, a compendium of

10 Wade, R, 'Bridging the digital divide: new route to development or new form of dependency?' (2003) 8(4) Global Governance 53.

11 DiMaggio, P and Hargittai, E, 'From the "digital divide" to "digital inequality": studying Internet use as penetration increases', Working Paper No 15, 2001, Center for Arts and Cultural Policy Studies, Princeton, NJ.

12 Intven, H, Oliver, J and Sepúlveda, E, Telecommunications Regulation Handbook, 2000, Washington, DC: infoDev Program of the World Bank.

13 DiMaggio and Hargittai, op cit fn 11.

14 The spate of innovations in digital mobile technologies in the late 1990s and early 21st century, however, are increasingly blurring the distinction between telephones and computers.

hardware and software, information flows, and human agents.[15] The significance of the distortions arising from such a view cannot be underestimated. Perceiving inter-networking as a specific 'thing' can lead policy-makers and practitioners to overestimate the potential benefits bestowed by Internet and Web access and to underestimate the scope of the challenges associated with adopting new technologies.[16]

Secondly, focusing excessively on technology access suggests the presence of uniform social and economic imperatives as well as uniform technological impacts. It presupposes that Internet access and use are one and the same. They are not. Although Internet penetration rates offer a means of quantitatively measuring the 'speed' of digitalisation, they do not account for how other factors influence Internet use and diffusion among different population segments and countries. It is socio-economic variables such as capability/skills, content, literacy, income and culture, as well as the nature of commercial and regulatory environments, that account for the absorptive capacity of societies toward technological innovations. By mediating imperatives for use, these meta-variables constitute the explanatory factors of digital disparities, including those that may be present even after the ability to access the Internet exists.[17] This highlights the need to transcend the binary conceptualisation of the digital divide toward recognition that this phenomenon encompasses multiple and varying dimensions.

Enter the issue of Internet use

Perhaps the greatest barrier to fostering inclusion in the knowledge-based economy is that the devil is in the detail. The starting point for developing policies to bridge digital disparities in developing and developed countries must be that there are variations in the configuration of issues that need to be addressed. It is equally important to recognise that the changes fostered by ICTs are not revolutionary. They are incremental and closely tied to broader social, economic, political and cultural factors. However, many well-intentioned initiatives continue to give priority to the 'digital' rather than to these other factors that may work to reinforce and possibly exacerbate 'divides'.

---

15 Benkler, Y, 'From consumers to users: shifting the deeper structures of regulation toward sustainable commons and user access' (2000) 52 *Fed Comm LJ* 561; Biegel, S, *Beyond Our Control?*, 2001, Cambridge, MA: MIT Press; Lessig, L, *Code and Other Laws of Cyberspace*, 1999, New York: Basic; Wu, T, 'Application-centered Internet analysis' (1999) 85 *Va L Rev* 1163.

16 Humphrey, J *et al*, *The Reality of E-Commerce with Developing Countries*, 2003, London School of Economics/Institute of Development Studies, University of Sussex; Kling, R, 'Can the "next-generation Internet" effectively support "ordinary citizens"?' (1999) 15 *The Information Society* 57; Paré, D, 'Does this site deliver? B2B e-commerce services for developing countries' (2003) 19 *The Information Society* 123; Paré, D, *Internet Governance in Transition*, 2003, Boulder, CO: Rowman & Littlefield.

17 Antonelli, C, 'The digital divide: understanding the economics of new information and communication technology in the global economy' (2003) 15 *Information Economics and Policy* 173; Corrocher, N and Ordanini, A, 'Measuring the digital divide: a framework for the analysis of cross-country differences' (2002) 17 *J Info Tech* 9; Martin, S, 'Is the digital divide really closing? A critique of inequality measurement in a nation online' (2003) 1(4) *IT & Society* 1.

In recent years, a growing number of scholars and practitioners have begun to embrace alternative conceptualisations of the digital divide that give pride of place to the processes associated with technological adoption as opposed to technology.[18] For example, Warschauer[19] argues that the central issue underpinning digital disparities is not access to ICTs, but rather the ways in which these technologies are used. Central to his framework is the notion of literacy, which he avers is a better analogy for considering the diffusion of inter-networking technologies than telephony because it focuses attention on issues affecting the adoption and use of ICTs. He points out that:[20]

- just as there are many types of literacy, there are many forms of online access;
- just as the meaning and value of literacy varies in particular social contexts, the meaning and value of access to ICTs varies in particular social contexts;
- both literacy and access to ICTs exist on a continuum, rather than in bipolar opposition;
- neither literacy alone nor access to ICTs alone bring automatic benefits; and
- the acquisition of both literacy and access to ICTs is a matter not only of education and culture, but also of power.

Using this framework to interpret the findings of a three-year case study of the diffusion of educational technology in Egypt, he concludes that the presence of computers and Internet connections without a corresponding emphasis on social mobilisation can lead to the squandering of resources and the perpetuation of existing inequalities. In his evaluation of the deployment of an Internet-based research network in a university capacity-building programme in Vietnam, Boyle[21] reaches a similar conclusion. He notes that:

> A separate question is whether or not the current discussion over bridging the 'digital divide' or promoting the 'information society' is orientated in a way that is sensitive to the diversity and complexity of the project such a discourse entails ... the accuracy and adequacy of that perspective, as a universal aspiration, is questionable. In this case, the intentions of individuals, as constituted in their local relations with others, emerge with a greater resonance and require closer attention.[22]

Focusing their attention on the case of the United States, DiMaggio and Hargittai[23] and Hargittai[24] also warn of the potential deficiencies arising from the adoption of a techno-centric outlook when addressing the complex social and economic changes

---

18 See, eg, the Digital Divide Network: www.digitaldividenetwork.org.
19 Warschauer, M, 'Reconceptualizing the digital divide' 7(7) *First Monday*, at www.firstmonday.dk/issues/issue7_7/warschauer/index.html; Warschauer, M, 'Demystifying the digital divide' (2003) *Scientific American*, August, p 42; Warschauer, M, 'Dissecting the "digital divide": a case study in Egypt' (2003) 19 *The Information Society* 297.
20 'Dissecting the "digital divide"', *ibid*.
21 Boyle, G, 'Putting context into ICTs in international development' (2002) 14 *J Int Development* 101.
22 *Ibid*, p 111.
23 DiMaggio and Hargittai, *op cit* fn 11.
24 Hargittai, E, 'The digital divide and what to do about it', in Jones, D (ed), *New Economy Handbook*, 2003, San Diego: Academic.

manifest in the deployment of inter-networking technologies. They suggest that the term 'digital inequality' better encompasses the various dimensions of Internet use than the term 'digital divide' because it encompasses factors beyond connectivity. Accordingly, they set out five dimensions of inequality which they propose directly influence whether and how the Internet and the Web are used:

- Equipment quality: outdated hardware/software and/or slow connection speeds can constrain the extent to which potential users derive benefits from using the Internet.

- Autonomy of use: locations from which potential users access the Internet (ie home, work, public libraries, etc) influence people's level of Web use and sophistication.

- Social support networks: individuals with the capacity to draw on social contacts for information tend to learn more quickly and are exposed to broader repertoires of online services.

- Experience: people investing time in using technology are likely to become sufficiently familiar with it for convenient and efficient use.

- Skill level: directly related to the four preceding variables insofar as together they directly influence an individual's ability to derive benefits from using ICTs.

It is important to note that neither DiMaggio and Hargittai nor Hargittai presume that the variables listed above operate in a vacuum. Echoing Warschauer's and Boyle's assertions about the importance of the social milieus within which ICTs are deployed and used, they point out that both access and use are continually being transformed through the interplay of social, economic, political and technological factors.

In the first study of its kind, Chen and Wellman[25] undertook a longitudinal comparative study of the digital divide in eight developed and developing countries.[26] Their findings suggest that while Internet penetration rates are increasing in many of the countries, specific aspects of the digital divide (eg gender, age) are actually increasing. They also found that the digital divide is shaped by reflexive interactions between social and technological factors so that 'the uneven diffusion and use of the Internet are shaped by – and are shaping – social inequalities'.[27]

Paralleling the perspectives outlined above, they conclude that policy initiatives aimed at bridging digital disparities need to move beyond promoting the greater use of computers and/or providing Internet connections to encompass strategies

---

25 Chen, W and Wellman, B, 'Charting and bridging digital divides: comparing socio-economic, gender, life stage, and rural-urban Internet access and use in eight countries', October 2003, AMD Global Consumer Advisory Board, at www.amd.com/us-en/assets/content_type/DownloadableAssets/FINAL_REPORT_CHARTING_DIGI_DIVIDES.pdf.

26 The authors examined national data for China, Germany, Italy, Japan, Mexico, South Korea, the UK, and the US.

27 Chen and Wellman, *op cit* fn 25, p 24.

that are premised on a more nuanced understanding of the many facets of digital inequalities within and between countries. To this end, Chen and Wellman propose an integrated framework for analysing Internet access and use (see Table 1).

Table 1: Framework for analysing digital disparities[28]

Access	Use
Technological access	**Technological literacy**
• ICT infrastructure • Hardware, software, bandwidth	• Technological skills • Social and cognitive skills
Social access	**Social use**
• Affordability • Awareness • Language • Content/usability • Location	• Information seeking • Resource mobilization • Social movements • Civic engagement • Social inclusion

The access component of their model calls attention to the ways in which different mechanisms for connecting to the Internet affect the volume, efficiency and diversity of use and to the economic, organisation and cultural variables influencing what users can gain from going online. The use component of their model highlights the skills required to make meaningful and productive use of the Internet as well as who uses the technology, for what purposes, and under what circumstances.

In the next section, Chen and Wellman's framework is used to structure a brief overview of the international business-to-business (B2B) e-commerce activities of SMEs in eight developing countries in Africa and in Asia and the Pacific.[29] The purpose of this exercise is to examine the role that motivations for technology access and use play in shaping the contours of digital inequalities when Internet connectivity already exists. By identifying the motivations for technology use it becomes patently clear that the imperatives for access and use are far from uniform. It also reveals that there may be substantial discrepancies between the anticipated ends of technology access and use as defined by those seeking to foster the wide deployment of ICTs and the purposes for which users actively engage with these technologies when they are present.

---

28 Chen and Wellman, *op cit* fn 25, p 38.
29 The eight countries are: Bangladesh, India, Kenya, Malaysia, Nepal, the Philippines, South Africa and Sri Lanka. For a full report of the findings, see Humphrey *et al*, *op cit* fn 16, and *B2B E-marketplaces: Current Trends, Challenges and Opportunities for SME Exporters in Developing Countries of Asia and the Pacific*, 2004, Geneva: International Trade Centre UNCTAD/WTO (ITC). I gratefully acknowledge the prior contributions of all my colleagues and research collaborators who participated in each study.

E-commerce and the digital divide

The key premise underlying much e-commerce-for-development discourse is that those in developing countries, especially SMEs, should uniformly welcome the shift to its use. Accordingly, policy-makers and practitioners are charged with two central tasks geared toward promoting use of the Internet and the Web. The first is raising awareness of the benefits to be derived from incorporating these technologies into day-to-day business activities (ie reduced transaction costs, greater access to new markets, improved organisational efficiencies, etc). The second is overseeing the implementation of legal and technical infrastructures to support their diffusion. In giving priority to technology and law, this strategy focuses on anticipated ends without giving sufficient consideration to the ways in which motivations for technology access and use mediate the outcomes of efforts to address digital equalities.

Technological access

In most developing countries the existing telecommunications infrastructure is unable to satisfy the demand for basic telecommunications services. In spite of large regional and national differences, businesses in developing countries are moving, albeit at varying speeds, toward implementing digital infrastructures that can be used for e-commerce purposes. SMEs using the Internet and personal computers for business-related activities are largely dependent upon using analogue networks and modem technologies. From their perspective, telecommunication service reliability and high connection charges are key impediments to potentially making greater use of the Internet. Further, they need a reliable source of electricity.

Although network connectivity is widely recognised as a valuable tool by SMEs that have Internet access, it is seen as having minimal impact on sales and purchasing efficiency by those producing non-standardised products. For these firms, a key motivating factor for using the Internet is the potential to benefit from reduced communication costs and enhance the speed of information exchanges. Despite high connection charges, it is cheaper to log onto the Internet to send/receive emails than to send/receive faxes and/or to make long-distance telephone calls.

SMEs in developing countries do not view their inability to fully engage with sophisticated B2B technologies as a major impediment to their competitiveness. Infrastructure constraints on technological access are not a principle concern, given their preferred uses and configurations of B2B e-commerce. Email remains the 'killer application' for facilitating their participation in international trade. There is no evidence that access to more sophisticated ICT infrastructures would significantly alter how SMEs in developing countries would engage with B2B e-commerce trading activities in the near to medium term. Even when sophisticated technologies are in place, firms often continue to encounter other trade-related infrastructure barriers such as poor transportation systems, inefficient customs procedures, and national currency regulations that offset many of the benefits they would derive from engaging in B2B e-commerce.

Technological literacy

Given that global buyers increasingly expect their suppliers to possess at least basic competencies in using Internet-related technologies, the issue of technological literacy is central to concerns of digital disparities. Low levels of awareness are key barriers to accessing Internet-related business applications. This lack of awareness exists at all levels of society and is particularly prevalent among SMEs.

A challenge to the acquisition of skills and capabilities in developing countries is the multitude of ways in which ICTs can be used to support electronically facilitated commercial interactions and transactions. This, coupled with the complexity of global value chain structures, creates barriers to the productive and meaningful use of e-business applications. For example, an important issue facing SMEs with high-speed network access is that standards for data exchange and formatting vary widely. These standards tend to be industry and/or even company specific. Moreover, the types of interfaces, platforms and e-business applications used may not be compatible or interoperable across multiple online trading venues. For SMEs this can make participating in B2B e-commerce an extremely expensive proposition, both financially and in terms of capabilities building.

While participating in B2B e-commerce can lead to cost savings and efficiency gains, this is not the whole story. Focusing on the use of technology as an end in itself, presuming that existing commercial practices are simply less efficient than electronically-based alternatives, and ignoring sector specificities, awareness-raising and training initiatives often create cynicism among the intended technology users. This can have the effect of further entrenching existing digital inequalities.

Social access

In numerous sectors and countries a preference for using existing personal networks and for face-to-face meetings to share certain types of information remains strong even when Internet connectivity is present. Trading relationships tend to be fostered over extended periods of time and are seen to be difficult to transfer to digital environments. This issue is not limited to developing countries.

Cost considerations also exert an important influence on motivating technology use. First, the cost of accessing the Internet in developing countries is widely recognised as being extremely expensive. In many instances this problem is further compounded by regional variations in connection speeds and the high tariffs associated with relying on telephone lines to connect to the Internet and the Web. Secondly, realising positive returns on investments in technology is neither a clear-cut nor short-term proposition. Beyond investments in hardware and software, other costs may actually increase because of the need to learn new skills, train staff, and maintain equipment. In many instances, domestic tariffs and taxes on computing and information systems serve to reinforce this problem. The willingness of developing country firms to incur the costs of engaging in electronic trading activities is directly linked to how the requisite technologies are seen to fit into their overall business strategies.

Social use

The received wisdom about B2B e-commerce is that it gives traders in developing countries the opportunity to sell their products and services more easily in external markets as well allowing the development of one-to-one trading relationships with buyers and sellers. For traders in developing countries specialising in small, one-off sales and those operating in highly fragmented product markets, the prospects of reaping such benefits can be a motivating factor in deciding to adopt particular technologies. However, there is no evidence to support the view that such benefits may be expected to diffuse uniformly across all economic sectors.

For most SMEs from developing countries engaging in B2B e-commerce, the primary benefits are not in the form of increased demand for their goods or the identification of new trading partners. Instead, they appear in the form of reduced communication costs with existing trading partners and potentially more efficient and effective information management with the organisation and the supply chain(s) within which they operate. The fact that these returns do not accrue over the short term can work to perpetuate digital discrepancies by acting as a disincentive for adopting ICTs.

National and sectoral business cultures also exert a major influence on the types of e-commerce technologies used by SMEs, and the extent to which these technologies are incorporated into their day-to-day business processes. In terms of motivating technology access and use, this is a double-edged sword. On the one hand, well-established business practices can foster inertia by locking firms into particular modes of production and distribution. This, obviously, can perpetuate disparities vis à vis the adoption and implementation of e-business activities, regardless of the levels of ICT awareness. On the other hand, business culture reflects the established commercial practices associated with particular market structures, the national and international value chains within which exporters operate, and the types of products being traded. These variables directly influence how the benefits of implementing e-commerce technologies are defined, and the extent to which they can be expected to materialise. They also influence the extent to which demand for using particular ICTs manifests itself in particular industry sectors.

Motivation, law, and the digital divide

It is often taken for granted that strong legal frameworks to support e-commerce contribute to reducing digital disparities by helping to nurture trust in online transactions and, thus, motivating greater participation in e-commerce activities. To this end, major international and regional efforts are underway to establish regulatory frameworks to bolster the diffusion and adoption of e-commerce.[30] Among other things, developing countries are being called upon to adjust their

---

30 The United Nations Commission on International Trade Law (UNCITRAL) has played a major role in the development of model laws for e-commerce transactions. The Organization for Economic Co-operation and Development (OECD) has been at the forefront of attempts to develop e-commerce related policies for such areas as telecommunications infrastructure and services, Internet taxation, consumer protection, network security, privacy, and data protection. The key body for Internet jurisdiction issues is the Hague Conference on Private International Law. Issues relating to e-commerce trade barriers are being considered by the World Trade Organization (WTO).

national legislative frameworks by incorporating the principle of electronic equivalence for information, documents and digital signatures.[31] The incorporation of this principle into a growing number of national e-commerce frameworks is leading to increasingly uniform laws for governing electronic transactions and electronic signatures.

While standardising legislation and rules for e-commerce is desirable, it is particularly striking that the same techno-centric logic which negates the importance of human experiences and purpose appears to exhibit itself in emergent frameworks aimed at providing legal security and predictability for electronically facilitated trading. This approach can be summarised as follows: *Technology makes online trading possible. However, even if the technology is present, companies are unlikely to engage with it in the manner envisaged by its designers and those deploying it because online business-related interactions and transactions do not enjoy the same legal protection as their offline counterparts. As a result, trust-related factors are a key obstacle to the 'take-off' of e-commerce. If laws are put in place to ensure confidence in online trading, use of the technology will be buttressed.* The risk here is that law may come to be viewed in some quarters as the foremost factor for motivating technology access and use once the technology is present. However, the evidence from recent studies suggests that national and international e-commerce legislation is not a key driver to the wider e-commerce diffusion and adoption by businesses in developing countries.[32] This can be explained, in part, by discrepancies between the legal frameworks being propagated to support e-commerce and the commercial practices employed by firms that engage in e-commerce activities.

The failure to take into account users' motivations for technology access and use is giving rise to multiple design–actuality gaps[33] that may actually reinforce digital disparities. Within the current context, two such gaps can be identified. First, emergent legal frameworks appear to be rooted in a vision of electronically facilitated trading that is premised on a business-to-consumer model rather than a B2B model. In the business-to-consumer setting, consumers cannot rely on the social cues and interactions that enable them to inspect products and to assess the trustworthiness of sellers when shopping offline. Although the online retailer's brand may help to establish trust, online consumers are often required to engage in a transaction with only minimal information about the merchant. Establishing trust in this context is dependent upon consumers being assured that:[34]

---

31 The principle of electronic equivalence grants information or documents in digital formats the same legal standing as their paper-based equivalents. The same holds true in terms of ensuring that digital signatures can be used with legal effect.

32 Gibbs, J, Kraemer, K and Dedrick, J, 'Environment and policy factors shaping global e-commerce diffusion: a cross-country comparison' (2003) 19 *The Information Society* 5; Humphrey *et al*, *op cit* fn 16; International Trade Centre, *op cit* fn 29.

33 A design–actuality gap refers to the 'match or mismatch between the local actuality (where we are now) and system design (where the design wants to get us)': Heeks, R, 'Information systems and developing countries: failure, success, and local improvisations' (2002) 18 *The Information Society* 101.

34 *Best Practice Examples Under the OECD Guidelines on Consumer Protection in the Context of Electronic Commerce*, OECD Paris, DSTI/CP(2002)2/FINAL: Directorate for Science, Technology and Industry Committee on Consumer Policy, at www.olis.oecd.org/olis/2002doc.nsf/43bb6130e5e86e5fc12569fa005d004c/3b2fd5f3ef38740ec1256bbc0050ec39/$FILE/JT00126337.PDF.

- they will be afforded the same levels of protection online as would be in place offline;
- the retailer will act in accordance with fair business, advertising and marketing practices;
- clear and obvious online disclosure mechanisms are in place.

Although they are not a substitute for social cues, legal infrastructures can go a long way to helping consumers trust online transactions in these instances by establishing legal principles to ensure that the above concerns are addressed.

In contrast, transacting online comprises only one dimension of B2B e-commerce. The other, more important dimension is exchanging online and offline transaction-related information to support co-ordination of supply chains. When it comes to the trading of non-standardised tangible products, B2B e-commerce seldom involves online transactions with strangers. For these products, ICTs of varying degrees of sophistication are primarily used to supplement conventional business practices. Therefore, the variables influencing motivations for accessing and using the technology are not restricted to the presence of legal and technological infrastructures. In failing to recognise how different motivating factors apply in different contexts, national e-commerce frameworks may actually dissuade potential users from accessing and using the technology by imposing additional costs on how firms do business with one another.[35] Secondly, a design–actuality gap is also evidenced in how obstacles to trust are perceived. The main trust-related obstacle to technology access and use in the B2B e-commerce domain is not the lack of legal infrastructures, but rather that the use of sophisticated electronic trust services comes at a very high price.

A key motivating factor for accessing and using some types of e-marketplaces (eg online bulletin board services)[36] is that they are relatively inexpensive to use and do not offer complex services. For some SMEs, this lack of sophistication and cheapness can act as an incentive for engaging with the technology, particularly if they are exporters of highly standardised products or if they operate in highly fragmented value chains. An important motivating factor for engaging with the technology is precisely that users are not mandated to use expensive electronic trust services. Instead, trust is a product of the types of social interactions normally associated with the negotiation of transactions offline. Likewise, for trade in many other products where information requirements are very complex, the technological and legal infrastructures that are in place may not sufficiently address the different types of trust associated with engaging in commercial trading activities. In this context, trust is fostered over time through social interactions between actors.

---

35 See, eg, s 3 of the Indian Information Technology Act 2000, which does not legally recognise digital certificates issued by Certificate Authorities that are not licensed in India. This means that owners of digital certificates issued by Certificate Authorities that do not maintain an office in India are unable to use their existing digital certificates for transactions in India. As a result, Indian certificate holders are not able to use digital means to enter into legally recognised electronic contracts with international buyers and sellers holding digital certificates issued outside of India.

36 The main 'service' offered by this type of B2B e-marketplace is the provision of trade-leads or classified ads that must be followed up using email, hyperlinks, the telephone, fax or the post.

While important, the mere presence of legal and technological infrastructures is unlikely to be the determining factor in motivating technology access and use. This conclusion parallels the findings of a recent OECD study on the impact of B2B e-commerce on supply chains in four different industry sectors. The authors of that study concluded that 'at the level of market systems, the "new economy" is in fact not very different from "business as usual"'.[37]

This suggests that the perceived lack of motivation of SMEs to engage with the Internet and the Web for e-business activities may actually be an appropriate, and effective, strategic response to both commercial and digital disparities. Indeed, the fact that SMEs are seen to be lagging behind may be an advantage in helping them to make better choices about the types of digital technologies they choose to engage with. This also suggests that, even if legal issues such as electronic signatures, privacy and data protection, intellectual property protection, and cyber-crimes are resolved, this is unlikely to foster reductions in digital disparities or to improve access to international markets for developing country exporters.

Conclusion

In spite of a growing body of research highlighting the need for a more nuanced, use-centred approach to tackling digital disparities, the paradigm guiding many efforts to bridge the so-called digital divide continues to be rooted in a binary distinction between haves and have-nots. One of the most unsatisfactory dimensions of this perspective is that it offers a misleading and overly simplistic portrayal of what is, in fact, an extremely complex and multi-faceted phenomenon. Overcoming digital disparities does not simply follow from providing access to technological and legal infrastructures.

The starting point for fostering inclusion into the network society must be that there are monumental variations in the configuration of issues to be addressed. This highlights the need for transcending the notion of 'the digital divide'. What people actually want to do with the ICTs at their disposal, and the ways in which they are using or want to use inter-networking technologies, can only be adequately assessed within this context. It is only after such a task has been undertaken that any effective judgment about policy priorities for bridging digital disparities can be made. Therefore, it is essential to establish a base of empirical knowledge about the diverse causes of disparities in the diffusion and uptake of digital technologies.

If national and international measures aimed at bridging these disparities are to succeed in the long run, they need to recognise the complex inter-play of a wide range of social, economic, political, cultural and technological factors that influence motivations for technology access and use. This means that policy choices and programmes must be made in accordance with the motivations of technology users, not on abstract assessments of technological potential and its supposedly uniform imperatives and impacts.

---

37 Desruelle, P *et al*, 'Techno-economic impact of e-commerce', report on a workshop held at the Institute for Prospective Technological Studies (IPTS), Seville, Spain, 5–6 June 2001. Report EUR 20123 EN: European Commission Joint Research Centre (DG JRC), 2001.

Chapter 8
Filtering, Blocking and Rating: Chaperones or Censorship?

Brian W Esler

The right to impart and receive information freely has long been a cornerstone of human rights law, and of democratic theory. On 26 August 1789, the architects of the French Revolution issued the Declaration of the Rights of Man, which secured the right of citizens to communicate ideas and opinions freely, and which right has been retained virtually unchanged throughout the history of France's democracy. Almost exactly a month later, the United States declared free speech to be fundamental to its nascent political structure by amending its recently adopted Constitution to protect that right explicitly. Over a century and a half later, the United Nations' Universal Declaration of Human Rights similarly recognised that '[e]veryone has the right to freedom of opinion and expression; [including] freedom to hold opinions without interference and to seek, receive and impart information and ideas through any media and regardless of frontiers'. Soon thereafter, Europe recognised a similar right (subject to explicit exceptions) in the European Convention on Human Rights. It can now be safely said that no modern democratic society fails to cherish and protect such fundamental rights.

It may be asked, though, whether free speech has any value if it cannot be heard. The prisoner shouting in his cell, or the hermit shouting on the mountain, may have much to say, but their words have no impact without an audience. As observed by Justice William Brennan almost four decades ago, 'The dissemination of ideas can accomplish nothing if otherwise willing addressees are not free to receive and consider them. It would be a barren marketplace of ideas that had only sellers, and no buyers'.[1]

Today, however, access to an Internet connection means that the hermit's hello can be heard around the world, along with the harangues of the hacker, the hajji, the hagiographer, the half-wit, the haves, and the have-nots. The true marketplace of ideas – theorised by Jefferson[2] and more recently Habermas[3] – has arrived. Or has it?

---

1   *Lamont v Postmaster General*, 381 US 301, 308 (1965) (Brennan J concurring) (holding unconstitutional a federal law that required the Post Office to detain and destroy unsealed mail from foreign countries that was determined to contain communist propaganda unless the addressee returned a reply card indicating his or her desire to receive such mail).

2   'No experiment can be more interesting than that we are now trying, and which we trust will end in establishing the fact, that man may be governed by reason and truth. Our first object should therefore be, to leave open to him all the avenues to truth. The most effectual hitherto found, is the freedom of the press. It is, therefore, the first shut up by those who fear the investigation of their actions.' Thomas Jefferson, 'Letter from Thomas Jefferson to John Tyler, 1804', in Lipscomb, J and Burgh, A (eds), *The Writings of Thomas Jefferson*, 1905, Washington, DC: Thomas Jefferson Memorial Association.

3   Jürgen Habermas laid out five conditions for what he calls 'ideal speech': (1) every subject with the competence to speak and act is allowed to take part in a discourse; (2) everyone is allowed to question any assertion whatever; (3) everyone is allowed to introduce any assertion whatever into the discourse; (4) everyone is allowed to express his attitudes, desires and needs; and (5) no speaker may be prevented, by internal or external coercion, from exercising his rights as laid down in (1) and (2). Habermas, J, 'Discourse ethics: notes on philosophical justification', in *Moral Consciousness and Communicative Action*, Lenhart, C and Nicholson, S (trans), 1980, Cambridge, MA: MIT Press, p 86.

Prejudice in its original sense – that is, to prejudge based on assumed similarities – is the fundamental basis of all rational thought. We all filter and categorise information to find that which is relevant to our needs. Internet search engines rise or fall on their ability to translate our queries into such useful information. Websites – especially commercial sites – utilise technology to move their sites to the top of search returns, and search engines respond in kind to counteract (or to allow in exchange for payment) such attempts.[4] Nonetheless, most Internet users have had the experience of finding a link buried in a site, which leads to another relevant link, and to another ... until we find ourselves down some pleasurable but unexpected informational rabbit hole, in a direction we did not intend to go, but one which broadens our perspectives nonetheless. This ability to explore the confines of the Internet freely, to use technology to aid our search, and perhaps to be surprised and challenged by what we find, is what makes the Internet such a revolutionary educational and political device. There is a reason that the technologies used to search the Internet are called 'browsers', rather than 'pinpointers'.

Nonetheless, because cyberspace is a virtual realm, technology can be used to attenuate, as well as illuminate, information.[5] The application of even seemingly neutral technologies may have a dramatic impact upon how we perceive this electronic space. For instance, a browser that orders search returns according to payment will lead users to information different from that which would otherwise be revealed. Similarly, technologies that can filter out certain Internet content – such as adult or other controversial sites – will also present the user with a very different virtual geography, but if all rational thought is based to some extent on such filtering, is there any reason to be concerned when technology can augment such natural prejudices?

Certainly some think so. As early as 1996, the passage of the US's Telecommunications Act, which in part attempted to prevent minors from accessing 'obscene or indecent' content, led cyber-libertarian John Perry Barlow to draft a Declaration of the Independence of Cyberspace. Like Thomas Paine reacting to Burke's calumnious criticism of the French Revolution, Barlow excoriates some of the earliest attempts to control access to certain materials on the Internet:

> In the United States, you have today created a law, the Telecommunications Reform Act, which repudiates your own Constitution and insults the dreams of Jefferson, Washington, Mill, Madison, DeToqueville, and Brandeis. ... In our world, all the sentiments and expressions of humanity, from the debasing to the angelic, are parts of a seamless whole, the global conversation of bits. We cannot separate the air that chokes from the air upon which wings beat.

> In China, Germany, France, Russia, Singapore, Italy and the United States, you are trying to ward off the virus of liberty by erecting guard posts at the frontiers of

---

4 http://computer.howstuffworks.com/search-engine.htm.
5 As noted by the American Civil Liberties Union: '[I]n the physical world, people censor the printed word by burning books. But in the virtual world, one can just as easily censor controversial speech by banishing it to the farthest corners of cyberspace using rating and blocking programs.' ACLU, 'Fahrenheit 451.2: Is cyberspace burning?', at http://archive.aclu.org/issues/cyber/burning.html.

Cyberspace. These may keep out the contagion for a small time, but they will not work in a world that will soon be blanketed in bit-bearing media.[6]

To a certain extent, Barlow's declaration has come true. Governmental attempts to cordon off cyberspace have not been entirely successful. However, failure to achieve perfect success does not mean that such attempts have failed completely. Simply by making access more difficult, the government may be able to achieve its objectives.[7] This chapter will explore some of those attempts in order to highlight how filtering, blocking and rating technologies can affect the right 'to seek, receive and impart information and ideas through any media and regardless of frontiers'.[8] Principally, this will be done by examining the experience of the United States in trying to mandate the use of Internet filters for pornography.

The basics of filtering technology and ratings systems

Broadly, filters are technologies that impose themselves between the computer's Web browser and its Internet connection to prevent objectionable content from appearing. The designers of filtering software generally use one of three approaches to determine whether a site merits blocking: (1) software analysis; (2) human analysis; and (3) site labelling.[9] Software analysis involves having the software scan a site for objectionable words or file names before displaying it. For instance, Google's SafeSearch function utilises software 'that checks keywords and phrases, URLs and Open Directory categories' to attempt to eliminate pornographic sites from search results.[10] A study done on the effectiveness of this technology found that SafeSearch eliminated such obviously non-pornographic sites as the United States' Congress' home page and the Israeli Prime Minister's Office.[11]

Human analysis involves having testers actually review the site before deciding whether to include it on a list of blocked sites. While undoubtedly a more accurate method of deciding when a site contains objectionable material, it is also the most expensive and time consuming. One of the more well known companies relying on human analysis is N2H2, which makes filtering technology for both employers, and schools and libraries.[12] However, even using such 'human filters', the links disabled

---

6 Barlow, JP, 'A declaration of independence for cyberspace', at www.eff.org/~barlow/ Declaration-Final.html.

7 For a more detailed discussion of state filtering see Deibert and Villeneuve, Chapter 9.

8 Universal Declaration of Human Rights, Article 19.

9 'Digital chaperones for kids', Consumer Reports (March 2001), at www.consumerreports.org.

10 www.google.com/safesearch_help.html.

11 Edelman, B, 'Empirical analysis of Google SafeSearch', at http://cyber.law.harvard.edu/ people/edelman/google-safesearch. Mr Edelman and Professor Zittrain of Harvard have an ongoing project 'to document and analyse a large number of web pages blocked by various types of filtering regimes, and ultimately to create a distributed tool enabling Internet users worldwide to gather and relay such data'. Zittrain, J and Edelman, B, 'Documentation of Internet filtering worldwide', at http://cyber.law.harvard.edu/filtering. For further discussion of N2H2 technology see Deibert and Villeneuve, Chapter 9, p 117.

12 www.n2h2.com/products/categories.php.

for the benefit of its 'younger visitors' include such seemingly innocuous sites as Ebay, Amazon.com, Hotmail, and CNN.[13] Moreover, as with most companies producing filtering technologies, N2H2 keeps confidential the details of its technology, as well as the sites it blocks, rendering it harder for both consumers and publishers to judge the effectiveness of the technology.[14]

Site labelling means that the filtering technology responds to voluntary labels used by some sites and promoted by various organisations.[15] One of the earliest of these rating systems is SafeSurf, which was introduced in 1995 and uses a 12-category system to rate websites according to age appropriateness and content.[16] Similarly, TRUSTe gives a kitemark to websites that have appropriate privacy protection principles, including a 'kids seal' for websites that require parental permission before collecting information from children.[17] The Entertainment Software Rating Board (ESRB), which already rates video and computer games, has also begun rating websites, chatrooms, bulletin boards and multi-player web-based games based on age appropriateness and content.[18] The international Internet Content Rating Association has one of the most ubiquitous rating systems, which relies on website authors to fill out a questionnaire giving information on the site's content regarding chat, language used, nudity or sexual content, violent content, and subjects such as gambling, drugs and alcohol.[19]

Technology enhances the utility of such labels. Specifically, the standards-setting body for the Internet – the World Wide Web Consortium (W3C) – has established a standard called the Platform for Internet Content Selection (PICS).[20] The above labelling systems are generally PICS compliant, which means that browsers and other technology designed to W3C standards can be programmed to recognise and respond to these labels. By creating a standard, W3C also ensured that rating would become more commonplace, by lowering the cost and complexity of implementing filtering technologies.[21]

As observed by Professor Lawrence Lessig:

> As envisioned by its authors, PICS would be neutral among ratings and neutral among filters; the system would simply provide a language with which content on the Net could be rated, and with which decisions about how to use that rated material could be made from machine to machine. ... Most people who first endorsed the system imagined

---

13 *Ibid.*

14 In 2002, Benjamin Edelman filed a lawsuit against N2H2 to obtain a declaratory judgment that he had the right to research N2H2's technology, including circumventing its encryption system and publishing its block list. In April 2003, the suit was dismissed as presenting no actionable case or controversy. See http://cyber.law.harvard.edu/people/edelman/edelman-v-n2h2.

15 The Internet Content Ratings Association in the US promotes such a voluntary regime, and Microsoft's Internet Explorer can be programmed to respond to such labels. See How Stuff Works, *op cit* fn 4.

16 www.safesurf.com/time.htm.

17 www.truste.org.

18 www.esrb.org.

19 www.icra.org/_en/about/#icraglance.

20 www.w3.org/PICS.

21 Shapiro, A, *The Control Revolution*, 1999, New York: Public Affairs, p 108.

PICS sitting on a user's computer, filtering according to the desires of that individual. But nothing in the design of PICS prevents organizations that provide access to the Net from filtering content as well. Filtering can occur at any level of the distribution chain – the user, the company through which the user gains access, the ISP or even the jurisdiction within which the user lives. Nothing in the design of PICS requires that such filters announce themselves. Filtering in an architecture like PICS can be invisible, and indeed, in some of its implementations invisibility is part of the design.[22]

PICS is a platform designed for the World Wide Web, and does not necessarily govern the technical specifications for other Internet-related communications technologies such as chatrooms, file transfer protocol servers, Usenet discussion groups, streaming audio and video, email, instant messaging and peer-to-peer file sharing networks.[23] Also, Lessig's apocalyptic vision of the effect of filters discounts the marketplace effect, ie, that most consumers will want less, not more, filtering, and will avoid products and services that hardwire these content solutions. Nonetheless, if the filtering is surreptitious, so that consumers are unaware, they will be unable to exercise such choice. Moreover, if filtering is mandated – either by governments or by private consortiums such as ISPs – consumers will also have no recourse. Thus, filtering technologies do raise legitimate free speech concerns.

Governmental attempts to encourage the use of filtering technologies

Governments have enthusiastically embraced the promise of Internet filtering, but have varied in their willingness to mandate such technologies. As discussed elsewhere in this book, many nations use technology to prevent all of their citizens from accessing content deemed by those governments to be unwholesome.[24] In general, Western governments have been less intrusive in their manner of achieving this aim.

For instance, the European Union's 1997 Action Plan on Promoting Safe Use of the Internet only called for industry self-regulation, including voluntary measures to develop filtering and rating systems.[25] Since then, the EU has showered over €8 million on at least 13 different filtering projects.[26] Almost €1 million have been spent on the NETPROTECT project, which seeks to develop and promote a

---

22 Lessig, L, *Code and Other Laws of Cyberspace*, 1999, New York: Basic, p 178 (footnotes omitted).

23 Akdeniz, Y and Strossen, N, 'Sexually oriented expression', in Akdeniz, Y, Walker, C and Wall, D (eds), *The Internet, Law and Society*, 2000, London: Longman, pp 220–21. However, other filtering or blocking technologies can be applied to those applications. For instance, Cisco, whose routers and other technologies are a critical part of the Internet's infrastructure, announced as early as 2000 that it was designing its product to include built-in filtering systems for use as defensive measures against security breaches and denial-of-service attacks: see Beigel, S, *Beyond Our Control?*, 2001, Cambridge: MIT Press, pp 251–52. A recent study on spam filters used by ISPs to filter out junk email found that '[t]op Internet service providers blocked 17 percent of legitimate permission-based email' through use of such filters. See www.internetnews.com/xSP/article.php/2247651.

24 See Deibert and Villeneuve, Chapter 9.

25 COM(1997) 582 Amended Proposal for a European Parliament and Council Decision adopting a multiannual Community Action Plan on promoting safer use of the Internet.

26 http://europa.eu.int/information_society/programmes/iap/projects/filtering/index_en.htm.

'European tool for Internet access filtering'.[27] Other projects, such as ICRASAFE, seek to develop and promote an international self-labelling system for websites.[28] The most funding, however, has been given to the PRINCIP programme, which seeks to develop a '[m]ultilingual system for the analysis and detection of racist and revisionist content on the Internet'.[29]

The cornerstone of the European approach has been the Safer Internet programme, which was put in place in 1999, and was recently extended to at least 2008.[30] The Safer Internet programme seeks to tackle issues of illegal, harmful and racist content on the Internet.[31] Primarily, it does so by attempting to develop co-ordinated approaches to those problems. With regard to developing filtering and rating systems, the programme's two main goals are to demonstrate the benefits of filtering and rating, and to develop international agreement on rating systems.[32] However, European uptake of rating and filtering systems has been low, primarily because 'existing filtering and rating systems are unsophisticated, as users cannot be sure that content will be rated appropriately and that perfectly innocuous content will not be blocked'.[33]

To date, the EU has been reluctant to mandate use of such filtering and rating systems, and may be described as taking a 'softly, softly' approach to regulation. Similarly, the UK has not mandated Internet filters, although the Home Office guidance to parents on safe use of the Internet promotes use of such filters,[34] as does the quasi-governmental Internet Watch Foundation.[35]

Across the Atlantic, however, the approach to controlling access to Internet content has been more aggressive. In 1996, the US enacted the Communications Decency Act,[36] which forbade the knowing transmission of 'obscene or indecent' content to minors, but provided a defence to those who took good-faith, effective actions – such as utilising labelling – to restrict access by minors. Responding to the Supreme Court's invalidation of that statute on constitutional grounds in *ACLU v Reno*,[37] Congress then passed the Child Online Protection Act in 1998, which prohibited any online communication 'for commercial purposes' that included 'any material that is harmful to minors'. This law was also immediately challenged on First Amendment grounds and, in February 1999, a District Court judge enjoined its

---

27 *Ibid.*
28 *Ibid.*
29 *Ibid.*
30 Decision No 1151/2003/EC of the European Parliament and of the Council of 16 June 2003, amending Decision No 276/1999/EC.
31 www.saferinternet.org/index.asp.
32 www.saferinternet.org/filtering/index.asp.
33 *Ibid.*
34 www.homeoffice.gov.uk/docs/childsafetyinternet.pdf.
35 See Akdeniz and Strossen, *op cit* fn 23, pp 223–25.
36 47 USCA § 223. It was this Act that inspired Barlow to draft his 'declaration of independence for cyberspace'. See Barlow, *op cit* fn 6.
37 521 US 844 (1997).

enforcement.[38] However, that court struck down this law partly on the basis that there were less restrictive alternatives available for accomplishing the government's objectives – namely, blocking and filtering technology.[39]

A year later, Congress pursued that 'less restrictive alternative' in the Children's Internet Protection Act (CIPA).[40] As cogently predicted by Nadine Strossen,[41] Congress chose to regulate indirectly by utilising its spending power to require recipients of its funds – in this case, public libraries – to install filtering software as a condition for receipt of funds. In the words of CIPA, public libraries must utilise a 'technology protection measure ... that protects against access' by anyone to 'visual depictions' constituting 'obscenity',[42] and by minors to 'visual depictions' that are 'harmful to minors'.[43] CIPA defines a 'technology protection measure' as 'a specific technology that blocks or filters Internet access' to such material.[44] Libraries may, however, disable the filter 'to enable access for bona fide research or other lawful purposes'.[45] These provisions affect the at least 16 million Americans whose sole access to the Internet is through library terminals, as well as the millions of others who utilise such Internet access on a situational basis.[46]

United States v American Library Association[47]

A group of libraries and Web publishers challenged CIPA as soon as it was signed into law by President Clinton, relying on similar arguments to those that were successful in *ACLU v Reno*. Initially, their challenge succeeded. The District Court

---

38 *American Civil Liberties Union v Reno*, 31 F Supp 2d 473 (ED Pa 1999); *affirmed* 217 F 3d 162 (3rd Cir 2000); *vacated and remanded sub nom Ashcroft v American Civil Liberties Union*, 535 US 564 (2002); *affirmed on remand* 322 F 3d 240 (3rd Cir 2003).

39 31 F Supp 2d, 497.

40 114 Stat 2763A-335, codified variously at 20 USC § 9134 and 47 USC § 254.

41 Akdeniz and Strossen, *op cit* fn 23, p 217. At the time, Ms Strossen was the head of the American Civil Liberties Union.

42 In the US, only depictions of sex can be obscene, and such communications are not protected by the First Amendment. The legal definition of 'obscenity' is material which, considered as a whole, appeals to a 'prurient' or 'shameful' interest in sex, which lacks any serious literary, artistic, political or scientific value, and which is 'patently offensive' according to local community standards. See, eg, *Pope v Illinois Municipal Court*, 481 US 297 (1987); *Paris Adult Theater v Slaton*, 413 US 49 (1973). Nonetheless, if obscene speech can be denied constitutional protection putatively because of the effect such speech has on the recipient, one must wonder why no similar exception has been developed for violent speech, especially as studies have shown a strong correlation between children's exposure to violent images and violent behaviour. See Rowell Huesmann, L *et al*, 'Longitudinal relations between children's exposure to TV violence and their aggressive and violent behavior in young adulthood: 1977–1992' (2003) 39 *Developmental Psychology* 201. Surely society should be more concerned about violence than about sex.

43 20 USC §§ 9134(f)(1)(A)(i) and (B)(i); 47 USC §§ 254(h)(6)(B)(i) and (C)(i).

44 47 USC § 254(h)(7)(I).

45 20 USC § 9134(f)(3); 47 USC § 254(h)(6)(D).

46 As at the end of 2002, the US had approximately 160,700,000 Internet users: www.etforecasts.com/pr/pr1202.htm. The District Court found that 10% of US Internet users obtained access only through library terminals: 201 F Supp 401, 422.

47 Case No 02-361, ___ US ___ (2003); 2003 US Lexis 4799.

ruled that CIPA was facially unconstitutional since 'any public library that complies with CIPA's conditions will necessarily violate the First Amendment'.[48] Significantly, the District Court reached that conclusion by finding that provision of Internet access at public libraries constituted a 'designated public forum'.[49] It concluded that unfettered access to the Internet in libraries was like 'traditional public fora ... such as sidewalks and parks' because such access 'promotes First Amendment values in an analogous manner'.[50] Hence, although the government had a compelling interest in protecting minors from exposure to inappropriate material, the use of software filters was not narrowly tailored to further that policy objective, especially as other, less overbroad means were available to accomplish the same goal (eg, enforcement of Internet use policies, requiring parental consent or presence for minors, and the use of privacy screens to protect other patrons from exposure).[51] The claimants' early success was not to last. Bypassing the Court of Appeals, the government took the case directly to the Supreme Court. In a plurality decision, a fractured Supreme Court held that CIPA did not fall foul of the First Amendment. How and why it did so bears scrutiny.

The simplest, most straightforward and least controversial approach to the problem came in Justice Kennedy's solo concurring opinion. Since this was a facial (rather than an 'as applied')[52] challenge, and the government had a compelling interest in protecting minors from inappropriate material, Justice Kennedy voted to reverse simply because there was as yet no evidence that any adult was actually prevented lawful access.[53] As he bluntly put it, 'If, on the request of an adult user, a librarian will unblock filtered material or disable the Internet software filter without significant delay, there is little to this case'.[54] Thus, Justice Kennedy advises a cautious, case-by-case approach as to whether (or when) mandatory filtering may raise First Amendment concerns.

Chief Justice Rehnquist authored the opinion that garnered the most votes, although his opinion did not attract a majority.[55] He concluded that this case presented a problem not of access, but rather of resource allocation, which means that the government must necessarily make choices. Without explicitly saying so, he seemed to argue that, without government intervention, unfettered access will lead to a tragedy of the commons,[56] overwhelming the limited resource of libraries (and,

---

48 201 F Supp 2d 401, 453 (ED Pa 2002).

49 *Ibid*, 457.

50 *Ibid*, 466.

51 *Ibid*, 410, 479.

52 Generally, facial challenges fail if circumstances can be put forward under which the statute would be constitutional, making these types of challenges the most difficult to sustain. However, facial challenges on First Amendment grounds are given more leeway than most. See Fallon Jr, R, 'As-applied and facial challenges and third party standing' (2000) 113 *Harv L Rev* 1321, pp 1327–59.

53 123 S Ct, 2309–10 (Kennedy concurring).

54 *Ibid*, 2309.

55 Justices O'Connor, Scalia and Thomas joined.

56 Hardin, G, 'The tragedy of the commons' (1968) 162 *Science* 1243. Of course, while the physical environment with which Hardin was concerned is often comprised of limited resources, man-made environments such as the Internet are not so naturally limited. For a critique on the dangers of applying such spatial metaphors to the Internet, see Lemley, M, 'Place and cyberplace' (2003) 91 *Calif L Rev* 521.

by extension, the government) to provide access at all. In Justice Rehnquist's view, since the government has no constitutional duty to fund access, its decision to put constraints on the access it does fund caused no constitutional problems. Most importantly, he contended that 'Internet access in public libraries is neither a "traditional" nor "designated" public forum',[57] thus meriting only a rational basis review:

> A library's need to exercise judgment in making collection decisions depends on its traditional role in identifying suitable and worthwhile material; it is no less entitled to play that role when it collects material from the Internet than when it collects material from any other source. Most libraries already exclude pornography from their print collections because they deem it inappropriate for inclusion. We do not subject these decisions to heightened scrutiny; it would make little sense to treat libraries' judgments to block online pornography any differently, when these judgments are made for just the same reason.[58]

Since Congress proceeded on a rational basis in protecting minors by mandating the use of filters, there was no First Amendment violation.

Justice Breyer's concurrence is both the most interesting of the decisions upholding the government's actions, and also the most significant for future Internet access cases. Although agreeing with Justice Rehnquist's opinion that Internet access does not constitute a public forum,[59] he nonetheless explicitly recognised that this is not a simple case, and that historical precedents may not provide the appropriate fit:

> In ascertaining whether the statutory provisions are constitutional, I would apply a form of heightened scrutiny, examining the statutory requirements in question with special care. The Act directly restricts the public's receipt of information. And it does so through limitations imposed by outside bodies (here Congress) upon two critically important sources of information – the Internet as accessed via public libraries. For that reason, we should not examine the statute's constitutionality as if it raised no special First Amendment concern – as if, like tax or economic regulation, the First Amendment

---

57 123 S Ct, 2304. Justice Breyer explicitly concurred in this conclusion, albeit for different reasons, thereby giving this portion of the opinion stronger precedential status.

58 Ibid, 2306. Justice Rehnquist's opinion evidences a misunderstanding of the nature of the technology at issue, inasmuch as he continually refers to libraries 'collecting' material from the Internet. The case was actually about patrons' ability to 'collect' such information (and the government's ability to control such access). The libraries served as nothing more than a gateway to such access, and no more 'collected' the information on the Internet than they 'collected' the articles in a magazine or newspaper made available to patrons. Indeed, if Justice Rehnquist's analogy is correct, libraries might find themselves liable for payment of copyright royalties on *all* Internet content, since, by logical extension, all works on the Internet would become part of their 'collection', and would seemingly infringe the law unless otherwise licensed (eg, 17 USC § 108(g)(i) limiting the ability of libraries to expand their collection without payment of appropriate royalties). Such liability is congruous with his further statement that the Internet is 'no more than a technological extension of the book stack': 123 S Ct, 2305 (quoting from Senate Report No 106-141, 7 (1999)).

59 Ibid, 2310. Note, however, that this analysis applies only to Internet *access*, and does not overrule the court's earlier cases stating unambiguously that content on the Internet itself is to be afforded the highest possible First Amendment protection. Eg, *Reno v American Civil Liberties Union*, 521 US 844 (1997). Significantly, Justice Breyer did not join in Justice Rehnquist's exhortation (123 S Ct, 2304) that public forums are limited to those places historically used for First Amendment expressive purposes.

demanded only a 'rational basis' for imposing such a restriction. ... At the same time, in my view, the First Amendment does not here demand application of the most limiting constitutional approach – that of 'strict scrutiny'. The statutory restriction in question is, in essence, a kind of 'selection' restriction (a kind of editing).[60]

Thus, Justice Breyer argued that the key question is whether mandating filters in libraries is a 'proper fit', ie a means narrowly tailored to achieve the government's legitimate ends without unduly burdening First Amendment values.[61] Although Justice Breyer noted that filter technology is at best imperfect – blocking some legitimate material and letting through some obscene material[62] – no clearly superior or better-fitting alternative is presently available, so for the moment such technology constitutes a 'proper fit'. By Justice Breyer's reasoning, however, failure to use the best-fitting technology – ie, the filter which blocks the least amount of legitimate material – may itself give rise to a later as-applied challenge to implementation of CIPA.

Justice Stevens – who authored the nearly unanimous opinion giving expression on the Internet the highest degree of constitutional protection in *ACLU v Reno* – gave a blistering dissent. While he agreed that libraries' uncoerced, individual decisions to install filters raised no First Amendment concerns, Congress' imposition of such a requirement raised a very different question. Justice Stevens first raised the commonsense point that existing filtering technology was literally incapable of complying with CIPA's requirements, as it filters only by searching text, while CIPA covers only 'visual depictions'.[63] For Stevens, the issue was less about patrons' access than libraries' judgments about their collections, which he would grant First Amendment protection against federal interference.[64]

Although Justices Souter and Ginsburg joined in Justice Stevens' dissent, they paradoxically further argued that CIPA was unconstitutional because the First Amendment would be violated even if the libraries took these actions entirely on their own:

A library that chose to block an adult's Internet access to material harmful to children (and whatever else the undiscriminating filter might interrupt) would be imposing a content-based restriction on communication of material in the library's control that an adult could otherwise lawfully see. This would simply be censorship.[65]

Moreover, Justice Souter pointed out that the scarcity rationale posited by Justice Rehnquist is inapplicable to the Internet, and that the plurality's limited vision of libraries' mission is undermined by the fact that the libraries themselves are complaining about CIPA's provisions. Most persuasively, however, Justice Souter argued that since filtering occurs *after* the decision to supply Internet access is made, mandatory filtering is less like a decision to not acquire a book, and more like a decision to rip the pages out of a book already acquired:

---

60 *Ibid*, 2310–11.
61 *Ibid*, 2311.
62 *Ibid*, 2310, 2312.
63 20 USC § 9134(f)(1)(A)(i); 47 USC § 254(h)(5)(B)(i).
64 123 S Ct, 2316.
65 *Ibid*, 2320.

Thus, there is no preacquisition scarcity rationale to save library Internet blocking from treatment as censorship, and no support for it in the historical development of library practice. To these two reasons to treat blocking differently from a decision declining to buy a book, a third must be added. Quite simply, we can smell a rat when a library blocks material already in its control, just as we do when a library removes books from its shelves for reasons having nothing to do with wear and tear, obsolescence or lack of demand. Content-based blocking and removal tell us something that mere absence from the shelves does not.[66]

The American government's success in mandating the use of filtering technology in libraries may be only the beginning of a slippery slope. Recently, libraries have also become concerned that § 215 of the Patriot Act,[67] which expands the federal government's authority to search under the Foreign Intelligence Surveillance Act (FISA), will lead to federal agents reviewing patrons' library records and monitoring their Internet activity at library terminals. Perhaps to protect against that possibility, Congress included an explicit injunction that any such investigation of an American cannot be 'based solely on the American's exercise of his or her First Amendment rights'.[68] Nonetheless, a majority of the US Supreme Court has now said that access to the Internet involves no First Amendment rights. One must wonder whether the plurality's reasoning in *American Library Association* will extend to nullify that Congressional intent by finding that FISA monitoring of a library patron's Internet access does not involve First Amendment rights at all.

Conclusion

Clearly, the issue of Internet filtering is not going to go away, and indeed may be pushed to the forefront of other countries' legislative agendas based on the result in *American Library Association*. That decision itself leaves open further challenges to the actual implementation of such filtering in public libraries. Moreover, filtering technologies are still in their infancy. As the accuracy of filtering technology improves, its adoption by Internet users will increase, especially among families with children. The actual effects of such propagation remain to be seen. The question is, will the Internet remain a true 'marketplace of ideas', a blowsy bazaar of the bizarre to the banal, or will filtering technology transform the experience of many users into something akin to a Communist department store, where choice is limited by central governance?

---

66 *Ibid*, 2324. Indeed, Justice Souter also provides precedential support for his instinctive olfactory jurisprudence: 'The difference between choices to keep out and choices to throw out is thus enormous, a perception that underlays the good sense of the plurality's conclusion in *Board of Ed, Island Trees Free School Dist No 26 v Pico*, 457 US 857 (1982), that removing classics from a school library in response to pressure from parents and school board members violates the Speech Clause.' *Ibid*.

67 PL 107-56, 115 Stat 272 (2001). Section 215's relevant provisions are codified at 50 USC § 1861–62.

68 50 USC § 1861(2). For further explanation of these provisions, see Doyle, C, 'Libraries and the USA Patriot Act' (26 February 2003), at www.ala.org/Content/NavigationMenu/ Our_Association/Offices/ALA_Washington/Issues2/Civil_Liberties,_Intellectual_Freedom,_ Privacy/The_USA_Patriot_Act_and_Libraries/CRS215LibrariesAnalysis.pdf.

Perhaps to ask the question is to overstate the choices. Mandatory filtering or rating of content very much raises free speech concerns, as even the plurality in *American Library Association* recognised. Nonetheless, few democratic governments are going to seek to mandate private filtering.[69] Similarly, given open protocols and the global distribution of Internet technology, it would be very difficult to impose any system of universal ratings. As demonstrated by the growth of the open source movement,[70] the evolution of peer-to-peer technology, and the success of viral political campaigns, attempts to reign in the Internet through rating, blocking and filtering are likely Sisyphesian tasks.

Perhaps the greater danger to the marketplace of ideas lies not in government interference, but in user preference. With so much information now available electronically, intelligent users necessarily need to filter out the wheat from the chaff, and are going to rely on some form of filtering technology to accomplish that task. However, as each of us programs our browsers to our own preferences, installs the Internet filter which will keep out that which upsets or disturbs us, and visits only the sites approved by our own personal kite-mark society, our ability to be surprised, to be challenged, and to learn, is reduced.[71] The marketplace will still be there, but our own prejudices, voluntarily embedded in technology, may keep us from browsing at all of its stalls.

---

69 See Deibert and Villeneuve, Chapter 9.

70 For a detailed look at the growth of this phenomenon, see Moody, G, *Rebel Code*, 2001, Cambridge: Perseus.

71 Sunstein, C, *Republic.com*, 2001, Princeton: Princeton UP.

Chapter 9
Firewalls and Power: An Overview of Global State Censorship of the Internet

Ronald J Deibert and Nart Villeneuve

The Internet has often been declared immune from state censorship and surveillance by virtue of its decentralised design. Originally designed to route around damaged nodes, the Internet's dispersed architecture has been heralded widely as a major force for freedom of communications and access to information. Underlying nearly all of the global initiatives to spread Internet technology is an assumed association between the Internet and liberalisation. Indeed, authoritarian regimes have faced a major challenge maintaining their controls over information and communication as their citizens have connected to the Internet. And without doubt, the Internet has been a central force in facilitating the rise of civil society actors, dissidents, and transnational social movements of all stripes.

However, the Internet is not beyond the power and control of the state. Just as physical borders demarcate the boundaries of state power, states are seeking to create informational borders in cyberspace. Expanding into the digital realm, states are developing and implementing strategies, both legal and technological, that seek to control information flows on the Internet. Known as Internet blocking and content filtering, technological mechanisms used to censor and control access to the Internet have been developed and deployed. Although the race between state control and freedom of communications on the Internet may still favour the latter, the means used to filter and monitor are becoming increasingly sophisticated.[1] Perhaps even more so than traditional mass media, the Internet's dependence on software and hardware routing mechanisms may provide unprecedented opportunities for authorities to parse out and eliminate those types of information flows that are deemed illegal or threatening. At the very least, the perceived association between the Internet and liberalisation cannot be taken for granted as a natural outcome of the technology itself.

In this chapter, we provide a detailed overview of the relatively new practice of Internet content filtering. We begin by describing the different methods and means by which filtering takes place. As will be explained in detail below, there is no one single method or technology that states use to undertake Internet censorship and surveillance. Any firewall, router, proxy server or other networking device can be configured for filtering and used in conjunction with one or more such technologies at any or all levels of Internet access within a country with varying degrees of centralised co-ordination and control. Indeed, there are a wide range of strategies, products and tools that are deployed in different circumstances, creating a kind of matrix of controls that when fully imposed (as in the case of China) create a formidable set of constraints. We then turn to a brief illustrative survey of some national Internet censorship practices. Although countries like China and Saudi

---

1 For a detailed analysis of filtering technology see Esler, Chapter 8.

Arabia are widely acknowledged to censor Internet communications, the practice is much more widespread, and growing. Finally, we conclude with some observations on the implications of Internet censorship and surveillance for global communications policy, the practices of civil society, and the relationship between the Internet and democracy and liberalisation.

Internet content filtering and blocking

Knowledge of Internet censorship and surveillance is very much in its infancy. Although there have been several media and non-governmental reports in recent years, the basic techniques by which censorship and surveillance are undertaken are poorly understood. The means by which content is blocked or filtered on the Internet vary widely in terms of complexity, effectiveness and intent. Furthermore, not all of the means by which states attempt to control the Internet are technological. In some cases, regulations are employed to supplement technical controls, which can create a climate of what might be called *self-censorship* among Internet users. In the following section, we define some of the central terms associated with Internet content filtering and surveillance before turning to a global survey of state practices.

Internet content filtering is a term that refers to the techniques by which control is imposed on access to information on the Internet.[2] Content filtering can be divided into two separate techniques. *Blocking* techniques refer to particular router configurations used to deny access to particular Internet Protocol (IP) addresses or specific services that run on particular port numbers. For example, a state may run a blocking filter at the international gateway level that restricts access from within the country to websites that are deemed illegal, such as pornographic or human rights websites. *Content analysis* refers to techniques used to control access to information based on its content, such as the inclusion of specific keywords. Because parsing mechanisms employ keywords to block access, they are often the source of mistaken or unintended blockages. Depending on need and circumstance, different approaches to filtering can be implemented:

- *Inclusion filtering*: users are allowed to access a short list of approved sites, known as a 'white list', only. All other content is blocked.
- *Exclusion filtering*: restricts user access by blocking sites listed on a 'blacklist'. All other content is allowed.
- *Content analysis*: restricts user access by dynamically analysing the content of a site and blocking sites that contain forbidden keywords, graphics or other specified criteria.[3]

Most of the products and techniques used in filtering have the capability to use one or all of these approaches. These approaches are not mutually exclusive and can be used in conjunction with one another. Inclusion filtering is quite limited and

---

2 See Esler, Chapter 8.
3 Greenfield, P, Rickwood, P and Tran, H, 'Effectiveness of internet filtering software products', September 2001, at www.aba.gov.au/internet/research/filtering/filtereffectiveness.pdf, p 5.

therefore not in wide use. It is far too restrictive, as it allows user access only to pre-approved sites. Using this technique, the majority of the content on the Internet is effectively blocked. Exclusion filtering is the most efficient and common approach to filtering. Using this approach, all requests for URLs on the 'blacklist' are blocked. Depending on the technology, the URLs can be specific to certain web pages as well as blocking entire domain names. In addition, IP addresses of blocked domains are also added to the lists to avoid user circumvention.

Content analysis is a fast growing approach. Previously considered too restrictive and unreliable, content analysis technologies are taking advantage of the massive growth of computing power. Using this approach, content is filtered when keywords or phrases are found within the request for content or within the content itself. Content analysis techniques provide a potentially powerful way for states to parse out fine-grained bits of information contained within sites, as opposed to filtering entire sites altogether. The practice might be likened to censoring out individual sentences within books, as opposed to censoring entire books themselves.

Content filtering technologies are prone to two inherent flaws: *underblocking* and *overblocking*. While these technologies can be effective at blocking specific content such as high profile websites, the technology cannot filter similarly categorised content that is spread out across multiple domains: websites, newsgroups, email lists, chatrooms and instant messaging. Underblocking refers to the fact that content filtering technologies are incapable of blocking all content deemed 'unacceptable' and often with minimal effort restricted content can be found and accessed. On the other hand, filtering technologies often block content that they do not intend to block. Many blacklists are generated through a combination of manual designated websites as well as automated searches. Thus, websites are often wrongly classified and end up on blocking lists. Studies have consistently shown that this occurs regularly, thus routinely blocking thousands of websites.[4]

Overblocking is a significant challenge to access to information on the Internet, for it can put control over access in the hands of private corporations and unaccountable governmental institutions. In addition, because the filters can be proprietary there is no transparency in terms of the labelling and restricting of sites. The danger is most explicit when the corporations that produce content filtering technology work alongside undemocratic regimes in order to set up nationwide content filtering schemes. Most states that implement content filtering and blocking build customised blocking lists that sit on top of commercially developed technologies and blacklists.

The implementation of content filtering technologies and techniques will depend heavily on context and location. Exactly where content filtering/blocking occurs can be broadly divided into three categories:

- The *local* category refers to content filtering software installed on a personal computer in a private home, a business or public terminal.

---

4   For details, see www.onlinepolicy.org/access/schoolblocking.shtml;
    http://cyber.law.harvard.edu/people/edelman/mul-v-us;
    http://peacefire.org/censorware/BESS; http://censorware.net/reports/bess.

- The *organisational* category refers to network-based content filtering and blocking technologies used in the workplace, schools, and ISPs.
- The *national* category refers to state-directed implementation of national content filtering and blocking technologies at the backbone level affecting Internet access throughout a country.

At the local level, content filtering is most often implemented through the use of commercially available software. Known as *client-based* filtering, this type of software is marketed primarily to parents seeking to restrict their children's access to pornographic and other objectionable Internet content. These products are customisable and can be configured to use the whitelist, blacklist and/or content filtering approaches. In addition to strictly personal use, this type of filtering software is used in Internet cafés worldwide. In many places, the cost of a personal computer and Internet services, along with the lack of Internet connectivity, places the Internet out of reach for the average citizen.[5] Therefore, Internet cafés are an extremely important point of access for Internet users in developing countries. In some countries, Internet cafés are required by law to install and maintain content filtering systems provided by state authorities.

Organisational content filtering technologies can be deployed in a variety of ways but are primarily implemented through the use of routers, firewalls, or proxy servers. Known as *server-based* filtering, these methods will vary widely depending on the size and need of the organisation, but will more often than not rely on the blacklist method. Organisations and corporations with competent IT departments can effectively implement this method and successfully block user access to all specified IP addresses or domain names. Server-based filtering is generally implemented through the use of proxy servers. Sitting between a client program (eg, a Web browser) and an external server, a proxy server can monitor and filter any and all requests exchanged between the client and the external server. Proxy servers can be easily configured to deny requests for blacklisted sites and can log all the requests of users. In addition, proxy servers, along with firewalls and routers, can be configured to block the ports required by certain Internet services, thus reducing the chance of users employing countermeasures to bypass the content filtering.

At the national level, the Internet backbone and gateway routers can be configured to deny access to specific IP addresses or domain names. One method of implementation is the use of packet filtering. Data travelling across the Internet is broken down into IP packets that contain the IP address of the source and destination of the packets as well as the source and destination port of the packet. Routers and firewalls can be configured to block every packet going to or coming from IP addresses on the blacklist. Furthermore, packet filtering technology can be configured to sniff for specific keywords and deny access to content that contains such keywords. When implemented at international gateway points, such forms of content filtering can very effectively restrict entire national populations from gaining access to content deemed objectionable, making it difficult, although not impossible, for citizens to circumvent.

---

5 For a detailed discussion of this issue, see Paré, Chapter 7.

State content filtering practices

Understanding that the Internet is a complex decentralised medium, states are beginning to develop strategies to bring the borders of the Internet under their control. Even if the content filtering and blocking is at a low level, some countries are putting into place the institutional and technological means to rapidly escalate the level of censorship, should the need arise. In some countries, all levels of access are targeted and overlapping technical and policy means have been deployed, each developed or targeted toward a particular access level.

Non-technical (self-censorship)

Not all of the methods of controlling Internet content involve software and hardware. In some countries, regulatory measures create a climate of 'self-censorship', of which the best example is probably China. Self-censorship in China emerges at both corporate and individual levels. The former is motivated by access to lucrative Chinese markets while the latter is disciplined through intricate surveillance mechanisms. Nina Hachigian explains the significance of self censorship:

> [T]he self-censorship that the regime promotes among individuals and domestic Internet content providers (ICPs) is the primary way officials control what Chinese viewers see.[6]

The institutionalised mechanism for formal self-censorship is realised through a commitment to the 'Public pledge of self-regulation and professional ethics for China Internet industry', issued by the Internet Society of China (www.isc.org.cn). The 'Public pledge' commits signatories to abide by state laws, promote ethical Internet use and competition, observe intellectual property rights laws, and protect consumer privacy. Along with these seemingly innocuous clauses, the 'Public pledge' urges signatories to refrain from publishing information that may 'disrupt social stability' or 'spread superstition', which are in effect euphemisms for information that is critical of the state and information on religious groups such as the Falun Gong. Moreover, the 'Public pledge' places responsibility on ISPs to 'inspect and monitor information on domestic and foreign websites' and to block access to websites that 'disseminate harmful information'.[7] This 'Public pledge' transfers responsibility for censorship enforcement to organisations that have voluntarily accepted such restrictions.

Since its introduction on 16 March 2001, the 'Public pledge' has been signed by over 300 organisations, including Yahoo! Inc, the US Web portal giant. Yahoo! Inc provides Web portal, search engine, online chat and forum, and other services to users worldwide in a variety of languages. Their voluntary and public pledge to engage in self-censorship prompted Reporters Without Borders and Human Rights Watch to issue public letters to Yahoo! Inc, asking them to reconsider. Noting that

---

6   Hachigian, N, 'China's cyber-strategy' (2001) 80(2) *Foreign Affairs* 118.
7   Internet Society of China, *Public Pledge of Self-Regulation and Professional Ethics for China Internet Industry*, at www.isc.org.cn/20020417/ca102762.htm.

China restricts freedom of expression online and routinely imprisons those who engage in 'public expression of views that differ from those of the state', Human Rights Watch charged that there is a 'strong likelihood that Yahoo! will assist in furthering such human rights violations'.[8] Reporters Without Borders suggests that by voluntarily and publicly agreeing to censor Internet content, Yahoo! is complicit in 'demolishing the very foundations of the Internet and of democracy'.[9] Yahoo!'s legal representatives answered by stating that voluntary restrictions 'impose no greater obligation than already exists in laws in China', and therefore do not impose self-censorship beyond that which Yahoo! is already legally bound to enforce.

Internet café content filtering

In many developing countries, the costs of owning a personal computer are high and many individuals turn to Internet cafés and public access terminals to access the Internet.[10] At this level of local access, the primary mechanism of content filtering is the installation of commercial filtering on software on the local computer itself. Many countries have adopted legislation and implemented initiatives to ensure that café owners implement some form of content filtering in cyber cafés. In Turkey, Internet café owners must agree in writing to block access to specific Internet content.[11] Taiwan has introduced regulations that require Internet cafés to block access to pornography and gambling websites.[12] In addition to regulations, some countries have stepped up surveillance and police presence in Internet cafés. It is reported that in Tunisia and Vietnam undercover agents frequently visit Internet cafés and check the content users have been viewing.[13] Still others have moved to restrict women's access to Internet cafés. In Yemen, recent regulatory changes have required café owners to remove partitions between terminals, ostensibly to dissuade people from viewing pornography, but resulting in women being unable to use the terminals.[14] The combination of technical and physical surveillance along with regulations is being used to ensure that Internet cafés are effectively controlled. The result is that a primary location of Internet access in the developing world is effectively filtered and controlled.

In China, domestic firms have developed content filtering software which is approved by the Ministry of Public Security. This software, acting like other commercially available products, blocks access to a wide variety of websites that contain pornographic, violent and other 'objectionable content' including politically sensitive topics. These products are marketed primarily to parents, schools and Web cafés. In addition to extensive website blocking, these products also monitor and

8 Roth, K, 'Yahoo! risks abusing rights in China', Human Rights Watch, at http://hrw.org/press/2002/08/yahoo-ltr073002.htm.
9 Ménard, R, 'Open letter to the Yahoo! Chairman', Reporters Without Borders, at www.rsf.org/article.php3?id_article=2959.
10 See Paré, Chapter 7.
11 www.rsf.org/article.php3?id_article=7146&Valider=OK.
12 www.taipeitimes.com/News/archives/2001/11/15/0000111605.
13 www.rsf.org/article.php3?id_article=7252&Valider=OK.
14 www.guardian.co.uk/elsewhere/journalist/story/0,7792,1016428,00.html.

store information on users' Internet browsing. Furthermore, the software can be set up to alert the authorities when attempts are made to access banned content.[15] A popular content filtering product in China is Filter King. Filter King is available in several versions, including an enterprise net management system, family version and campus gateway. Filter King claims to block more than 500,000 websites which fall into categories such as pornography, gambling, narcotics, violence and reactionary doctrines. It contains keyword filtering options and can be set up to transmit users' attempts to reach banned information to a centralised police database.[16]

Organisational and business content filtering

Organisational filtering of schools, libraries and workplaces can be controlled through a combination of technical means. The most common is the implementation of proxy servers that deny access to particular blacklisted websites. The United States passed the Children's Internet Protection Act (CIPA) which required schools to implement 'Internet safety measures' in order to receive federal funding from the 'E-Rate' programme, which subsidises Internet access in schools. In effect, CIPA requires schools in the United States to have content filtering and blocking technology installed.[17]

While there are a variety of commercial content filtering products currently deployed in American schools, N2H2, the maker of the BESS system, has a dominant 40% market share.[18] BESS, like other commercial products, relies on a combination of blacklists and content analysis filtering. There are numerous configurable, categorised groupings of websites that can be blocked. In addition, BESS has configurable options that allow the filtering by keyword. This restricts the keywords that users can enter into various search engines.[19] However, testing of BESS and other commercial content filtering software indicates that these solutions are affected by both overblocking and underblocking. Due to a reliance on automated categorisation and slow and costly human review, content filtering software is unable to block all access to targeted content and also blocks access to legitimate content that it has inaccurately categorised.

The constantly growing Internet and the speed with which new content is created and old content modified renders content filtering software unable to keep pace, resulting in the flawed application of filtering.[20] Moreover, there is a complete lack of transparency and public review due to the fact that the block lists are the intellectual property of the company that created the software. Parents and educators are removed from the decision-making process and replaced with unaccountable corporations that rely on automated processes to determine content

---

15 For a variety of Chinese commercial content filtering products, visit www.1218.com.cn; information is also available at www.infosec.gov.cn.
16 Information on Filter King is available at www.zetronic.com.cn.
17 www.k12usa.com/cipa.asp.
18 For further discussion of N2H2 technology, see Esler, Chapter 8.
19 www.n2h2.com/products/bess.php.
20 http://cyber.law.harvard.edu/people/edelman/pubs/aclu-101501.pdf.

that is acceptable. This results in a democratic deficit in which there is no public scrutiny in determining what is and what should be blocked.

Whitelist filtering (Myanmar)

Internet access in Myanmar (Burma) is subject to tight restrictions and pervasive censorship. Internet access is available for a privileged few, including entrepreneurs and selected officials. However, the majority of users are confined to a government sanctioned intranet, an internal network of approved content. Understanding that there are numerous technical challenges to blocking all undesirable content, Myanmar has opted to allow in only information from previously approved websites. In some cases, users must request access to websites on the Internet for approval before they can be accessed. Other locations of access are subjected to 'blacklist' filtering. Myanmar uses an open source Web content filtering proxy, DansGuardian, loaded with customised lists of opposition websites, to implement a national censorship strategy. Users attempting to access banned content are presented with a special web page indicating that the website is blocked. Use of Internet and email services is heavily monitored and people who violate these strict policies face severe penalties.

Intermittent filtering

In some cases, filtering is deployed in an intermittent manner, often to coincide with specific events or politically sensitive time periods. During the 2001 presidential election in Belarus, the websites of major opposition newspapers, political candidates and civil society organisations were temporarily blocked.[21] For example, in response to the circulation of articles critical of the government, the Uzbek authorities temporarily blocked some Russian-language news and discussion web sites in January 2003.[22] Perhaps the most well known act of intermittent filtering occurred in September 2002 when access to the popular Google search engine was blocked in China for a period of two weeks.[23] By its very nature, intermittent filtering is perhaps the most difficult to detect.

Low-volume filtering, high-impact filtering

Some countries have opted for less intrusive national systems of content filtering and blocking. By focusing on specific 'high impact' websites, some countries seek to establish symbolic control, indicating that they will implement broader forms of control if people do not voluntarily censor themselves. This method also allows states to develop the technological and institutional infrastructure necessary to promptly implement far greater restrictions in a short period of time. Although the blocking at this point in time may be insignificant, the capacity is in place to respond rapidly to any new developments that may prompt the state to act swiftly and implement a far more extensive censoring regime.

---

21 www.cpj.org/news/2001/Belarus21sep01na.htm.
22 www.rferl.org/features/2003/01/31012003182158.asp.
23 http://news.bbc.co.uk/1/hi/technology/2231101.stm; http://web.amnesty.org/library/print/ENGASA170072002.

Recent developments in India have shown the difficulties involved in the implementation of a national content filtering capacity as well as the value that many countries see in being prepared for such an event. The government of India took particular exception to one Yahoo! Group, Kynhun, which had been posting material calling for independence from India. The government promptly ordered all ISPs in the country to block access to this particular Yahoo! Group. Unable to technologically implement this directive, many ISPs simply blocked access to the entire Yahoo! Groups domain (http://groups.yahoo.com), inadvertently preventing access to around 12,000 Yahoo! Groups.

Internet access is readily available in Jordan through ISPs and Web cafés and it is often reported that Jordan does not censor citizens' access to the Internet. However, at least one website – the *Arab Times Newspaper* (www.arabtimes.com) – is blocked, indicating that the capacity for backbone Internet content filtering is in place.[24]

In Singapore, ISPs are required to block a list containing 100 'high impact' websites – mostly pornography – at a national level. (Thailand appears to be following this model as well.) When accessing these sites, such as www.playboy.com, visitors are directed to a special web page that informs the user that the site has been blocked. Most reports indicate that these high impact sites are almost exclusively pornographic. The government also encourages ISPs to provide options and tools that users can install or access which censor the Internet. In this way, users are educated and encouraged to voluntarily submit to various censoring regimes.

National political filtering

A variety of other countries have adopted national level filtering systems that prevent access to Internet content that is specifically related to the country itself. In these cases, the websites of opposition groups, independent media, foreign media and human rights websites are routinely blocked. Users are not given any reason for the blockage, and instead receive generic 'file not found' or 'connection timeout' errors generally indicative that the website was not reachable although the website is in fact active. In an interesting case, Syria similarly blocks opposition and human rights websites but additionally blocks all domains with a .il (Israel) domain suffix. Thus, Syrian citizens are unable to access many Israeli websites. This is the only known instance in which one country has attempted to block all web content from another country.

In order to achieve superior filtering results, some countries have developed filtering solutions based on modified commercial systems. The expertise and dependable technology are purchased from foreign firms, many US-based, and implemented on a countrywide basis. All incoming and outgoing Internet traffic in Saudi Arabia is filtered through a proxy form system enabled with content filtering software. Pornography and sites considered to be in 'violation of Islamic tradition' are blocked. In addition, political websites identified by a security committee chaired by the Ministry of the Interior are blocked. The Internet Services Unit provides web-based forms through which users can suggest sites to be blocked and unblocked by authorities. Users accessing banned content are presented with a

---

24 For a full discussion of backbone filtering, see below.

special web page indicating that the website is blocked. The content filtering technology used in Saudi Arabia is developed by Secure Computing Corporation, the makers of SmartFilter.

Although Internet access in Yemen can be obtained through two ISPs, the majority of Yemenis access the Internet in Web cafés. Both ISPs employ server-based filtering systems in order to block pornography sites. Users trying to access banned content are presented with a special web page indicating that the website is blocked. The content filtering technology used by YNET Teleyemen, which accounts for 73% of Internet subscriptions in Yemen, is developed by Websense. This commercial technology allows countries to deploy more sophisticated blocking systems that can block by individual web page as opposed to blocking by entire domain or IP address. Through this technology, access to specific port numbers can also be blocked, as Saudi Arabia has done with specific ports that proxy servers are known to run on. In this way, anti-circumvention methods can effectively be deployed.

China's national content filtering system is probably the most ambitious, entailing a system of controls reaching down to the backbone level. The national backbone is a series of routers that connect China's internal networks to each other and to the international Internet. An Internet user's request for content or a service is routed through a series of backbone network routers. In China, these routers are configured to contain tables of banned IP addresses and they simply do not forward requests to the banned addresses, thus denying the user access to the requested Web content and services. At the user's end only a generic error message appears, indicating that the content cannot be accessed; it does not give reasons why. These error messages are generally the same as those received when a Web server is unavailable or there is some other networking problem. The user does not specifically know that they are accessing a website that has been deliberately blocked.

Recently, China has added increased packet filtering capabilities to the national gateway routers. Not only can Internet content be blocked by blacklisting domain names and IP addresses, but it can also be blocked by keyword. When requesting Web content that contains a banned keyword, the gateway routers block the request and deny connection between the requesting and responding IP addresses for up to 20 minutes. Domain names are also included as keywords, which indicates that overlapping techniques of filtering are being implemented at various levels to effectively control the information flow on the Internet.

Email is also being filtered in China. The filtering is occurring on two levels. The first is at the national backbone, where email traffic is filtered by subject line. Emails with subject lines that contain banned keywords are bounced back to the sender and do not reach the intended recipient. The next level occurs at the ISP. ISPs have begun to use spam filters to filter both the subject and body of emails. Emails containing banned words are bounced back to the sender with a message indicating that it has been blocked as spam. The message never reaches the intended recipient.[25]

---

25 The authors are currently engaged in a study of email filtering in China and have noted that it appears to be both intermittent and subject to variation depending upon the ISP.

Filtering Matrix – Countries currently being researched by the Citizen Lab. Note that this is not a comprehensive list, but is meant to be illustrative of the different scope of national content filtering schemes.

Limited: Access is restricted to a small number of websites.

Distributed: Access is restricted to a significant number of sites, but sporadically implemented by different ISPs.

Comprehensive: Access is restricted to a number of sites within a comprehensive national framework.

	Distributed		Limited
Iran	Iranian ISPs filter access to pornography, news, religious and dissident websites. However, some ISPs have not implemented filtering measures at all.	**France**	French courts have ordered Yahoo! to block access for French Internet users to auction sites that sell Nazi memorabilia.
Pakistan	Pakistani ISPs filter access to pornographic websites and at least one news website (www.satribune.com). However, filtering behavior differs across multiple ISPs.	**Germany**	ISPs in the German state of North Rhine-Westphalia block several foreign Nazi/hate websites.
USA (Bess-K12)	The Children's Internet Protection Act (CIPA) requires schools to implement 'Internet safety measures' (40% use BESS) to be eligible for 'E-Rate' funding. Tests show that BESS overblocks and underblocks.	**India**	Indian ISPs filter access to the Yahoo! Group Kynhun; some block access to the entire groups.yahoo.com domain; others simply do not implement blocking at all.
Vietnam	Some Vietnamese ISPs use proxy servers with an Access Control List system to filter Internet access to news, human rights and dissident websites.	**Jordan**	Jordan filters access to one website (www.arabtimes.com) at the national level.
Comprehensive			
Bahrain	The Bahraini state-controlled ISP, inet, uses proxy servers to filter access to dissident websites and pornography.	**Singapore**	Singapore requires ISPs to filter access to 'high impact' pornographic websites.

China	China has sophisticated technology deployed at the national backbone level that filters access to news, human rights, and dissident websites. China also has content analysis technology that filters by keyword.	**Syria**	Syrian ISPs use proxy servers to filter access to human rights websites and the entire .il (Israel) domain.
Cuba	Cuba filters access to dissident websites at the national backbone router level.	**Tunisia**	Both private and publicly owned ISPs have backbone connections through the Agence tunisienne d'Internet (ATI), which filters access to human rights, news, dissident websites and pornography.
Kazakhstan	Kazakh ISPs filter access to news and dissident websites using router access control lists.	**UAE**	In the United Arab Emirates Internet access is filtered through a network of proxy servers that block access to pornography and dissident websites.
Myanmar	Myanmar (Burma) uses DansGuardian to filter access to dissident websites and pornography.	**Uzbekistan**	Uzbekistan's ISPs filter access to the websites of opposition and Islamic political parties along with some news sites using router access control lists.
Saudi Arabia	Saudi Arabia uses technology developed by Secure Computing Corporation, the makers of SmartFilter, at the national level to filter access to human rights, dissident, gambling sites and pornography.	**Yemen**	Both Yemeni ISPs use server-based content filtering systems to filter pornographic content. YNET Teleyemen, which accounts for 73% of Internet use, uses technology developed by Websense.

Conclusion

In some respects, the increasing state control over Internet communications represents a natural maturation process. Like other means of communication, such as printing, radio and television, the 'Wild West frontier' period of innovation is gradually giving way to greater regulation and oversight as the technologies deeply permeate society with increasingly significant consequences for a wide spectrum of interests. As these interests come to depend on the Internet for vital concerns, the pressures to reign in the technology and shape the ways in which it is employed grow. Whereas once governance of the Internet was largely a technical concern, questions of Internet design and security have become increasingly politicised.

As described above, the Internet is certainly not immune to state intervention, as authorities have increasingly intervened in shaping the constraint environment within which global communications take place. Although there was once a time when the Internet was largely 'free' and unregulated, states have begun to adopt a myriad of measures to filter content and monitor communications. These measures range from very aggressive multi-spectrum controls, such as those implemented in China, to more simple methods of narrowly defined controls, as in Singapore and Thailand. Additionally, technological solutions to content filtering and surveillance are being provided by private corporations – a market sector that is likely to continue to grow worldwide in coming years.

These content filtering practices have a number of important implications for global politics, civil society and democracy. First, as the practice of Internet content filtering and surveillance is largely new territory, the rules by which states implement such controls are poorly defined, not well known among the general public, and very rarely subject to open debate. There may be circumstances where states may legitimately seek to circumscribe certain forms of speech and communication over the Internet, but as it stands now such decisions are typically taken behind closed doors through administrative fiat. Adding to the problem is the fact that the technologies implementing the content filtering are often commercial products with proprietary protections that conceal the methods used to filter content. Given that many of the countries engaged in content filtering practices are signatories to the United Nations Declaration of Human Rights, Article 19 of which protects access to information and freedom of speech and communication, at the very least these practices contradict important principles. At worst, they are being undertaken without a clear understanding of the costs and consequences for their societies of doing so.

Secondly, Internet content filtering places considerable constraints on civil society organisations, from business, to academia, to activists, restricting their ability to communicate worldwide and access information vital to their operations. It has long been assumed that one of the primary reasons for the rise and spread of civil society actors worldwide has been the Internet. If this assumption is true, one must begin to question what effects the strangulation of that environment will have for their activities, their operations, and their ability to network. Moreover, the subterranean ways in which such content filtering activities take place create considerable challenges to civil society actors, who may be completely unaware that information that exists on the Internet has otherwise been concealed from their view.

Lastly, the rise and spread of state censorship on the Internet raises important questions of public policy concerning the global communications infrastructure. Certainly the emergence of a global commons of information has been widely seen as an important collective good. Insofar as states begin to chisel away at that global commons, the 'network effects' generated by the interaction of individuals and organisations worldwide will almost certainly diminish along with it. From this perspective, the practice of individual states restricting access to information and freedom of speech and communications goes beyond national sovereignty concerns to affect the well being of individuals worldwide. In this respect, state censorship of the Internet must be considered a truly global issue for consideration by citizens of every country.

Chapter 10
Cyber Property
James Couser

... a wise man creates laws, but a foolish man is controlled by them.[1]

This chapter focuses on what will become the central question about the way in which virtual communities develop; namely the manner in which they are controlled. The Wild West of the early Internet has been tamed and in its place we have reached a cross section of paths, each representing a possible future along which the law in this area could develop. The question of which path is taken will, without some radical groundswell of public opinion to the contrary, ultimately depend upon which route will enable profits to be maximised. That may be an unpopular conclusion, yet, if the history of capitalism has taught us anything, it is that the greed that motivates the powerful few invariably triumphs over the inertia of the masses in the end. This chapter seeks to describe the manner in which the future may be shaped, and in particular to consider whether that is a good, bad or indifferent thing for the wider public generally.

Part of the difficulty faced by those who would place the boundaries of control differently, particularly where software is concerned, is that whilst any success they might enjoy resounds to the benefit of us all, they will receive little if any credit for that success. It is for this reason that, in the view of the author anyway, inertia will ultimately triumph. If proof of that assertion is required, ask yourself this question: we all know that the billionaire Bill Gates is the person behind Windows, but can you name the programmers responsible for the open source Linux operating system or the free email program, Pegasus? If you can you will doubtless also know that you are in the minority.

The nature of property

Property is a term that has been manipulated for centuries. This is not the place for a general discourse on all of the various forms of property, but it is important to set out a brief outline of the law in order to lay to rest what is perhaps the most enduring of all of the ghosts that haunt this area – the notion that copyright is somehow *necessarily* different from other forms of property regime. It is certainly different as we presently structure things, but that may have nothing to do with the fundamental nature of copyright interests, and everything to do with the economic goals of those who wish to protect such interests. Once it is accepted that there is nothing to prevent us structuring our intellectual property regimes differently, it becomes possible to begin addressing what ought to be the central issue: what should our response be to what is presently regarded as copyright infringement, and in particular to software piracy?

---

1 Kung-sun Yang, cited in *The Book of Lord Shang*, trans by Duyvendak, J, 2003, Clark, NJ: Lawbook Exchange.

Property is a term which, to lawyers anyway, describes the relationship each of us has with the things we encounter. It describes not just the thing itself, but also the relationship that the owner, and to a lesser extent the person in possession of the thing, has with it. It is this duality of meaning that has been manipulated by lawyers. By way of example, were I to loan my brother my car, I might properly speak of my property in it notwithstanding the fact that he is presently sat behind the steering wheel. Equally, the fact that I am presently driving my brother's car does not, without more, mean that I have rights of ownership over or to it. English law deals with this duality of interest by drawing a distinction between ownership and possession. Professor Goode describes this as meaning that English law recognises two interests in property: title and second best title; ownership and possession, in other words.[2]

To make this more manageable, and in an attempt to avoid the confusion that has often occurred in this area, I shall use the term 'asset' when referring to the thing itself, and 'interest' when referring to the various rights that an asset's stakeholders may assert. It is absolutely vital to be clear about the terminology in this area, because it is unconfined use of the term 'property' that has enabled the propagation and perpetuation of the myth that copyright is *necessarily* different. It may not, or at the very least need not, be. Very clearly, there are differences between intellectual property and the other property regimes, but then there are also differences between personal property and real property, but that should not lead us to assume that our response to those differences ought *necessarily* to be conceptually different. However, this is what occurs where copyright is concerned, and it is only by removing these blinkers and surveying the area afresh that we are able to discern what the proper response ought to be.

The rights of the interest holder of a piece of land who has parted with possession of it are, generally speaking, protected by the system of registration which, since 1926, has resulted in 70% of all the land in England and Wales being registered. Similarly, the rights of the interest holder of a car or some other piece of personal property are protected through the rules relating to *nemo dat*, yet where copyright is concerned the response is quite different. There the rules relating to ownership[3] are jettisoned altogether in favour of a scheme of granting a limited monopoly for a set period of time. This limited monopoly gives the right holder the power to control not just who may use the asset, but also the manner in which it may be used.

Now, to a certain extent it is true to say that copyright is no different from real or personal property in this respect. The interest in the asset is owned by x who then parts with possession on terms to y. If the asset is a piece of land, those terms might include restrictive covenants;[4] if it is a car, it might include a contractual term that

---

2 Goode, R, *Commercial Law*, 2nd edn, 1995, Harmondsworth: Penguin, pp 35–37.

3 As a matter of English law, only personal property is susceptible to ownership, with real property ultimately vesting in the Crown. However, for the purposes of this chapter I am disregarding this aspect of the doctrine of tenure, on the basis that it does not in any way alter the argument being made, and it is in any case arguably somewhat anachronistic as we move towards full registration of real property; see, eg, the Land Registration Act 2002.

4 In this respect, consider in particular Part 1 of the Commonhold and Leasehold Reform Act 2002.

the vehicle will not be re-sprayed in certain shades of colour.[5] In that respect, what the copyright holder does is no different from what x does in the above scenarios; it is simply a matter of utilising the contractual relationship between the parties to regulate the use to which the asset may be put. However, the key point is that intellectual property is designed to do this quite aside from any contractual relationship that might exist; its rationale is to enable the interest holder to retain control over the asset long after it has left his possession. Only intellectual property has this feature as its aim, its *raison d'être*. Where other forms of property are concerned, the usual situation is that a house or a car may have a succession of owners, each of whom has absolute freedom to treat the asset as they please. They cannot infringe the intellectual property rights of whoever designed the asset – assuming that those intellectual property rights are still extant – but they are perfectly at liberty to alter or modify it as they see fit, just so long as they don't reverse engineer the asset and begin selling their own version. As we shall see, even that restriction is open to criticism, but it at least allows the competing interests to be balanced by allowing the person who has paid for it to improve their asset if they believe themselves able to, whilst providing protection for the research and development costs that went into creating the asset. However, where software is concerned there is no such right of improvement, because copyright protection provides a monopoly, and whereas the car comprises both intellectual property interests *and* a physical asset, a computer program essentially comprises *only* intellectual property interests.[6]

There are numerous justifications for allowing some element of control in this way, but it is not so easy to justify copyright as it is presently formulated, and in particular for the length of time it is granted. The principal rationale for this markedly different response is intuitively fairly straightforward. The other forms of property regime all relate to tangible matter. I can touch a car or a book or a house or an apartment, whereas I obviously cannot touch a copyrighted expression of an idea. What is seldom addressed, however, is whether this is a valid reason for drawing such a distinction; whether what appears to be intuitively straightforward is capable of withstanding more considered scrutiny. The nature of the asset may be different, but does that mean that the nature of the interest is necessarily different also? For example, a green car (asset) is different from a blue car (asset), because one is green and one is blue, but the interest in each is the same: ownership or possession or whatever of a car. The question then is why should copyright *necessarily* be any different? We have chosen to structure our systems this way, but are those structures a good thing, or do they hamper innovation? Even if they were a good thing when we originally set the structures up, are they still a good thing now? And if they do hamper innovation, what, if anything, can we do about that? These are questions that the remainder of this chapter will seek to address.

---

5   As was apparently once the case with Rolls Royce motor cars.
6   The objection that even software must have some tangible component (in the form of its carrier medium) has now been eroded by the ability to download programs direct from websites.

Is copyright necessarily different?

We are, and have been for some time, encouraged to view copyright as different. We are frequently told that software piracy is evil, and that it is not just those that are involved in the wholesale commercial exploitation of copyrighted material who are pirates. It was instructive to note the lengths that the music industry in particular went to in order to shut down the peer-to-peer file serving website, Napster. What's more, having shut Napster down, the industry threatened individual users of the Gnutella network, which had sprung up in Napster's place, with prosecution.[7] The student or law professor who downloaded music on their home computer became, in the eyes of the copyright lawyers, pirates.

To a certain extent it is possible to see why those tasked with protecting intellectual property rights have adopted such a draconian attitude towards their work. It is well documented how those who would never dream of taking a piece of software from a shelf at their local store without paying for it will happily download the same piece of software for free via Gnutella or one of its clones. Furthermore, the paradox of that attitude is lost on the majority who, in short, regard downloading software as, somehow, different from stealing it from a shop.[8]

The difficulties that such attitudes throw up should not be ignored, because it is in all our interests that programmers should keep on programming, and the manner in which we presently make that worth their while is by offering incentives to innovate; in other words, the chance to exploit their ideas and make a little, or in some cases a lot of, money. If the opportunity to make money is undermined completely then the rationale for putting in the hard work which they will have to devote to a particular project is removed.[9] To this extent software piracy *is* different, because as matters presently stand there is little interest in the paperless office, and so people do not tend to download books, for example, in the same way that they do software. Furthermore, software is particularly vulnerable to perfect reproduction, so that a pirated version of Windows will be identical to the real thing. These difficulties have to be acknowledged and some form of incentive to innovation maintained yet, notwithstanding that fact, the system of copyright protection as it is presently structured goes too far where software is concerned.

The notion of copyright, as it was originally enacted in 1710, provided a right to control copying for a period of 21 years, which would automatically be renewed, or 'returned' to the author as the Act put it, for a further 14 years if he was still alive at

---

7   See, eg, *A & M Records, Inc v Napster, Inc*, 239 F 3d 1004 (9th Cir, 2001); *MGM et al v Grokster et al*, Summary Judgment, District Court (CD Calif), 25 April 2003, at www.techlawjournal.com/courts2001/mgm_grokster/20030425.asp; *RIAA v Verizon*, US Court of Appeals (DC Cir), 19 December 2003, at www.eff.org/legal/cases/RIAA_v_Verizon/.

8   See, eg, Couser, J, 'Software piracy and the Doris Day syndrome' (1999) 7 *Int J Law and IT* 1, pp 3–4, and in particular the citations given in fn 5.

9   This assumes that what motivates programmers is financial gain, and as such is open to the objection that that is unlikely to be universally true. However, even the creators of 'free' software, such as the Pegasus email program, have to eat. The man behind Pegasus, David Harris, finances himself by selling the operating manuals to those who want them, and so my argument – whilst admittedly not perfect – seems acceptable enough.

the end of the first period.[10] Copyright was intended to grant a right of limited duration. Most importantly, it was essentially a personal right, in that death prevented renewal beyond the original 14 year period. That is in stark contrast to the period of protection provided for today, where the primary period of protection is the life of the author, with a secondary period of protection for a further 70 years arising upon the author's death – life plus 70, as it is generally referred to. Where, for example, books or other forms of copyrightable material are concerned, this is difficult enough to defend. On philosophical grounds the justification for copyright is usually given as being that, as an author expresses himself through his work, so, as a manifestation of the author, the author ought to be able to control his work for the duration of his life, just as he is able to control other aspects of his life. However, the plus 70 years aspect of the protection provided makes no sense on this basis. Equally, a justification predicated on unjust enrichment has difficulty making sense of what is effectively in many instances the compulsory nature of the contractual relationship between the author and some third party. For example, whilst it may be James Couser who has written this chapter, the copyright has been assigned elsewhere. Of course I am 'free' to decline to accept this condition of publication, but that would simply result in the non-publication of my work, which is the sort of 'freedom' last seen elsewhere in the dark days of the *laissez-faire* contract cases where travellers were found to have 'agreed' to exclusion clauses in the train companies' terms and conditions that excluded liability for every conceivable ill that could occur. The fact that a traveller was only able to work if he first reached his place of work, and the fact that the only way to reach his place of work was by travelling by train, were considered to be irrelevant to the question of whether the passenger had 'freely' agreed to the exclusion clause.[11] The analogy with copyright is not, admittedly, a precise one, as what was being excluded in the ticket cases was, generally speaking, liability for death and personal injury. However, one way of viewing those cases is as examples of exploitation, as the traveller was essentially in a take it or leave it scenario in which leave it was not really an option at all, and that clearly is far more analogous with the copyright scenario set out above. This deeply manipulative aspect of copyright is barely addressed by the present legislation in this area, beyond the frankly toothless implementation of the *droit moral* in Chapter IV of the Copyright, Designs and Patents Act 1988.

However, whilst these arguments make the period of copyright protection difficult to defend generally, there are additional objections where software is concerned. A book may be read and re-read hundreds of years after its author's death, although admittedly only a tiny minority of books are read even 10 years or so after their first publication. With software, however, the period during which it will remain relevant and usable is always going to be quite limited. It is a truism that repays reconsideration that there is more computing power in a modern digital watch than in the craft that accomplished the first moon landing, the point being that this is a fast moving area, with computers doubling in capacity every 18

---

10 Statute of Anne, 1710.
11 See Atiyah, P, *An Introduction to the Law of Contract*, 1995, Oxford: Clarendon, pp 282–312.

months or so.[12] A program written even 20 years ago would seem hopelessly outdated, so that protection for such an enormous period of time is pointless. The period of time granted has been defended on the basis that copyright does not provide a monopoly, protecting only the expression of the idea rather than the idea itself,[13] yet one has to question whether that is in fact correct. A book about a teenage wizard might refer to Harry Potter, or to any number of less commercially successful works, but a piece of software will always have far less room for what is probably best described as dramatic licence; there are simply only so many ways of efficiently utilising information, and once all of them in a particular area have been programmed – and protected – that is the end of the matter until 70 years after the deaths of the programmers.

What we see from this is that the law in this area finds itself attempting unsuccessfully to reconcile competing tensions. On the one hand, we clearly do want to allow those who innovate to have some form of control over their creations, as it is that incentive to innovation that begets further innovation. On the other hand, the protection presently on offer is a blanket, one-size-fits-all solution, when that is patently not appropriate. One way of dealing with this would be to refuse copyright any special status, and to treat it as any other form of property, liable to be bought and sold once and for all, with no ability in the creator to control its subsequent use.[14] Such a response would in effect be to say that intellectual property is not *necessarily* different from the other property regimes discussed above, and to treat it as one would a piece of real or personal property. However, this would ultimately be to the detriment of society as a whole, particularly where software is concerned, because computer programs are uniquely susceptible to perfect reproduction. The very feature that enables software programmers to bypass retail outlets and market their creations direct to the public over the Internet also means that anyone who wishes to can copy the program perfectly and, usually, without fear of corruption. The only thing preventing them from doing so presently is the normative force of the law in this area. In the absence of such laws, the software programmer, knowing that his work is susceptible to being copied perfectly with there being nothing he can do to prevent that, will either have to make the initial unit price prohibitive in order to recoup his outlay and make a profit, or look for some alternative source of employment. Yet the present solution to this quandary ignores the fact that whilst the expression of the idea may be the work of the copyright holder, the idea itself is ownerless. However, as was explained above, the breadth of copyright means that where software is concerned it is in effect not just the expression of the idea, but also the idea itself that receives protection.

---

12 This is an application of Moore's Law. In 1965 Gordon Moore, who was then Director of Research and Development Laboratories at Fairchild Semiconductor, a Division of Fairchild Camera and Instrument Corp, predicted that the number of transistors on a printed circuit would roughly double every couple of years. Today, Moore's Law still holds true. For Gordon Moore's original paper, see ftp://download.intel.com/research/silicon/moorespaper.pdf.

13 See, eg, Bainbridge, D, *Introduction to Computer Law*, 5th edn, 2004, London: Longman, p 16.

14 Subject, of course, to their ability to impose contractual stipulations on those they sell to.

The commons and a continuum approach

What, then, is the answer to all of this? One solution, perhaps even the solution that will ultimately prevail, is to do nothing, to accept the status quo and prepare for a world in which, at least for the foreseeable future, ownership of the building blocks of code that make up the various software applications that govern our online lives is concentrated in the hands of a small bunch of businessmen. This is probably not so dystopian as it presently sounds. We have seen it all before with the railroads and coal mines that were the economic drivers of the 19th century and we know that, however unassailable the position of the rights holders may presently seem, they will, like Ozymandias, ultimately fade to nothing. That is the nature of a capitalist society, even assuming that capitalism is the future of society. The other side of that coin, however, is that without some external impetus such change is unlikely to occur in the lifetime of anyone reading this chapter, and that is something that ought to trouble anyone who cares about the issues that this discussion throws up.

For example, freedom of expression is a meaningless concept unless one also possesses the tools with which to communicate in the first place.[15] At one level this can be taken to refer to the email and chat programs that enable speech in the digital environment, as without these one is effectively mute. I can tap away at my keyboard endlessly, but without the relevant software running in the background I am speaking to myself. However, the point runs deeper than this. When I wrote the first sentence of this chapter, copyright automatically arose in my choice of words, so that the manner in which I expressed the arguments I am conveying received protection for the remainder of my life and an additional 70 years thereafter. However, the right I enjoy is over the manner in which I express the sentiments contained in this chapter; the ideas themselves are no more mine than the air I breathe. Following on from that, whilst the particular formulation of words may be mine, in the sense that – at the time of writing, even if not by the time of publication – I own the copyright in them, it is only the manner in which the words are arranged over which I have any control, rather than the words themselves. Others remain free to use those words as they please. That at first seems a rather trite point, but in fact it is central to understanding what is wrong with the law in this area when it is applied to software. The reason that I have no right to prevent others from utilising the words themselves is intuitively so obvious that we seldom stop to consider what its rationale might be. It is self evident that we cannot allow language to be gradually whittled away on a first-come, first-granted-copyright basis, as allowing that to happen would be simply farcical. It would, for no particularly good reason, provide a monopoly of extended duration over the words used solely because I happened to have been the first to use them. We would never allow that to happen, and yet that is in effect what allowing software the protection it is presently afforded does. For example, there are only so many ways of electronically moving money from one bank account to another. Once all of them have been reduced down into the form of software, there is no longer any free way of achieving that end. Whereas you are still free to use the words of my opening

---

sentence in your everyday speech, once others have programmed the various pieces of code that comprise a program in every conceivable way that they can be used for a particular purpose those pieces of code become off limits, as the only environment in which you would wish to utter them is a digital one. In other words, the effect of intellectual property as it is presently formulated is to limit your ability to speak code freely, as any attempt to do so will be an infringement of the programmer's copyright.

What the present rules are incapable of taking into account where software is concerned is that many of the interests in respect of which protection is sought are societal in nature. By this I mean that these interests cannot and should not ever be owned outright by one individual. It will be recalled that this chapter began by asking whether intellectual property rights are *necessarily* different from other forms of property regime. The answer to that enquiry was that they are, and yet the nature of the protection that such interests presently attract is curiously hybrid in its composition, resembling the ownership of the other forms of property regime when viewed from the perspective of the rights holders, but looking far more like a licence or other secondary form of right when it is the consumer's use of the software that is under consideration. It is instructive to return to the example of the first sentence of this chapter in order to see why this is an inappropriate response on any level. My use of the words I have employed may be the product of many hours' consideration. It may even be that I am some tortured genius, slaving over dictionaries and thesauruses for months, perhaps even years, on end, seeking out the perfect formulation of words. However, no matter how thickly I spread the hyperbole I will never acquire rights over the words themselves, only the use to which I have put them. The reason for this has most recently been explained by Professor Lessig in an account that is deceptively accessible.[16] Lessig draws upon the theory that certain things are common to us all,[17] the commons as they are known, pointing out that language is one such common. No one can own language; it belongs to us all equally but, courtesy of copyright, programming language abides by a different set of rules. It can effectively be curtailed, owned and controlled. It is, in short, not free, but no one consulted us on whether this was an acceptable state of affairs. It has simply been allowed to happen. Yet if programming language ought to be seen as just that, a form of language, then how is that recognition to be reconciled with the need to provide an incentive to innovation that it has already been conceded must be a necessary feature of the framework in this area?

One solution is to accept that the one-size-fits-all approach of copyright as it is presently formulated is simply inappropriate. The difficulty with this is that, whilst it has been suggested before, actually formulating a scheme within which it would operate has proved more elusive, yet that is not to say that it is impossible to do so. One possibility would be to insist upon registration of all copyrights before they take effect. So, for example, the opening sentence of this chapter would only acquire

---

16 Lessig, L, *The Future of Ideas*, 2001, New York: Random House.
17 In fact, part of the beauty of Lessig's account is that he supplements commons theory by inserting what he refers to as 'layers' into it: *ibid*, pp 19–25.

protection once I applied for protection for it. Alternatively, it would be equally possible to treat software as a class apart, such that copyright would continue to arise in other mediums in the manner that presently applies, but only in software once protection had been applied for. The advantage of this approach would be that the response to the fact of the computer programmer's work could be tailored to fit the specific circumstances of the case. Thus, a truly innovative program, such as the original Windows operating system, might well receive a degree of protection akin to that presently available. More humble programs, however, could not expect anything like the same level of protection. The real question that this approach would raise would be that of who would decide which programs warranted what protection. At first glance this seems a hopelessly subjective exercise, and it is certainly the case that it would involve a revision of the manner in which we presently view copyright. Instead of the process of registration being characterised as a principally administrative question of filling in the appropriate forms and paying the requisite fee, it would assume a qualitative aspect in which those charged with the task would be called upon to assess the relative merits of competing programs in order to decide what level of protection ought to be provided. Such an approach has the distinct advantage of allowing the level of protection provided to fit the need for protection in order to foster innovation, and is not entirely without precedent, as this is effectively what occurs where patents are concerned. The downside, however, is that there would most likely be lingering doubts about the ability of those responsible for this assessment to properly undertake it, just as there are such concerns in respect of the patent system itself.

However, despite such misgivings, we should not simply sit back and do nothing. The system as it is presently structured provides a blanket degree of control that is defective in almost every scenario it is possible to envisage. The proper approach ought to be to accept that any degree of control over the commons, however slight, must be justified on the very highest scale, and with a precision that has hitherto been lacking. Accepting this is necessarily also to accept that the degree of protection provided depends upon where on the continuum between commons and control any given piece of software happens to lie. It is only once this occurs that the scattergun, one-size-fits-all approach of the present set-up can be jettisoned.

Chapter 11
Virtual Sit-Ins, Civil Disobedience and Cyberterrorism

Mathias Klang

> Those who profess to favor freedom, yet deprecate agitation, are men who want crops without plowing up the ground ... This struggle may be a moral one; or it may be a physical one; or it may be both moral and physical; but it must be a struggle. Power concedes nothing without a demand. It never did and it never will.[1]

Introduction

The purpose of this chapter is to investigate the foundations justifying denial of service (DoS) attacks. The main thrust of this examination is whether or not such attacks may be seen as an acceptable form of civil disobedience.

In order to accomplish this, the concept of civil disobedience must be explored further, with a focus on its role in contemporary political activism. The term itself carries many ideas and concepts and is by no means straightforward. Within online civil disobedience the metaphor of the sit-in has been used by those who carry out attacks, and therefore this chapter will explore the mechanics of DoS attacks and compare them to the basics of the sit-in as a valid tactic of disobedience.

In the attempt to search for truth, legal academics and philosophers are both prone to the same mistake: attempting to ascertain the true meaning of a word in order to find out what the concept really means. Popper called this exercise nominalism[2] and, while this is an interesting and, at times, individually educational exercise, it may sometimes seem to be rather futile. The temptation is to follow the advice of Humpty Dumpty, who claimed: 'When I use a word it means just what I choose it to mean – neither more nor less.'[3] However, it is important to observe that in the discourse on online activism today one of the terms being used with alarming regularity is cyberterrorism.

When invoking the spectre of terrorism it is important to remember that today the relevance of the correct label in this case is far from academic. If the action of DoS is seen to be disobedience the courts may show tolerance; if it is seen to be criminal the courts will punish it; but if it is seen as terrorism then society will neither tolerate the actions nor forgive the proponents.

Terrorism and cyberterrorism

In his thesis on political terrorism, Bauhn notes that defining terrorism often hinges on the innocence of the victim. While he disagrees that the act should be defined by

---

1 Douglass, F, 'The significance of emancipation in the West Indies' [1857] in Blassingame, J (ed), *The Frederick Douglass Papers, Series One: Speeches, Debates and Interviews*, Volume 3: 1855–63, 1985, New Haven, CT: Yale UP, p 204.

2 Popper, K, *The Open Society and its Enemies*, 1966, London: Routledge and Kegan Paul.

3 Carroll, L, *Through the Looking Glass*, 1999 [1872], Mineola, NY: Dover.

the victim's innocence, he sympathises with previous authors' attempts to define the actions of the politically motivated terrorist. His own definition is founded upon an understanding of the difficulties of definition. He defines the terrorist as the perpetrator of terror, and states that 'political terroristic acts are violent, intimidatory and ... have political purpose'.[4]

While in the main the negative connotation remains, the general concept of terrorism has been under development, particularly so since 2001. The political discourse on terrorism has shifted the focus from the methodology of violent action to the descriptive term for those who would oppose the established order. The main change is that whilst in the past a violent political group was not necessarily terrorist, today a terrorist group does not necessarily have to have committed an act of violence.

The liberation of the terms terrorist and terrorism from the actual act of terror has allowed for a more flexible use of the label. Those who fight against terrorism are justified since terrorism is something reprehensible. This legitimacy is important since the violence perpetrated by the counter-terrorist can at times be greater than the violence carried out by the terrorist.[5]

While the removal or reduction of the need for violent activity[6] from the definition of terrorist has made it easier for the counter-terrorist to legitimise violence in the name of combating terrorism, it has also allowed for the creation of a more confusing concept of cyberterrorism, which is defined by Denning as the convergence of terrorism and cyberspace. Since the attacks are online, Denning's terrorist has to be redefined as one who attacks or threatens to attack information; she also adds the requirement that the attack should 'result in violence against persons or property, or at least cause enough harm to generate fear'.[7] This final part is worrying, since the attack need not cause devastation for the label of cyberterrorism to apply; it is enough if the attack generates fear. The qualification of fear has not been a necessity when defining or discussing offline terrorism. Whether the government or populus is afraid has little bearing upon the justification in applying the term terrorism to a political action. This addition of fear may be due to the fact that there have been few cyberterrorism attacks of any dignity, if indeed there have been any at all.[8] Despite the publicity and discussions of the vulnerability of the information society, the cyberterrorist remains a ghost in the machine rather than a serious threat.

---

4   Bauhn, P, 'Ethical aspects of political terrorism' (1989) 1 *Studies in Philosophy*, Lund: Lund UP.

5   Gearty, C, 'Terrorism and morality' (2003) *EHRLR* 377.

6   Gearty talks of 'the deliberate or reckless killing of civilians, or the doing of extensive damage to their property, with the intention of thereby communicating a political message of some sort to a third party, usually but not necessarily a government'. *Ibid.*

7   Denning, D, 'Cyberterrorism: Testimony before the Special Oversight Panel on Terrorism Committee on Armed Services, US House of Representatives', May 2000, at www.cs.georgetown.edu/~denning/infosec/cyberterror.html.

8   Vegh, S, 'Hacktivists or cyberterrorists? The changing media discourse on hacking' 7(10) *First Monday*, at http://firstmonday.org/issues/issue7_10/vegh/index.html.

Civil disobedience and the sit-in

There is a *prima facie* moral duty of the individual to follow the law. To some, this obligation to obey the law is absolute. Socrates, for example, believed in following the rules of society. So firm was his belief that even when Crito suggested that an escape could be arranged he refused, took his penalty and drank the fatal poison. Socrates expanded his position by explaining that he was obligated to the state and had accepted its rules, and it would be wrong to disobey those rules; therefore there could never be justification for doing wrong.[9] For most, this duty to obey the law is based upon the belief that without this obedience either the state would be unable to function or without total obedience some would gain unfair advantages.[10]

Whilst the rigour of Socrates' position may well be admired, it is seldom emulated. The discussion of whether there is a duty to obey the law is rarely taken to this extreme. However, the question of whether there is a duty of obedience towards the law and the state is an active one, since the question of when disobedience is valid remains. Practitioners of civil disobedience tend to justify their actions by pointing to the fact that they are fighting a larger injustice and in this role they have the right, some would even claim the duty, to break the law. Therefore, the disobedients are doing what they believe to be morally right despite the fact that their actions unfortunately come into conflict with the enforced rules. The term civil disobedience itself contains two important parts: civil action and disobedience. Dr King needed four criteria for his action to be legitimate: documented injustice, negotiation, self-purification, and direct (non-violent) action.[11]

Opposing the state on a large scale tends to border upon rebellion or revolution. Opposing parts of the state – or more correctly opposing certain of the state's commands – has become known as civil disobedience. It is important to bear in mind that there is a fine line between rebellion and civil disobedience. In what is probably the most famous protest against the social effects of technology, the Luddites, protesting against the mechanisation of the textile industry, destroyed factory machinery. The Luddites were defeated by armed soldiers, and the leaders were either executed or deported in 1813. On a smaller scale, but with an enduring legacy, Henry David Thoreau felt that his country was acting immorally and reached the conclusion that once a government no longer behaved morally, its citizens no longer had an obligation to support it. He recommended that citizens withdraw from their obligations towards the state. In England, Emmeline Pankhurst and her daughters formed the Women's Social and Political Union, whose purpose was to speed up the enfranchisement of women. Its members, commonly known as suffragettes, believed that their cause needed publicity and to further this goal they committed illegal acts (eg, chaining themselves to railings and setting letterboxes alight) to shine the light of publicity on their cause. Such violence and destruction of property is not accepted by all activists.

---

9   Plato, *Five Dialogues*, Grube, GMA (trans), 2002, Indianapolis: Hackett.
10 These positions have been challenged by legal academics: see, eg, Raz, J, 'Obligation to obey: revision and tradition', in Edmundson, W (ed), *The Duty to Obey the Law*, 1999, Boulder, CO: Rowman & Littlefield; Smith, M, 'Is there a *prima facie* obligation to obey the law?' (1973) 82 *Yale LJ* 950; Wolff, R, *In Defence of Anarchism*, 1970, Berkeley, CA: University of California Press.
11 King, M, 'Letter from Birmingham City Jail', in Bedau, H (ed), *Civil Disobedience in Focus*, 1991, New York: Routledge.

Mohandas Gandhi was a great believer in non-violent protest. His ideas were formulated at the onset of the South African campaign for Indian rights and can be best seen in the Indian struggle for independence from the British Empire. One of the most impressive non-violent campaigns was the Salt campaign, in which 100,000 Indians were jailed for deliberately violating the Salt Laws. Since the creation of the doctrine of non-violent resistance formulated by Mohandas Gandhi, the term 'civil disobedience' regularly includes non-violence as an additional qualification. Spurred on by the success of non-violent resistance, the methodology was adopted by Martin Luther King in his successful campaign to bring an end to racial segregation laws. While the origins of the sit-in are difficult to locate, a popular point of origin stems from 1960 when four African American college students in Greensboro, North Carolina protested against the whites-only lunch counter by sitting there every day. After the publication of an article in the *New York Times* they were joined by more students and their actions inspired similar protests elsewhere.

The concept of disobedience as conceived by Gandhi and developed by Dr King was to draw attention to the injustice and in this manner to commence a political discussion that would lead to the creation of more just society, which is the purpose of civil disobedience.[12] For many, the implementation of information and communications technology (ICT) for the same end was inevitable. The earliest formal connections seem to be made as early as 1996, when the Critical Art Ensemble published a book containing a chapter on the topic of Electronic Civil Disobedience.[13]

Distributed denial of service

The DoS attack is usually described as an incident which prevents a legitimate user or organisation from accessing a systems resource or the delaying of systems operations and functions. The incidents or attacks can be related to a specific network service such as email, or to the domain name of the target. Attacking the domain name has the added advantage for the attacker of tending to diminish all the victim's online functions since the domain name cannot be resolved. This means legitimate users attempting to access a web-based service are unable to connect to the server, since they are unable to acquire the necessary IP address to do so. This is due to the fact that the server under attack is busy responding to its attackers' requests and is unable to reply to legitimate users' requests. The legitimate user, unaware of the ongoing attack, will only receive an error message from her browser that the server is unavailable.

Traditionally, the distributed DoS attack entailed the co-ordination of traffic to a designated website; this first required the marshalling of many protesters to be prepared at their computers to send information at a given time to a specific target. These attacks were complex affairs, and required a great deal of social cohesion and organisation amongst the protesters, who sat alone in front of their computers with only the virtual presence of others. To overcome some of these organisational

---

12 Rawls, J, *A Theory of Justice*, 1999, Oxford: OUP.

13 Critical Art Ensemble, *Electronic Civil Disobedience and Other Unpopular Ideas*, 1996, New York: Autonomedia.

problems, co-ordinating software may be used by protestors. Such attacks are known as co-ordinated point-to-point DoS attacks. In these kinds of attacks the attackers may use software with the same effects as that used in the point-to-point DoS attacks. Naturally, the more users and the more sophisticated the software, the more efficient the attack. The important issue with this type of attack is that it still requires a user to be involved in the attack, and to be efficient it requires the gathering of a large group of people who have the time, technology and will to carry out the attack.

While there are different forms of DoS attack, such as TCP SYN flooding, ICMP flooding, UDP flooding and ping of death, the most common is TCP SYN flooding, which will be explained briefly here.

When attempting to view a web page, the browser attempts to establish a contact with the server upon which the information is stored. The initial contact is made up of the client and server exchanging a set sequence of messages known as the three way handshake:

1   The browser (client) begins by sending a SYN message to the server.
2   This is acknowledged by the server by sending a SYN-ACK message to the client.
3   The final message is an ACK message sent by the client.

After the handshake, the connection between the client and server is established. The required data can thereafter be exchanged between the client and the server, whether it is email, a web page or any other TCP-based service.

This system is at its most vulnerable when the SYN-ACK message has been sent by the server since, at this stage, the server is awaiting the final ACK message. At this point the connection is half open. Since the memory of the server is finite and the system requires the server to save to memory any half-open communications awaiting the final ACK message, the system can be caused to overflow if too many unfinished connections are made. In order to intentionally create the half-open connection, a technique known as IP spoofing is used. This technique entails the sending of SYN messages to the server with non-responsive client systems, ie systems which are unable to respond to any SYN-ACK messages received. The effect of too many half-open connections is that the server's memory will be filled and the system will be unable to accept any new SYN messages until the list of awaiting half-open connections have been completed or timed out. Existing or outgoing connections will in most cases not be affected. When the attackers stop sending spoofed IP messages the server will time out those messages awaiting response and recover; however, for this to occur the attacker must stop sending the messages.

These types of attack that still involve the physical intervention of the user have sometimes been called client-side DoS, to differentiate them from server-side DoS. While the client-side DoS requires the active participation of many like-minded individuals, the server-side DoS has no such requirement. To be effective the server-side DoS attack requires only one individual and the creation of an army of zombies. In this context, a zombie is a computer containing a hidden software program that enables the machine to be controlled remotely. For the purpose of the DoS this remote control of other people's computers is done with the intent of attacking a specific victim server.

The most efficient method of introducing software into other people's computers with the capability of taking control of them at a specified date is either by hacking into the computer and installing the software directly, spreading the program in the form of a virus, or including the code within a piece of desirable software that the user will download and install himself.

Two well publicised examples of server-side DoS attacks are the Mafiaboy attack, where a 15 year old known only as Mafiaboy successfully attacked websites operated by Yahoo!, eBay and Amazon.com,[14] and the 13 year old who used a DoS attack to take down a California-based computer security site.[15]

The advantage of using zombies to carry out the attack on a server is that the attacker does not need to disadvantage himself by persuading and co-ordinating other users in participating in the attack. There is an added advantage of increased anonymity, since the attacker's machine is not directly involved in the DoS attack but acts only via its unwitting intermediaries – the zombies. With adequate time and effort in preparation, the number of zombies created can be sufficient to create havoc with even the most sophisticated of servers. Naturally, the more time spent in preparation, the more likely it is that the plans will be uncovered prior to the attack and defences will be created that will limit the effects of the attack.

Online activists: the electrohippies

There has been insufficient research into hacker culture and psychology to create a nuanced picture of what motivates people to carry out DoS attacks. This has left the field open for simplification, generalisation and the creation of the image of the hacker as a technically sophisticated but naïve young man who is driven by ignorance, a desire for destruction or purely criminal impulses. This image is the one most often used in media and has been mirrored in films from *WarGames* (1983) to *Swordfish* (2001).

However, when attempting to comprehend the driving forces behind the hacker, it is important to look beyond our own media imposed images. In his research into hacker culture, Taylor[16] identifies six main driving forces that motivate hackers (addiction, curiosity, boredom, power, peer recognition and opposition); within the section on peer recognition, Taylor includes politically motivated actions. The book is an excellent starting point for those wishing to understand the hacker; however, it is important to recognise that it is based upon research carried out prior to the growth of online activism. Today, a book on hackers must recognise the effects of a larger group of politically motivated online activists.

---

14 Jaffe, J, 'Attacks fell an online community', 27 January 2003, at www.wired.com/news/infostructure/0,1377,57392,00.html.

15 Gibson, S, 'The strange tale of the denial of service attacks against grc.com', Gibson Research Corporation, at http://iso.grc.com/dos/grcdos.htm.

16 Taylor, P, *Hackers*, 1999, London: Routledge.

The actions of DoS attackers are, or are rapidly becoming, illegal. The question which therefore needs to be addressed is what it is that drives these people to carry out such actions. If they are merely criminals, then we need hardly proceed any further. The question is whether there can be any legitimacy in their actions. In order to explore this further, we must take a closer look at the motives underpinning online activists. However, this is not as simple as it may sound, since the current legal environment does not promote the development of an open dialogue between attacker and society.

A group of activists dedicated against the trend of clandestine action is the *electrohippies collective*. This group uses client-side DoS as a protest method and it does so in an open manner. They write: '... we do not try to bury our identities from law enforcement authorities; any authority could, if it chose to, track us down in a few hours. However, because some of us work in the IT industry, we do not make our general membership known because this would endanger our livelihoods.'[17] Furthermore, the group has taken pains to publish its views in a series of publications available online.

In an attempt to create a dialogue on the subject of the use of DoS as a political activism tool, the electrohippies have employed the sit-in as a metaphor and they term their attacks virtual sit-ins. Since they use the client-side method they do not employ zombie machines, and without zombies their actions must be supported by those willing to carry them out. One of their claims of legitimacy is that they have the popular support of the protesters: 'Our method has built within it the guarantee of democratic accountability. If people don't vote with their modems (rather than voting with their feet) the action would be an abject failure.'[18]

Since they are dependent upon popular support, in order to have any effect their actions must be deemed worthy of support by the protesting individuals. To obtain this support, the collective established four principles, which govern any action they undertake. The principles are proportionality, speech deficits, openness and accountability. Proportionality refers to the insight that it is not acceptable to disrupt communications without justification; the attack itself must not be the focus. The tactic is a means and not an end: it brings publicity to an event which *is* the focus of the action.[19] The action can only be legitimate if a speech deficit exists, ie a lack of equality between the actors within the public discourse. The attack must therefore be used to draw attention to this inequality and is not in itself the intended goal. The principles of openness and accountability refer to the legitimacy of the attack, since without these it would be difficult to argue that the ultimate goal is an open discourse.

The electrohippies' views are not unopposed; another group of activists argue that since DoS attacks are a violation of people's freedom of expression and

---

17 DJNZ and the Action Tool Development Group, 'Client-side distributed denial-of-service: valid campaign tactic or terrorist act?' (2000) *The Electrohippies Collective Occasional Paper No 1*, February 2000, at www.fraw.org.uk/ehippies/papers/op1.html.

18 *Ibid.*

19 As an example, they cite their actions against the WTO, which coincided with the offline protests in Seattle. *Ibid.*

assembly, 'No rationale, even in the service of the highest ideals, makes them anything other than what they are – illegal, unethical, and uncivil'.[20] The electrohippies are aware of the paradox of using DoS attacks for the purpose of promoting open and free speech since they are curtailing the speech of others, but they maintain that their actions are justified if their principles are adhered to.[21]

In March 2003, virtual sit-ins organised by the electrohippies against the war in Iraq managed to disrupt the Prime Minister's website (www.number-10.gov.uk), causing it to be unavailable on several occasions. In response to criticism, they argued that their actions did not prevent any communications between the allies but were intended to show the use of official websites as a part of the propaganda directed at 'seeking to sanitise their violation of International human rights law. Action by the Collective is therefore valid in order to highlight their violation of fundamental rights by a method that seeks to restrict their misuse of the right to freedom of expression under the UN Universal Declaration'.[22]

Denial of service and law

The Computer Misuse Act (CMA) 1990 provides no remedy against DoS attacks. It creates three offences: unauthorised access to computer material, unauthorised modification of such material, and unauthorised access with intent to commit or facilitate commission of further offences. This means that the CMA can only be applied in server-side DoS attacks since these attacks require the use of zombies.

The UK realised that legislation in this area needed to take technological developments into account, and in May 2002 an amendment to the CMA was introduced to the House of Lords, which *inter alia* dealt with DoS attacks. It defined what DoS is, and the terms under which a DoS action is a criminal offence. The amendment also included changes to ensure that a person could be prosecuted for a DoS attack where proof of the action was available within the jurisdiction of the United Kingdom. However, the Bill was never passed. Legislation which can be used against DoS attacks includes the Terrorism Act 2000, which defines terrorism in this context as the use or threat of action that is designed to seriously interfere with or seriously disrupt an electronic system for the purpose of advancing a political, religious or ideological cause.

Internet-based crime led to calls for harmonisation of the substantive and procedural security laws of EU Member States, and for the UK to ratify the European Cybercrime Convention and the European Commission's proposal for a Council Framework Decision on attacks against information systems.[23] Article 4 of this Decision deals directly with the criminalisation of DoS attacks.

---

20 Oxblood Ruffin, Cult of the Dead Cow (17 July 2000) Response to Electrohippies, at www.cultdeadcow.com/archives/000865.php3.

21 *Op cit* fn 17.

22 Electrohippies Collective's online protest against the Iraq War, 2003, at www.internetrights.org.uk/casestudies.shtml.

23 COM(2002) 173 final. Adopted in April 2002, it provides a general framework to approximate and increase judicial and police co-operation in relation to attacks against information systems. Member States had until 31 December 2003 to implement the proposed framework.

These developments have had the effect of criminalising DoS attacks. Additionally, the Convention on Cybercrime reinforces the legal position that these acts are criminal offences or should be criminalised, leaving little room for interpretation of DoS as a tool of protest. In the case of DoS attacks, actions which hinder the functioning of a computer system by suppressing computer data are criminalised by Article 5 of the Convention.[24] However, despite the increase in legislation in this area, several issues of legal interpretation remain unresolved[25] and this creates an unsatisfactory position vis à vis the predictability of the law.

Toleration of disobedience

In the press conference presenting the Commission's proposal for a Framework Decision on attacks against information systems, the Commissioners created clear links between DoS and terrorism.[26] Since September 2001, as we have seen, discourse on the response to terrorism has become increasingly harsh. This has led to greater calls for the criminalisation of DoS attacks with little attention being paid to their role as a method of peaceful democratic protest.

It is often pointed out that freedom of expression is the foundation upon which any democracy stands, since without the ability to freely spread and collect ideas there cannot be a functioning democracy. Naturally, even this right must be balanced so as not to seriously hamper the rights of others. In the physical world, we tolerate (to a varying degree) our lives being occasionally disrupted. Animal rights protesters may hamper our ability to enter fast food restaurants; anti-war demonstrators may hinder our ability to travel through city centres as we normally do. Our daily lives are also hampered by jubilant rugby supporters cheering the homecoming team, crowds viewing royal pageants, or roadblocks and diversions set up to protect visiting politicians. Around the world on New Year's Eve there is mass disobedience in the streets as the New Year is ushered in. These events are tolerated by society since they are deemed important to society.

Most protesters believe in the importance of their actions. To the rest of society, these actions are annoyances. Despite this, such annoyances are important since they are the voice of dissent, and it is only through the growth of dissent into mainstream thought that social development can take place. Despite the fact that we today feel that the causes people such as Dr King and Gandhi fought for were just and their methodology is seen as being worthy of our admiration, this does not mean that civil disobedience is commonplace and acceptable in society. The goals and methods of civil disobedients in the past are always easier to accept than the goals of those protesting against the status quo today.

---

24 *Ibid.*
25 Kerr, O, 'Cybercrime's scope: interpreting "access" and "authorization" in computer misuse statutes' (2003) *NYU L Rev* 1596.
26 Commissioner Vitorino (Speech/02/174) and Commissioner Liikanen (Speech/02/175), 23 April 2002.

On the surface it would seem that society cannot create a right of civil disobedience since there can be no permission to disobey. Those who fear civil disobedience see a state of anarchy where individuals disobey rules on a whim. Fear of this anarchy maintains the status quo: a belief in the ideals of civil disobedience, a respect in the past practitioners, but no desire to create a toleration of disobedience.

A common position adopted by those who oppose disobedience is that civil disobedience has no place in a democratic society. This argument is based upon the belief that democracy is the ultimate form of self-rule, which allows the greatest amount of input from the individual on the rule of law.[27] Therefore, disobedience against the system is not the answer since the system itself is meant to be self-correcting and inequalities can be changed from within.

It is important to make the distinction that while the state may be democratic, it does not necessarily follow that all practices therein are just. To be able to redress an injustice within this system, those who are affected by it must appeal for change. This appeal is the process of bringing the injustice under the gaze of those who have the ability to create change. Singer has defined the process of disobedience as one method for a minority to appeal to the majority to reconsider an injustice.[28] The need for disobedience in such an appeal is necessary when the democratic process itself prolongs the injustice. Disobedience is therefore not intolerance towards the system but the view that allowing the democratic process to run its course perpetuates the injustice. Dr King goes further and states that there is an obligation to disobey in the situation where the law is unjust:

> For years now I have heard the word 'Wait!' It rings in the ear of every Negro with piercing familiarity ... We must come to see, with one of our distinguished jurists, that 'justice too long delayed is justice denied'. ... You express a great deal of anxiety over our willingness to break laws. This is certainly a legitimate concern. Since we so diligently urge people to obey the Supreme Court's decision of 1954 outlawing segregation in the public schools, at first glance it may seem rather paradoxical for us consciously to break laws. One may ask: 'How can you advocate breaking some laws and obeying others?' The answer lies in the fact that there are two types of laws: just and unjust ... One has not only a legal but a moral responsibility to obey just laws. Conversely, one has a moral responsibility to disobey unjust laws.

This still does not resolve the concern about what would happen if everyone disobeyed. Thoreau and Gandhi argue that disobedience is not a bad thing; they base this conclusion on their conception of anarchy as an equitable form of government. However, this argument does not put most of us at ease. The fear is that the legitimate actions of people like Dr King will be copied by the less scrupulous. While Dr King ensured the justification of his actions by using four stages[29] and also insisting upon non-violence from his supporters, it is often

---

27 Harrison, R, *Democracy*, 1995, London: Routledge.
28 Singer, P, *Practical Ethics*, 2nd edn, 1993, Cambridge: CUP.
29 Determining whether injustices exist; negotiation; self-purification; and direct action. *Op cit* fn 11.

assumed that copycats will be less thorough. This increase in lawlessness due to the acceptance of disobedience has, however, been disputed.[30]

There is another problem: if we are to objectively accept that disobedience is justified for a certain group, then how may disobedience be limited for others? This type of argument is often referred to as the slippery slope, the idea being that we cannot allow any disobedience since the moment we accept any form of disobedience we will rapidly slide to the bottom of the slope and be required to accept all disobedience.

Those who argue that the slippery slope will lead us to anarchy would prefer that no disobedience be allowed. This is a simple and elegant solution which provides us with an easily remembered rule. However, the problem of disobedience is already complex, and attempting to simplify it with absolute rules is not an equitable solution. Using the slippery slope to create a feeling of insecurity is not an acceptable solution. Such arguments have been used and abused over a long period of time;[31] their complexity may create a desire to simplify. Let us not deny justice for the sake of simple arguments.

If the protest, even the DoS, is an appeal from a minority group to the majority to reconsider and to pay attention to what is occurring within a certain situation, then it fulfils a worthwhile purpose. If the effects of DoS attacks are ephemeral, the purpose also justifies the cost. Therefore, the creation of legislation with the intent of criminalising protest under the guise of terrorism is to minimise the openness we presently enjoy in society.

Conclusion

The politically motivated online disobedient is actively partaking in a political discourse, the goal of which is to create a more equitable society. The disobedient is exercising fundamental rights of expression (and virtual assembly). Traditionally such rights are not limited without serious cause. The present legislative trends which criminalises DoS attacks in the name of terrorism are much too far reaching and seriously hamper the enjoyment of individuals' civil rights.

The blanket limitation of civil rights within a society should only be tolerated if the limitation also has the effect of removing a serious threat to the society which faces those limitations. The threat of cyberterrorism has been greatly overstated and is founded upon a lack of understanding of the technology, or even technophobia. If the threat comes not from terrorists but rather from criminal use of the DoS technique, then the legislation goes too far in its attempts to create order.

---

30 Dworkin, R, 'Civil disobedience', in *Taking Rights Seriously*, 1978, Cambridge, MA: Harvard UP.

31 Volokh, E, 'The mechanisms of the slippery slope' (2003) 116 *Harv L Rev* 1026.

Chapter 12
Privacy: Charting its Developments and Prospects

Rebecca Wong

Introduction

Since the publication of the influential paper 'The right to privacy' by Samuel D Warren and Louis D Brandeis, the study of privacy has evolved into a topical discussion of the development of the subject, ranging from its philosophical foundations to its legal development.[1] How privacy has been interpreted depends on the context, but its interpretation has been the subject of divergent opinion, ranging from those who take a reductionist approach to those who hold that privacy is unique in its own right. The legal protection of privacy under the European Convention on Human Rights has, however, taken a wider approach, preferring to detach itself from the very definition of 'privacy' as a concept, and focusing its attention instead on the aspects that form part of private life and balancing this with the provision on freedom of expression. This will be the subject of discussion later in this chapter. To begin with, the question that arises is: what legal developments have arisen following Warren and Brandeis' seminal paper?

In their article, Warren and Brandeis considered whether the existing US law afforded a principle, which could properly be invoked to protect the privacy of the individual, and the nature and extent of such protection, by examining the role of property law, tort law and copyright. Although specifically concerned with the legal interpretation of privacy in the US, the article levelled its criticisms generally at media intrusion into people's lives: a case not dissimilar to recent UK examples involving the privacy of celebrities.[2] Furthermore, the article implicitly identified a new right of privacy that ought to be protected by US tort law.[3] The issues arising from the Warren and Brandeis article were by no means harmonious. On the contrary, it raised concerns over the extent to which privacy can be applied as a tortious remedy in US law.

In response to Warren and Brandeis, Dean Prosser identified and elaborated four distinct torts on privacy, further stating that Warren and Brandeis had focused their attention solely on the second tort.[4] The four torts are:

---

1   Warren, SD and Brandeis, LD, 'The right to privacy' (1890) 4 *Harv L Rev* 193. See Kalven, H, 'Privacy in tort law – were Warren and Brandeis wrong?' (1966) 31 *Law and Cont Prob* 326; Prosser, W, 'Privacy' (1960) 48 *Cal L Rev* 338; Bloustein, E, 'Privacy as an aspect of human dignity: an answer to Dean Prosser' (1964) 39 *NYU L Rev* 962; Leebron, D, 'The right to privacy's place in the intellectual history of tort law' (1991) 41 *Case Western Reserve L Rev* 769.

2   It was argued that the article was prompted by the newspaper's interference in Warren's wedding. This has been disputed in Barron's article: 'Warren and Brandeis, "The right to privacy" (1890): demystifying a landmark citation' (1979) 13 *Suffolk UL Rev* 875. See also Leebron, *op cit* fn 1.

3   Leebron, *op cit* fn 1.

4   Prosser, *op cit* fn 1.

1 Intrusion upon seclusion or solitude.
2 Public disclosure of private facts.
3 False light in the public eye.
4 Appropriation.

A subsequent article by Bloustein,[5] in response to Prosser's paper, reiterated the nature of a single tort in privacy and argued that Warren and Brandeis were concerned with the notion of 'inviolate personality'. The term 'inviolate personality' includes other notions such as individual dignity and integrity, personal uniqueness and personal autonomy.

There are numerous commentaries on the legal protection of privacy within the US,[6] and it is not the purpose of this chapter to examine the nature of such developments, nor is it to provide an exhaustive definition of privacy, which would prove to be counterproductive. Rather, its purpose is to consider the main definitions given by privacy scholars to the concept of privacy, paying particular attention to the issues and arguments involved in such definitions. This will be followed by an examination of the legal protection of privacy through Article 8 of the European Convention on Human Rights, the Data Protection Directive and the common law of confidentiality. Finally, I will examine the case, if any, for the tort of privacy in the UK and whether *de facto* privacy has been implemented through the law of confidence and the Human Rights Act 1998.

Concepts of privacy

Given its importance as a political value,[7] the concept of privacy has nevertheless presented numerous difficulties for privacy scholars in defining what is perceived to be an ambiguous term.[8] Definitions have ranged from the right to be let alone,[9] to 'development of personality',[10] to the right to control information about oneself.[11] It would, however, be a fallacy to take the view that privacy consists primarily of 'the

---

5 Bloustein, *op cit* fn 1.

6 Reidenberg, J and Schwartz, P, *Data Privacy Law*, 1996, Dayton, OH: Michie; Rotenberg, M, *The Privacy Law Sourcebook 2003*, 2003, Washington, DC: EPIC; Solove, DJ and Rotenberg, M, *Information Privacy Law*, 2003, New York: Aspen.

7 See Bennett, C, *Regulating Privacy*, 1993, London: Cornell UP; McCloskey, H, 'The political ideal of privacy' (1971) 21 *Philosophical Quarterly* 303; Thompson, J, 'The right to privacy' (1975) 4 *Philosophy & Public Affairs* 295, where it is commented that 'nobody seems to have a clear idea what privacy is'.

8 Davis, F, 'What do we mean by "right to privacy?"' (1959) 4 *South Dakota L Rev* 1; Wacks, R (ed), *Privacy, Vol 1*, 1993, Aldershot: Dartmouth, p xii; Wacks, R, 'The poverty of privacy' (1980) 96 *LQR* 73. See also Laurie, G, *Genetic Privacy*, 2002, Cambridge: CUP, which provides a comprehensive definition of privacy by differentiating between spatial and informational privacy.

9 Cooley, T, *A Treatise on the Law of Torts*, 1907, Chicago: Callaghan & Co. Justice Cooley's definition can be found in Warren and Brandeis' seminal article, *op cit* fn 1.

10 Strömholm, S, *Right of Privacy and Rights of the Personality*, 1967, Stockholm: Norstedt.

11 Fried, C, *An Anatomy of Values*, 1970, Cambridge, MA: Harvard UP, p 141; Wasserstorm, R, 'Privacy: some assumptions and arguments', in Bronaugh, R (ed), *Philosophical Law*, 1978, London: Greenwood.

right to be let alone'.[12] Privacy is, by no means, an absolute right.[13] This can be evidenced by looking at the jurisprudence of the European Court of Human Rights, which qualifies the right to privacy with derogations such as the interests of national security and the rights and freedoms of others.[14] Westin examines the argument by taking the view that 'the constant search in democracies must be for the *proper boundary line* in each specific situation and for an over-all equilibrium that serves to strengthen democratic institutions and processes'.[15] What needs to be clarified from the outset is how privacy has been described. As Schoeman argued, there is a difference between a claim, entitlement or right to privacy and a measure of control (control-based definition).[16] A claim asserts the status of privacy, but does not provide the reasons for its importance. Some commentators have preferred to describe the condition of privacy rather than give a definition.[17] Privacy has also been described as a state of limited access to a person, which is the corollary of a control-based definition.[18] The question that arises is: what are the elements characterising a control-based definition of privacy?

Control-based definition

In his book on *Privacy and Freedom*, Westin takes an anthropological perspective on the concept of privacy. He provides a twofold definition of privacy, holding that it is a 'claim of individuals, groups, or institutions to *determine for themselves when, how, and to what extent information about them is communicated to others*'.[19] Viewed in terms of the relation of the individual to social participation, privacy is the voluntary and temporary withdrawal of a person from general society through physical or psychological means, either in a state of solitude or small-group intimacy, or, when among larger groups, in a condition of anonymity or reserve.[20] Westin's definition refers to a control-based definition. A further criticism of the control-based definition is its emphasis on individual autonomy, which has been identified as a weakness in formulating a policy to protect privacy.[21]

In rejecting the individualistic approach, Regan argues that greater recognition should be given to the 'broader social importance of privacy'. She suggests three grounds for this, namely, privacy as a common value in which all individuals value

---

12 Diffie, W and Landau, S, *Privacy on the Line*, 1998, Cambridge, MA: MIT Press, p 150. Here the authors took the view that the 'right to be let alone' was not realistic in a modern society.
13 See Murray, Chapter 15.
14 European Convention on Human Rights, Article 8(1), (2).
15 Westin, A, *Privacy and Freedom*, 1967, London: Bodley Head, p 25 (emphasis added).
16 Schoeman, F, *Philosophical Dimensions of Privacy*, 1984, Cambridge: CUP, pp 2–4.
17 See, eg, Parent, W, 'Privacy, morality and the law' (1983) 12 *Phil & Pub Affairs* 269, who preferred to describe privacy as a condition.
18 Schoeman, *op cit* fn 16, p 3.
19 See Westin, *op cit* fn 15, p 8 (emphasis added).
20 Westin, *op cit* fn 15, p 7. See also Murray, Chapter 15.
21 Regan, P, *Legislating Privacy*, 1995, Chapel Hill, NC: University of North Carolina Press, p 212.

some degree of privacy; as a public value, which is not merely of value to the democratic political system; and finally as a 'collective value' in the light of technological developments and market forces, requiring a similar minimum level of privacy. Indeed, the final category is particularly pertinent where privacy is a particular concern in the context of 'unsolicited commercial communications'.[22] These views do bring a different perspective to the concept of privacy and underline the need to be clear about what privacy entails.

A further argument against the control-based definition is that individuals may not necessarily have lost control over their personal information, where they willingly give up their privacy in certain respects.[23] In rejecting the control-based definition, Parent preferred to describe privacy as:

> the condition of not having undocumented personal knowledge about one possessed by others. A person's privacy is diminished exactly to the degree that others possess this kind of knowledge about him.[24]

Parent also develops the idea of personal information as 'facts which most persons in a given society choose not to reveal about themselves ... or ... facts about which a particular individual is acutely sensitive and which he therefore does not choose to reveal about himself'.[25]

The restriction or control of personal information has been partially achieved through the data protection legislation, which restrains organisations from collecting or processing personal information without the individual's consent, and this is particularly the case with special categories of information.[26] The term 'partially' is used because there are a number of exemptions from consent that are covered under the Data Protection Directive 95/46/EC and national legislation implementing the Data Protection Directive (DPD).

Reiman, however, found that the control-based definition of privacy was inadequate:

> Privacy must be a condition independent of the issue of control ... the right to privacy is not my right to control access to me – it is my right that others be deprived of that access ... having this right will protect my ability to control access to me.[27]

The control-based definition, however, does not take into consideration instances where personal information may be obtained without the knowledge of the

---

22 Reference is also made to 'unsolicited commercial communication' in Article 7 of the E-Commerce Directive 2000/31/EC. This should be interpreted in conjunction with the Directive on Privacy and Electronic Communications 2002/58/EC, which prohibits the sending of unsolicited mail without the consent of individuals, preferring the opt-in approach (see Article 13).

23 Parker, R, 'A definition of privacy' (1974) 27 *Rutgers L Rev* 280.

24 Parent, *op cit* fn 17.

25 *Ibid*, p 270.

26 Special categories of information require explicit consent under Article 8 of the Data Protection Directive 95/46/EC. These are racial/ethnic origin; political opinions; religious or philosophical beliefs; trade union membership; and data concerning health or sex life.

27 Reiman, J, 'Driving to the Panopticon' (1995) 11 *Santa Clara Computer & High Technology LJ* 27, p 31.

individual through surreptitious means, data mining techniques and online profiling.[28] This would leave the individual with no control over their information and the only means of redress would be through the protection of legislation such as data protection legislation. Thus, although the control-based definition does not solve all the problems in defining privacy, it can be described as one of the main features characterising privacy.

The philosophical definition of privacy

Two schools of thought predominate in the interpretation of privacy: the reductionist approach, which takes the view that privacy is not unique and can be reduced to other interests; and the view that privacy is unique in its own right.

In support of the reductionist theory, Thompson argued that the right to privacy is derivative, in the sense that it can be explained in the case of each right without the need to mention the right to privacy:

> For if I am right, the right to privacy is 'derivative' in this sense: it is possible to explain in the case of each right in the cluster how come we have it without even once mentioning the right to privacy. Indeed, the wrongness of every violation of the right to privacy can be explained without even once mentioning it.[29]

This argument has been attacked by scholars such as Rachaels,[30] who took the view that privacy was distinctive and important as a value. It does, however, raise the issue of whether the UK has adopted a derivative stance in the legal protection of privacy by holding the view that it can be protected through other rights such as the law of confidentiality and defamation without the need for an explicit privacy right.[31]

Another view contributing to the reductionist approach was advocated by Posner, who took an economic perspective on the analysis of privacy. He argued that while 'personal privacy seems to be valued more highly than organizational privacy, a reverse ordering would be more consistent with the economics of the problem'.[32] He also argued for the maximisation of investment in the production and communication of socially useful information. Gavison, however, took the view that privacy is a unique concern and should be given weight in balancing values.[33] She recommended that the law should make an explicit commitment to privacy. Such a commitment would, in her view, affirm that privacy was not just a convenient label, but a central value. However, she did not uphold the view that this equates with the absolute protection of privacy. Reiman also favoured privacy as a unique. He contended that:

> The right to privacy is the right to the existence of a social practice which makes it possible for me to think of this existence as mine ... The right to privacy, then, protects

---

28 Bygrave, L, *Data Protection Law*, 2002, The Hague: Kluwer Law International, pp 301–57.
29 Thompson, *op cit* fn 7, p 313.
30 Rachaels, J, 'Why privacy is important' (1975) 4 *Phil & Pub Affairs* 323.
31 I will return to this point later in the chapter.
32 Posner, R, 'An economic theory of privacy', in Schoeman, *op cit* fn 16, p 333.
33 Gavison, R, 'Privacy and the limits of law' (1980) 89 *Yale LJ* 421.

the individual's interest in becoming, being and remaining a person. It is thus a right which all human individuals possess, even those in solitary confinement.[34]

It is important to understand the two views, which will form the basis of any arguments in favour of or against a legal right to privacy.

Legal definition of privacy

Having considered some of the theoretical arguments underpinning the definition of privacy, the question arises as to the legal protection offered to protect privacy. This chapter considers the protection of privacy in the United Kingdom through Article 8 of the European Convention on Human Rights (ECHR), data protection provisions and confidentiality.

Inspired by the UN Declaration of Human Rights 1958,[35] the ECHR was adopted and ratified by all the Member States of the European Community. Article 8 expressly provides that:

1 Everyone has the right to respect for his private and family life, his home and his correspondence.

2 There shall be no interference by a public authority with the exercise of this right except such as is in accordance with the law and is necessary in a democratic society in the interests of national security, public safety or the economic well-being of the country, for the prevention of disorder or crime, for the protection of health or morals, or for the protection of the rights and freedoms of others.

Unlike the UN Declaration of Human Rights, it does not expressly refer to 'arbitrary interference' and does not forbid attacks upon honour and reputation.[36] It is couched in terms of 'respect' rather than actual reference to privacy itself. *Prima facie*, it appears to be wider in scope than the term of privacy. The question then arises as to how far privacy can be and is protected through this provision. Is privacy synonymous with the notion of 'private life'? The European Court of Human Rights provided some guidance on the concept of 'private life', extending it to business, but refraining from giving an exhaustive definition:

... it would be too restrictive to limit the [notion of private life] to an 'inner circle' in which the individual may have his own personal life as he chooses and to exclude therefrom entirely the outside world not encompassed within that circle. Respect for private life must also comprise to a certain degree the right to establish and develop relationships with other human beings.[37]

---

34 Reiman, J, 'Privacy, intimacy and personhood' (1976) 6 *Phil & Pub Affairs* 26, p 44.

35 Protected under Article 12 of the Universal Declaration of Human Rights 1948, which provides that 'no one shall be subjected to arbitrary interference with his privacy, family, home or correspondence, nor to attacks upon his honour and reputation'.

36 Velm, J, 'The European Convention on Human Rights and the right to respect for private life, the home and communication', in Robertson, A (ed), *Privacy and Human Rights*, 1973, Manchester: Manchester UP, p 15.

37 *Niemietz v Germany* (1992) 16 EHRR 97, p 111.

In *Botta v Italy*[38] it was held by the European Court of Human Rights that the notion of 'private life' includes a person's physical and psychological integrity; the guarantee afforded by Article 8 of the ECHR is primarily intended to ensure the development without outside interference of the personality of each individual in his relations with other human beings. This was reiterated in the case of *X v Iceland*,[39] which concluded that the right to respect for private life 'comprises also to a certain degree the right to establish and develop relationships with other human beings, especially in the emotional field for the development and fulfilment of one's own personality'.

Article 8 does not simply impose negative obligations which must be adhered to, but also entails positive obligations, as in *X and Y v The Netherlands*, which held that 'there may be positive obligations inherent in an effective respect for family life. These obligations may involve the adoption of measures designed to secure respect for private life even in the sphere of the relations of individuals between themselves'.[40] In addition, the interpretation of 'respect' under Article 8 also imposes a positive obligation to comply with Article 8 and this can be exemplified in *Marckx v Belgium*.[41]

Where Article 8(1) has been breached, Article 8(2) can only be invoked if such interference was in accordance with the law, necessary in a democratic society, and for the furtherance of one of the aims listed in Article 8(2). 'In accordance with the law' has been interpreted to mean that there must have been some form of legal basis for such interference (*Eriksson v Sweden*):

> The phrase 'in accordance with the law' requires, *inter alia*, that if the law confers a discretion, its scope and manner of exercise must be indicated with sufficient clarity to afford a measure of protection through arbitrary interference.[42]

Interference must also be necessary in a democratic society. Such measures must have been proportionate to the aims and not exceed the means necessary to achieve the aim (*Olsson v Sweden*).[43] It will also take into account the margin of appreciation.[44] In *Hatton and Others v UK*,[45] it was held that there must have been less onerous ways of achieving the aims. The body of case law that has been built up to encompass a wide range of rights under Article 8 reflects the diversity and extent to which this provision can be invoked: it includes freedom from surveillance (*Malone v UK; Niemietz v Germany; Huvig v France; Kruslin v France*),[46] access to personal records (*Gaskin v UK*)[47] and right to family life (*Olsson v Sweden; Eriksson v*

---

38 (1998) 26 EHRR 241.
39 Application No 6825/74, 5 D & R 86.
40 (1986) 8 EHRR 235, p 240.
41 (1979–80) 2 EHRR 330.
42 (1990) 12 EHRR 183, p 184.
43 (1989) 11 EHRR 259.
44 The doctrine of margin of appreciation gives Member States discretion as to how to perform their obligations (*Handyside v UK* (1976) 1 EHRR 737).
45 (2002) 34 EHRR 1.
46 (1991) 13 EHRR 448; (1992) 16 EHRR 97; (1990) 12 EHRR 528; (1990) 12 EHRR 547, respectively.
47 (1989) 12 EHRR 36.

Sweden).[48] The major issue that arises is whether the incorporation of the ECHR through the Human Rights Act 1998 (HRA) has effectively created a statutory right to privacy and whether it creates rights between private parties (horizontal effect). Space does not permit an in-depth analysis of this issue, but suffice it to say that the academic debate has been to decide whether to grant full horizontal rights or whether the HRA has created indirect horizontal rights. There is no universal consensus and the issue remains unresolved.[49]

The protection of privacy through the law of confidentiality

The lack of consensus over the concept of privacy can also be explained by its relationship with confidentiality.[50] In the absence of a UK privacy right,[51] the law of confidentiality has frequently been invoked as a possible legal avenue for invasions of privacy.[52] To find a claim for breach of confidentiality, there must be a relationship which imparts an obligation of confidence, and there must have been unauthorised use of such information.[53]

The extension of the law of confidentiality to cover instances normally considered to be within the domain of privacy has led to a state of confusion and uncertainty over the scope of the law of confidentiality and whether it should be utilised as a ground for protecting privacy *per se*. In the light of recent judgments such as *Douglas v Hello!*[54] and *Wainwright v Home Office*,[55] it does appear that the courts' approach to the issue of privacy has been to use the law of confidentiality to provide a remedy for an invasion of privacy. Indeed, in the case of *A v B and C*,[56] the Court of Appeal overturned an injunction granted to prevent the disclosure of a footballer's adulterous liaisons with two other women in order to protect his private and family life. The court held that 'in the majority of situations, if not all situations, where the protection of privacy was justified, an action for *breach of confidence now would, where appropriate, provide the necessary protection*'.[57]

However, recent comments made by the judiciary appear to relax the second limb of the confidentiality criteria, that there must be a relationship imparting an obligation of confidence.[58] In *Attorney General v Guardian Newspapers Ltd*, Lord Goff

---

48 (1989) 11 EHRR 259; (1990) 12 EHRR 183, respectively.

49 Eg, Wade, W, 'Human rights and the judiciary' [1998] *EHRLR* 520; Wade, W, 'Horizons of horizontality' (2000) 116 *LQR* 217.

50 Wacks, R (ed), *Privacy, Vol II*, 1993, Aldershot: Dartmouth.

51 See *Kaye v Robertson* [1991] FSR 62.

52 See, eg, *A v B* [2002] 3 WLR 542; *Douglas v Hello!* [2001] QB 967, CA; *Venables and Another v News Group Newspapers* [2001] 1 All ER 908.

53 *Coco v AN Clarke (Engineers) Ltd* [1969] RPC 41.

54 [2003] 3 All ER 996.

55 [2003] UKHL 53.

56 [2002] EWCA Civ 337.

57 *Ibid* (emphasis added).

58 Phillipson, G, 'Transforming breach of confidence? Towards a common law right of privacy under the Human Rights Act' (2003) 66 *MLR* 726.

stated that 'it is well settled that a duty of confidence may arise in equity independently of [a transaction or relationship between the parties]'.[59] Further, in *WB v H Bauer Publishing Ltd*, the court articulated the view that:

> English common law [is] moving towards greater protection for privacy; the means by which this is being achieved would appear to be by the *development of the law of confidence*. One of the inhibiting factors about this aspect of the law hitherto has been that it was traditionally necessary to establish a duty of confidence – most frequently associated with a prior relationship of some kind. It is becoming easier now, however, to establish that an obligation of confidence can arise (in equity) without the *parties having been in any such prior relationship*. The obligation may be more readily inferred from the circumstances in which the information came to the defendant's attention.[60]

Another case that comes to mind is *Campbell v MGN*, where the information was obtained not through a confidential relationship, but rather through the covert operation of a photographer in taking photographs of model Naomi Campbell leaving a Narcotics Anonymous meeting. The Court of Appeal found that an obligation of confidence arose in this situation.[61] However, the House of Lords decided by a majority of 3:2 that Campbell retained a right to privacy, overturning the Court of Appeal's decision. Lord Nicholls took the view that the time had come to recognise that the values enshrined in Articles 8 and 10 are now part of the cause of action for breach of confidence. Lord Hoffmann, however, expressed the view that 'what human rights law [had] done [was] to identify private information as something worth protecting as an aspect of human autonomy and dignity'.

Other views include Phillipson, who has argued that the law of confidence appears to 'implicitly endorse the radical view of confidence, whereby the obligation can be imposed solely through the nature of the information concerned' rather than through a pre-existing relationship of confidentiality.[62] This was further amplified in the *Douglas v Hello!*[63] case, where the two famous complainants brought a claim *inter alia* for breach of confidence as well as breach of privacy. The case is significant because the Court of Appeal examined the issue of privacy in some depth. Lord Justice Sedley took the view that privacy itself as a legal principle could be drawn from the fundamental value of personal autonomy. Sedley LJ considered that there were 'perceived needs of legal policy' for a new cause of action in tort:

> What a concept of privacy does, however, is accord recognition to the fact that the law has to protect not only those people whose trust has been abused but those who simply find themselves subjected to an unwanted intrusion into their personal lives. *The law no longer needs to construct an artificial relationship of confidentiality between intruder and victim:*

---

59 [1990] 1 AC 109, p 281.

60 [2002] EMLR (emphasis added).

61 [2003] QB 633.The claim of confidentiality arose out of the fact that MGN had obtained and made public information about Campbell which was not intended for the public domain. The Court of Appeal held that MGN could rely on the defence of public interest in order for the press to put the record straight, if a public figure chose to make untrue pronouncements about his or her private life. The case has recently been decided by the House of Lords. The decision may be found at [2004] 2 WLR 1232.

62 *Op cit* fn 58, p 746.

63 [2001] QB 967.

it can recognise privacy itself as a legal principle drawn from the fundamental value of personal autonomy.[64]

These comments have been the subject of interpretation in a recent case, *Wainwright v Home Office*. The case concerned the strip search of a woman and her son in accordance with rule 86(1) of the Prison Rules 1964.[65] The claimants instigated legal action on the basis of an invasion of their privacy, arguing that in order to enable the UK to conform to its international obligations under the ECHR, the court should declare that there was a tort of invasion of privacy under which the searches of both claimants were actionable. The Court of Appeal rejected any claim to a common law right to privacy, a decision later affirmed by the House of Lords,[66] where Lord Hoffmann regarded the comments made by Sedley LJ as merely advocating the extension of the law of confidentiality, rather than supporting a view in favour of a general principle of privacy. According to Lord Hoffmann, the protection of privacy should be introduced by legislation rather than through the existing common law. In addition, it was argued that ss 6 and 7 of the HRA were sufficient to fill the gaps in existing remedies. Though it is acknowledged that there is no right to privacy at common law, there is a view that the protection of privacy has been statutorily created through the HRA, and this issue appears to have been sidestepped in this case, which might have provided a stronger ground for the argument in favour of legal protection of privacy.[67]

What are the arguments, if any, against the extension of the law of confidentiality to protect privacy? As Wright argues, the law of confidence cannot simply be used to address the invasion of privacy arising not from disclosure, but from publicity given to damaging material that is in the public domain.[68] In addition, Wacks took the view that the law of confidence was inadequate to protect a claim to privacy on the basis that it was concerned with '(a) *disclosure* or use rather than publicity, (b) the *source* rather than the nature of the information, and (c) the *preservation of confidence* rather than the possible harm to the plaintiff caused by its breach'.[69]

There are, however, a number of obstacles to be overcome before the law of confidence can be invoked – not least satisfying the criteria provided by *Coco v Clarke Engineers*.[70] One case that has illustrated the inadequacy of the law of confidentiality is *Peck v UK*.[71] In this case, the complainant had attempted to commit suicide and this was captured on CCTV operated by Brentwood County Council, which was subsequently passed on to numerous broadcasters. The law of confidentiality could not apply to this case, because there was no duty of confidentiality arising between the complainant and Brentwood County Council. A

---

64 *Ibid*, p 1001 (emphasis added).

65 Now the Prison (Amendment) Rules 1998 (SI 1998/23).

66 [2003] UKHL 53.

67 Beyleveld, D and Pattinson, S, 'Horizontal applicability and horizontal effect' (2002) 118 *LQR* 623.

68 Wright, J, *Tort Law & Human Rights*, 2001, Oxford: Hart.

69 Wacks, R, *Personal Information*, 1989, Oxford: OUP, p 134 (emphasis added).

70 [1969] RPC 41.

71 (2003) 36 EHRR 41.

claim was brought before the European Court of Human Rights on the ground that there was a breach of his right to respect for private and family life under Article 8 of the ECHR. It was held by the court that his rights were infringed. One argument submitted was that Peck had no right to privacy in a public place. The European Court of Human Rights rejected this argument on the basis that the fact it happened in public did not deprive Peck of his right to respect for privacy. There is 'a zone of interaction of a person with others, even in a public context, which may fall within the scope of "private life"'.[72] It should be remembered that if consent had been obtained from Peck or the video was anonymised, then there would have been no violation of Article 8.[73]

Later, in the case of *Douglas v Hello! (No 5)*, Lindsay J reviewed the case of *Peck* and acknowledged the difficulties of adopting the law of confidentiality to protect privacy. He stated:

> [the] inadequacy will have to be made good and if Parliament does not step in then the courts will be obliged to. Further development by the courts may merely be awaiting the first post-HRA case where *neither the law of confidence nor any other domestic law protects an individual who deserves protection*. A glance at a crystal ball of, so to speak, only a low wattage suggests that if Parliament does not act soon the less satisfactory course, of the courts creating the law bit by bit at the expense of litigants and with inevitable delays and uncertainty, will be thrust upon the judiciary. But that will only happen *when a case arises in which the existing law of confidence gives no or inadequate protection*; this case now before me is not such a case and there is therefore no need for me to attempt to construct a law of privacy and, that being so, it would be wrong of me to attempt to do so.[74]

Though the question was not addressed in any depth, the judgment reiterates the view that the law of confidentiality cannot solely be used to protect privacy.

One is inclined to agree with the views advocated earlier: that through the HRA, a statutory right to privacy has been created and the question should not be whether there is a right to privacy at common law, but whether the HRA has created a statutory right to privacy through its incorporation of the ECHR.[75] However, in the recent case of *Campbell*, Lord Hoffmann has questioned the disparity and limitations of the HRA by arguing that its 'recognition [had] raised inescapably the question why it should be worth protecting against the state, but not against a private person'. A settled response on the horizontal effect of the HRA is needed to resolve the issues arising from this debate.[76]

---

72 *Ibid*, para H5(a).
73 Thanks to Professor Brownsword for highlighting this point.
74 [2003] EMLR 31, para 229 (emphasis added).
75 One question that has arisen is how far s 3 of the HRA can be interpreted. It provides: 'So far as it is possible to do so, primary legislation ... must be read and given effect in a way which is compatible with the Convention rights.' In the House of Lords' decision in *Re S and Others* [2002] UKHL 10, Lord Nicholls took the view that s 3 'was obligatory [and not] an optional canon of construction'. Suffice it to say that the scope of the HRA and its application are likely to result in debate on the implications of a statutory right to privacy.
76 See Beyleveld and Pattinson, *op cit* fn 67.

Privacy through the data protection legislation[77]

One of the major pieces of legislation concerned with the protection of personal information or 'personal data' is the DPD, enacted in 1995, and national legislation implementing the DPD.[78] The philosophy behind the development of data protection differs between the US and Europe. It was eloquently stated by Reidenberg that 'Europe treats privacy as a political imperative anchoring in fundamental human rights. European democracies approach information privacy from the perspective of social protection'.[79]

Article 1 of the DPD does not expressly limit the scope of its protection to privacy, but rather takes a broad approach to include the protection of 'fundamental rights and freedoms'. This is taken to mean that the DPD protects the rights as elaborated under the ECHR. This is then qualified by the second part of Article 1 on the free movement of personal data.[80] Under the Directive, an individual's consent is required before personal data can be processed, unless it falls within the exemptions under Article 7 or, in the case of sensitive personal data, Article 8. The Directive places an obligation upon the organisation to maintain appropriate security for the processing of personal data under Articles 16 and 17.

Although the Directive is concerned with the protection of information relating to an identified or identifiable natural person (Article 2(b)), countries such as Austria and Denmark have extended the scope of protection to 'legal persons'. Legal persons are those bodies that are incorporated under company legislation and have the same rights, duties and liabilities[81] as natural persons. In a study compiled by Korff,[82] it was recommended *inter alia* that processing be extended to personal data of legal persons in specific areas, including credit reference agencies, direct marketing and decisions which 'significantly affect' them (by public or private bodies). The European Commission has not, as yet, taken up these recommendations.

---

77 For further discussion of the DPD and the Data Protection Act 1998, see Christie, Chapter 13, this volume.

78 For more information on developments prior to the implementation of the Directive, see Charlesworth, A, 'Information privacy law in the European Union: *e pluribus unum or ex uno plures?*' (2003) 54 *Hastings LJ* 93; Lloyd, I, *A Guide to the Data Protection Act 1998*, 1998, London: Butterworths.

79 Reidenberg, J, 'Testimony before the hearing on the EU Data Protection Directive: implications for the US privacy debate before the Subcommittee on Commerce, Trade and Consumer Protection of the House Committee on Energy and Commerce, 107th Congress, 1st Session, 8 March 2001', at http://reidenberg.home.sprynet.com/Reidenberg_Testimony_03-08-01.htm. As elaborated by Reidenberg and Schwartz in *Data Privacy Law, op cit* fn 6, the US uses the term 'information privacy' rather than 'data protection', because of the possibility of the latter term being linked to intellectual property rights.

80 Article 1(2) of the DPD states that 'Member States shall neither restrict nor prohibit the free flow of personal data between Member States for reasons connected with the protection afforded under paragraph 1'.

81 See *Seita SA v Consorts Gourlain* [2002] II JCP 10133 in which the company concerned was held not to be corporately liable for cancer that the individual developed as a result of smoking.

82 Korff, D, 'Study on the protection of the rights and interests of legal persons with regard to the processing of personal data relating to such persons', at http://europa.eu.int/comm/internal_market/privacy/docs/studies/legal_en.pdf.

Some of the changes introduced by the DPD include the following:

- An extended breadth of application: extending to manual documents retained in a filing system as well as automated files.
- An exclusion for processing in the course of a purely personal or household activity.[83]
- An exclusion for activities outside the scope of Community law.[84]
- Exemptions for the processing of personal data for literary, artistic or journalistic purposes ('Special purposes').[85]
- Data subjects can access their own information subject to exemptions.[86]
- A requirement that organisations notify individuals of any processing activities relating to personal data, unless they are exempt in cases where individuals' rights and freedoms are unlikely to be adversely affected.
- Provision for the appointment of 'in-house' data protection officials.
- The transfer of personal data outside the EEA is subject to Article 25, which prohibits the transfer unless it is deemed adequate by the European Commission. Derogations are provided under Article 26.

The UK implemented the DPD through the Data Protection Act 1998 (DPA). Recent cases such as *Campbell*[87] and *Douglas v Hello! (No 5)*[88] have shown that the DPA has been used in conjunction with other legal grounds, such as the common law of confidentiality in order to protect individual privacy. The remedies for infringement of the DPA are, however, limited. In most cases the only applicable remedy after the fact will be an award of damages. There is a possibility that legal proceedings will be instituted for an offence committed under s 60(1) of the Act, but this is of limited scope as such proceedings may only be brought by the Information Commissioner or Director of Public Prosecutions.

With the exception of criminal proceedings, the question that arises is: can any infringement of privacy be quantified in monetary terms? What financial value will be sufficient to recompense an individual's loss of privacy? Although the DPD and the DPA provide for damages to be paid, damages, in my view, are wholly inadequate and should extend to criminal sanctions, and power to bring proceedings should not be restricted to the Director of Public Prosecutions.

The other criticism of the DPD is that it was implemented at a time with no consideration of major technological developments such as the use of personal data on web pages and possible profiling techniques used and aggregated by companies

---

83 DPD, Article 3(2).
84 *Ibid*, Article 13.
85 *Ibid*, Article 8.
86 *Ibid*, Article 10.
87 [2003] QB 633.
88 [2003] EMLR 31.

such as clickstream data.[89] For example, in the case of *Lindqvist*,[90] the European Court of Justice had to consider two questions: first, whether reference to individuals on web pages including their working conditions and hobbies constituted the processing of personal data within Article 3 of the DPD; and secondly, whether the process of uploading pages onto the Internet constituted the transfer of personal data to third countries, which was not permitted under Article 25. The European Court of Justice held that reference to individuals constituted the processing of personal data under Article 3, and it did not constitute the transfer of data to a third country under Article 25:

> Given, first, the state of development of the Internet at the time Directive 95/46 was drawn up and, second, the absence, in Chapter IV, of criteria applicable to use of the Internet, one cannot presume that the Community legislature intended the expression transfer [of data] to a third country to cover the loading, by an individual in Mrs Lindqvist's position, of data onto an Internet page, even if those data are thereby made accessible to persons in third countries with the technical means to access them.[91]

Although the decision contradicts the view of Advocate General Tizzano, it is, in my opinion, the correct interpretation. It must be remembered that if consent has been obtained from the individuals referred to on the web pages, then legal proceedings would not have arisen.

Unless consent has been obtained, companies and individuals are likely to fall foul of the data protection legislation implementing the DPD unless they can show that the exemptions provided by the DPD and national legislation implementing the DPD apply. The other issue that is not considered in the judgment, but which is interesting to examine, is the anonymisation and pseudonymisation of individuals on web pages. The German Federal Data Protection Act 2001, which implements the DPD, makes explicit reference in its provisions to these techniques:

> The organisation and choice of data-processing systems shall be guided by the objective of collecting, processing and using as little personal data as possible. In particular, use shall be made of the possibilities of *anonymisation* and *pseudonymisation* where possible and where the effort entailed is proportionate to the interests sought to be protected.[92]

In Sweden, however, the Data Inspection Board[93] took the view that where there is no possibility of identifying the individual through anonymisation, it will not fall under the data protection legislation (Personal Data Act).[94] This was qualified by stating that if a person can be identified, not necessarily by name but by any information, then it will fall under the legislation. It is likely that even with the use

---

89 This was partially remedied by the Directive on Privacy and Electronic Communications 2002/58/EC, which replaced Directive 97/66/EC. The UK has implemented this Directive through the Privacy and Electronic Communications Regulations 2003 (SI 2003/2426), which took effect on 11 December 2003.

90 Case C-101/01 [2004] 1 CMLR 20.

91 *Ibid*.

92 Federal Data Protection Act 2001, § 3a, at www.datenschutz-berlin.de/recht/de/bdsg/bdsg01_eng.htm#sec3a (emphasis added).

93 See www.datainspektionen.se/in_english.

94 The question was raised through personal correspondence with the Data Inspection Authority in September 2003.

of anonymisation and pseudonymisation techniques to conceal the identity of the person, processing of personal data will still fall under the DPD, so long as individuals can be identified.[95] The breadth and scope of the DPD are likely to impel countries outside the EEA to stringently meet the adequacy standards required under Articles 25 and 26, and this is particularly the case for web pages.[96]

Conclusion

In tracing the developments of privacy from Warren and Brandeis to the present day, issues such as media intrusion and misuse of personal information continue to be a current and pervasive problem. More often than not, the concept of privacy has been approached from an individualistic perspective. Given society's level of concern about privacy intrusion, particularly in respect of the protection of personal information at a European level, the data protection legislation has been seen as one possible response to this (though perhaps not an ideal response). The case of *Lindqvist*[97] further demonstrates the pervasive influence of Europe's data protection legislation and its implications for countries outside the EEA that do not have data protection laws in place.

The protection of privacy within the UK has come about through a myriad of grounds, ranging from the law of confidentiality to data protection legislation. As demonstrated by the case of *Peck*,[98] privacy cannot be protected solely through the law of confidentiality.[99] The recent House of Lords decision in *Campbell* has reiterated the nature and gradual development in the law of confidentiality by extending it to protect human autonomy and dignity, which are terms referred to by Lord Hoffmann to mean the right to control the dissemination of information about one's private life and the right to the esteem and respect of other people.

The HRA is likely to be invoked by individuals to recognise Convention rights, most notably Article 8. The *Campbell* case, however, has raised further questions about the anomalous situation in which the HRA is only applicable against the state. It is time to call for a proper debate on such limitations and to remedy this anomaly. Though Article 8 is not an absolute right, the case of *Re S and Others*[100] is a further confirmation that the road to a statutory right to privacy will not be long.

95　Recital 26 of the DPD states that 'the principles of protection shall not apply to data rendered anonymous in such a way that the data subject is no longer identifiable; whereas codes of conduct within the meaning of Article 27 may be a useful instrument for providing guidance as to the ways in which data may be rendered anonymous and retained in a form in which *identification of the data subject is no longer possible*' (emphasis added).

96　To date, Hungary, Switzerland, Argentina and Canada have met these requirements. The US has a 'Safe Harbor approach' whereby companies in the US self-certify a set of principles similar to those under the DPD.

97　C-101/01 [2004] 1 CMLR 20.

98　(2003) 36 EHRR 41.

99　See *Coco v AN Clarke (Engineers) Ltd* [1969] RPC 41.

100　[2002] UKHL 10. The case did not rule directly on privacy, but illustrates the interplay between ss 3, 6 and 7 of the HRA and its relationship with the ECHR.

Chapter 13
Employee Surveillance
David Christie

Introduction

Information and communications technology can be a great enabler of human rights. It allows ideas and opinions to travel almost instantaneously across digital networks to every corner of the planet. At the same time, it weakens the ability of states and organisations to control the spread of information. It is at least arguable that, thanks to modern communications technology, there has never been a time in human history when we have enjoyed so much freedom of thought and expression.

However, technology can also be used as a powerful instrument of surveillance.[1] In this sense, it can be used to undermine human rights and fundamental freedoms. This idea was brilliantly depicted by George Orwell in his novel, *1984*, where advances in communications technology were used to keep an entire society under constant surveillance. Orwell's novel was primarily concerned with surveillance by the state but, in our own world, it is not just surveillance by government and law enforcement agencies that poses a threat to our liberty. Surveillance by our employers may also intrude on communications that we would rather keep private.

While there is nothing new about employers monitoring their employees, what is new is the relative ease with which employers may use technology to carry out covert and intrusive surveillance operations. Indeed, modern employers have access to a bewildering array of surveillance technology, far beyond anything that Orwell's Thought Police had at their disposal. All aspects of an employee's behaviour at work can now be monitored, often without the employee knowing that the surveillance is taking place. In the last few years, employee surveillance has become more sophisticated, more insidious and more pervasive than ever before.[2]

Monitoring employees' telephone calls, email and Internet use is a particularly emotive and controversial issue. Not only is it one of the emerging legal issues of our time, but it is also a pressing practical problem in the day-to-day management of employment relationships. Many employees seem to regard their ability to make private telephone calls or to send private emails from their work as an unassailable right. On the other hand, many employers think that they have an unfettered right to information about what their employees are doing during their working hours.

This chapter is about how the law in the UK attempts to reconcile these two different perspectives.[3] The last few years have seen the introduction of several

---

1   For a general discussion of surveillance technology, see Klang, Chapter 14.
2   See Castells, M, *The Internet Galaxy*, 2001, Oxford: OUP, pp 170–82.
3   The law is stated as at 1 September 2004.

major pieces of legislation in the UK, which have had a direct impact on this issue. As we shall see, these pieces of legislation do not provide a unified or coherent system of regulation. The legislative provisions are confusing, and at times even conflicting. In an attempt to provide some guidance on the matter, the Information Commissioner has published a Code of Practice on Monitoring at Work, which we shall consider towards the end of the chapter.

We begin our analysis by considering the common law. Despite an enormous amount of statutory intervention over the last 30 years, the employment relationship is still essentially one of contract and is regulated at common law by various implied terms. These terms operate independently of legislation and the content of any written statement of employment terms and conditions. Some of these terms may have an impact on the way in which employers can use technology to monitor their staff.

The implied terms of an employment relationship

Under UK law, whenever a contract of employment is formed, rights and obligations are created on both sides. Over and above anything provided in a written contract of employment, a myriad of terms will be implied at common law. Many of these would be deemed to be too obvious to be worth stating in a written contract, but some are of fundamental importance to the operation of the relationship. One of the most obvious implied terms is the idea that the employee is engaged to further his employer's business.[4] This term requires that the employee uses his time at work (and the facilities that have been provided to him) for his employer's benefit, rather than his own. It follows that an employee who surfs the Internet to check football results, or to download pornography or to look for alternative employment, is technically in breach of contract. Whether or not such conduct merits disciplinary action or dismissal will depend on the circumstances and the position which the employee holds. It will also depend on the terms of any policy on Internet use which the employer operates.

The employee is also under an implied obligation to serve his employer honestly and faithfully.[5] Consequently, an employee who deliberately misuses his employer's communications systems to further the interests of a competitor (by, for example, emailing the employer's customer database to a rival organisation) has breached the employment contract in a fundamental way. Such conduct may well result in the employee being dismissed.

So far, we have considered how implied terms of the employment relationship may restrict the actions of employees. Other implied terms impose limits on employers. For example, both parties in an employment relationship are under an obligation not to act in such a way as to destroy the relationship of mutual trust and confidence that should exist between them.[6] This may restrict the ability of

---

4 See, eg, *Wessex Dairies Ltd v Smith* [1935] 2 KB 80; *Sanders v Parry* [1967] 1 WLR 753.

5 See, eg, *Hivac Ltd v Park Royal Scientific Instruments Ltd* [1946] 1 All ER 350, CA; *Faccenda Chicken Ltd v Fowler* [1986] IRLR 69, CA.

6 *Malik v Bank of Credit and Commerce International SA* [1997] IRLR 462, HL; *Johnson v Unisys Ltd* [2001] IRLR 279.

employers to carry out covert surveillance operations. While case law has not developed this concept to any great extent to date, it is not difficult to envisage a scenario where an employee who has been subjected to an unjustified surveillance operation takes the view that his employer's actions amount to a breach of trust and confidence. In some circumstances, the employee may be entitled to resign and claim that he has been constructively dismissed.

While the implied term of mutual trust and confidence may provide employees with some protection against oppressive surveillance, the common law does not presently provide employees with any general right to privacy in the workplace. However, it has been speculated that the introduction of the Human Rights Act 1998 may enable the judiciary to develop a limited right to employee privacy through the case law. In order to understand how such a right might come about (and what the limits on it are likely to be), it is necessary to widen our focus to international law and consider the provisions of the European Convention on Human Rights and Fundamental Freedoms (ECHR).[7]

The European Convention on Human Rights

Article 8(1) of the ECHR provides that 'Everyone has the right to respect for his private and family life, his home and his correspondence'. This right is qualified by Article 8(2), which provides:

> There shall be no interference by a public authority with the exercise of this right except such as is in accordance with the law and is necessary in a democratic society in the interests of national security, public safety or the economic well-being of the country, for the preservation of disorder or crime, for the protection of health or morals, or for the protection of the rights and freedoms of others.

The scope of Article 8 has been explored in the case law of the European Court of Human Rights. The decisions are not binding, as the Court does not formally observe the doctrine of precedent. However, the Strasbourg case law does cast valuable light on how the right to privacy is applied in practice. For example, the Court has held that the right to privacy is not limited to a person's home, but may extend to his place of work.[8] The notion of 'correspondence' has been widely interpreted by the Court to include telephone conversations,[9] as well as written correspondence. While there are no decisions as yet that deal explicitly with the interception of email or the monitoring of Internet use, it seems clear that these activities would be caught within the ambit of Article 8. As the Court has observed, the ECHR is a 'living instrument',[10] which must be re-interpreted in light of changing conditions and technological developments.

---

7 Council of Europe (1950), Strasbourg.
8 *Niemetz v Germany* (1993) 16 EHRR 97; *Malone v UK* (1984) 7 EHRR 14.
9 *Malone, ibid.*
10 *Tyrer v UK* (1978) 2 EHRR 1.

Halford v United Kingdom[11] is, to date, the only decision of the European Court of Human Rights that deals expressly with the question of electronic monitoring of an employee in the workplace. The claimant in this case was the Assistant Chief Constable of Merseyside Police. She alleged that she had been refused promotion because of her gender and she brought a complaint of sex discrimination before an employment tribunal. The employer provided her with a private telephone line in her office and assured her that calls made on this line would not be monitored. The claimant believed that the telephone calls she made from her office were indeed being intercepted by her employer for the purposes of obtaining information that could be used against her in the employment tribunal case. Although the tribunal case settled without a hearing, the claimant then brought fresh proceedings before the European Court of Human Rights, claiming that the interception of her telephone calls infringed her right to privacy under Article 8.

The Court found that, in the particular circumstances of the claimant's case, she had a 'reasonable expectation of privacy' in respect of the telephone calls which she made from the private line in her office. The Court accepted that telephone calls made from business premises may be covered by the concept of private life and correspondence within the meaning of Article 8 and rejected an argument put forward by the UK government to the effect that an employee has no right to privacy in respect of any communications made from the workplace.

Halford was based on an unusual and specific set of circumstances.[12] As a result, the case cannot be cited as authority for the proposition that all covert surveillance of employees is contrary to Article 8. It has been suggested that the decision in *Halford* hinged on the fact that the complainant had been given a reasonable expectation of privacy by virtue of her employer's assurances that her telephone line would not be monitored. When the Court found that those assurances were probably wrong, it was able to hold that the employee's rights under Article 8 had been breached.

While the decision in *Halford* went in favour of the employee, the corollary of the decision seems to be that where an employer has taken steps to remove an employee's expectation of privacy, the employer is free to carry out surveillance. This has become a cause for very considerable concern. If an employee's right to privacy is dependent on the extent to which the employer allows it to exist, those most in need of privacy protection may not receive any at all.[13]

What is not clear from the *Halford* decision is the extent to which an employer may attempt to justify a surveillance operation by reference to the qualifications in Article 8(2). The Court simply does not address this point. However, it would appear from the wording of Article 8(2) that there is considerable scope for employers to argue that their monitoring or recording activity is justified by at least one of the exceptions. Indeed, the wording of Article 8(2) is sufficiently wide that it

---

11 (1997) 24 EHRR 523; [1997] IRLR 471; [1998] Crim LR 753; 94 LS Gaz R 24, ECtHR.

12 See Oliver, H, 'Email and Internet monitoring in the workplace: information privacy and contracting out' (2002) 31 *ILJ* 321, p 336.

13 See Ford, M, 'Two conceptions of worker privacy' (2002) 31 *ILJ* 135.

is difficult to think of any legitimate monitoring or recording that could not, in principle, be covered by one of the exceptions.

This point is perhaps illustrated by *Mohammed v First Quench Ltd*,[14] a case involving a company that had set up a secret surveillance camera system following a number of thefts on its premises. The secret camera caught the applicant having sex with another employee and the applicant was dismissed. An employment tribunal held that the dismissal was unfair. On appeal to the Employment Appeal Tribunal (EAT), it was argued that the surveillance system introduced by the employer contravened the applicant's human rights. While the appeal was rejected on other grounds, the EAT observed that where there was evidence of theft, a limited covert surveillance operation may not breach Article 8.

The extent to which Article 8 offers privacy protection to employees in respect of their email and Internet use has still to be authoritatively determined. Perhaps future case law from the European Court of Human Rights will help to provide some answers. In the meantime, questions about employees' rights under Article 8 have assumed much more immediacy in the UK, thanks to the introduction of the Human Rights Act 1998.

The Human Rights Act 1998

Until 2 October 2000, the rights guaranteed under the ECHR were beyond the reach of most individuals in the UK. While it was possible for a UK citizen to petition the Strasbourg authorities, the cost and time involved in bringing such a complaint were usually prohibitive. The Human Rights Act 1998 (HRA) was introduced in an attempt to remedy this problem by allowing individuals to enforce their Convention rights before domestic courts and tribunals.

Strictly speaking, the HRA does not incorporate the ECHR into UK law. However, it does give further effect under domestic law to almost all of the rights contained in the Convention. From the outset, it was clear that the Act was no ordinary piece of legislation, but one of profound historic and political importance. As well as adjusting the historic balance of power between the executive, legislative and judicial branches of government, the HRA has energised and transformed the UK legal system by exposing it to international human rights standards.

The HRA came fully into effect across the UK on 2 October 2000.[15] It requires that UK courts and tribunals take account of the Convention rights and case law when determining any question that arises from a Convention right.[16] All UK legislation must, as far as possible, be given effect in such a way as is compatible with the rights guaranteed under the Convention.[17] It is unlawful for public authorities

---

14 2001, unreported.
15 Scotland had a foretaste of things to come from May 1999, when the Scotland Act 1998 made it unlawful for the Scottish Executive and the Scottish Parliament to act incompatibly with the Convention rights.
16 HRA, s 2.
17 *Ibid*, s 3.

(including courts and tribunals) to act in a way which is inconsistent with the Convention rights.[18]

Only public authorities are directly bound by the Act. As a result, the HRA provides more protection to employees who work in the public sector. However, there is scope for the HRA to affect employment in the private sector too. This is because the definition of 'public authority' within the HRA expressly includes courts and tribunals. Therefore, courts and tribunals are bound to give effect to the Convention rights in their decisions, even if the dispute does not involve a public authority.

One way in which the HRA may make an impact in the field of employee surveillance is through the interpretative obligation imposed on courts and tribunals. All legislation (irrespective of whether it came into force before or after the HRA) must now be read and given effect in such a way that is compatible with the Convention rights, so far as possible. This obligation extends to familiar concepts in employment legislation, such as 'reasonableness' (or otherwise) of an employer's decision to dismiss in unfair dismissal law.[19] In practice, many unfair dismissal claims turn on the nature and extent of the employer's investigations prior to the employee's dismissal. The HRA exposes these investigations to more scrutiny than before. Investigations that contravene an individual's human rights are susceptible to challenge and may lead to a finding of unfair dismissal.

Another way in which the HRA may curtail employers' surveillance methods is through the development of the common law. We noted earlier the speculation that the judiciary may seek to develop a right to privacy as a new implied term in the employment contract. While such a right would probably be limited in nature, there is some support for this idea, for example, in the way in which the courts and tribunals have developed the concept of mutual trust and confidence over the last 25 years. The HRA would give judicial attempts to forge a common law right to privacy in the employment relationship at least a standing start.

Any progress here, however, is likely to be incremental in nature. In the short term, a major limitation on the impact of the HRA is that the legislation provides only limited means of enforcement.[20] An employee whose rights under Article 8 have been violated by his employer will only be able to bring a direct action against his employer if his employer is a public authority.[21] If the employee works in the private sector, a breach of his Convention rights will only be relevant if he can refer to the breach as part of another claim (for example, a complaint of unfair dismissal or sex discrimination).

Where the HRA has already had an impact in the field of employee surveillance has been in terms of the other legislation that it has prompted. It is this legislation that we must now consider.

---

18 *Ibid*, s 6.
19 The relevant provisions are contained in Part X of the Employment Rights Act 1996, as amended by the Employment Relations Act 1999 and the Employment Act 2002.
20 See Ewing, KD, 'The Human Rights Act and labour law' (1998) 27 *ILJ* 275.
21 HRA, s 7.

The Regulation of Investigatory Powers Act 2000

The defeat of the UK government in the *Halford* case, coupled with the introduction of the HRA in October 2000, required a major overhaul of the UK's statutory regime for the interception of communications. The government's response was the Regulation of Investigatory Powers Act 2000 (RIPA), a statute designed to provide a single legal framework for the interception of communications in the UK, whether by government agencies or by private employers. The stated aim of the legislation was to provide a statutory regime in which investigatory powers could be exercised in accordance with human rights. RIPA came into force at the same time as the HRA and was intended to be consistent with the rights guaranteed under the ECHR.

RIPA makes it a criminal offence, without lawful authority, to intercept a communication in the course of its transmission by post or by a public or private telecommunications system.[22] This includes the monitoring and interception of telephone calls made by employees. It also includes the monitoring and interceptions of employees' emails and Internet use.

However, RIPA also provides that interceptions may be lawful if the sender or intended recipient has consented to the interception, or where there are reasonable grounds for the belief that the sender or intended recipient has consented.[23] This raises the possibility that an employer may be able to argue that their employees had consented to such an interception: for example, by virtue of them agreeing to a contract or policy which made provision for such interceptions to take place.

RIPA allows employees to take an action for damages against an employer if they believe the employer has unlawfully intercepted a telecommunication made to a third party on the employer's network. At first glance, this may seem to be quite a substantial protection for the employee. However, there are potentially major problems with enforcement. How is an employee to know that a particular communication has been intercepted? How is the employee's loss to be quantified? Is it realistic to expect an employee to bring an action for damages against an organisation upon which he depends for his income? In this respect, it could certainly be argued that these provisions in RIPA ignore the realities of the employment relationship and are therefore of little practical use to employees.

The Telecommunications (Lawful Business Practice) (Interception of Communications) Regulations 2000

Section 4(2) of RIPA gave the Secretary of State the power to introduce regulations authorising certain types of interception and record-keeping. This provided the authority for the introduction of the Telecommunications (Lawful Business Practice) (Interception of Communications) Regulations 2000 (LBP Regulations),[24] which

---

22 RIPA, s 1(1) and (2).
23 *Ibid*, s 3. Interceptions may also be lawful if the interceptor has a warrant, or, in certain circumstances, without a warrant: for example, to comply with the EU Convention on Mutual Assistance in Criminal Matters. Interception is also permitted when done by the postal or telecommunications provider for purposes connected with the operations of the service.
24 SI 2000/2699.

came into force on 24 October 2000. According to the government, the Regulations were an attempt to provide that legitimate monitoring and recording activities by businesses would not be prohibited by RIPA. They were also intended to give effect to the EU Telecommunications Data Protection Directive.[25]

Essentially, the Regulations provide a list of circumstances where it is lawful for an employer to monitor or record certain types of communications without the consent of the caller, sender or recipient. As they were drafted largely in response to employers' concerns about the effect of RIPA, it has been argued that the interests of employees were largely ignored. The Regulations allow employers to monitor or record all communications transmitted over their systems, without the consent of the persons making the communications, for any of the following purposes:[26]

- To establish the existence of facts that are relevant to the business (for example, for recording evidence of business transactions).

- To ensure compliance with regulatory or self-regulatory practices or procedures relevant to the business (this may involve checking that communications comply with both external and internal rules, such as the employer's policies on email and Internet use).

- To ascertain or demonstrate standards which are or ought to be achieved by the person using the system (eg, for staff training or quality control purposes).

- To detect or prevent crime (this may legitimise surveillance where an employee is suspected of misusing drugs or using the Internet for criminal purposes, eg, downloading child pornography).

- To investigate or detect unauthorised use of the system (again, this could be used to enforce an employer's internal policy on email or Internet use).

- To ensure the effectiveness of their communications systems (eg, to prevent viruses).

Monitoring but not recording is permitted in two specified circumstances:[27]

- To check whether the communications were relevant to the employer's business (eg, opening an employee's email when the employee is away from the office).

- To monitor communications to a confidential anonymous counselling or support helpline (although only to protect or support helpline staff).

There are some limited safeguards.[28] First, the interception must be for a reason that is relevant to the employer's business. Only business communications or those that directly affect the business in some way are likely to be relevant. A communication that is clearly personal or private is unlikely to be relevant to the business: therefore, monitoring of such communication may be unlawful. A second safeguard is that it is necessary under the Regulations for employers to take reasonable steps to inform employees that their communications might be monitored. Employees should

---

25 97/66/EC.
26 LBP Regulations, reg 3(1)(a).
27 *Ibid*, reg 3(1)(b) and (c).
28 *Ibid*, reg 3(2).

therefore be informed before they begin to use the system. Individuals from outside the organisation who send information to the employer's business should also be informed in some way.

The LBP Regulations have been severely criticised. The purposes for which monitoring may be lawfully carried out have been very widely defined, while the safeguards for employees and others are so limited that they are likely to provide little protection against an unscrupulous employer. For example, it is difficult to see how an employer could determine which emails are relevant to the business and which are not without examining their content. There is no compulsion on employers to obtain consent before they intercept a communication. All that is required is that every reasonable effort is made to inform system users of the fact. It is difficult to disagree with Hazel Oliver when she argues that the Regulations have 'watered down the restrictions placed on employers by RIPA to such a large extent that it could now be said that RIPA hardly limits employer monitoring practices at all'.[29]

The Data Protection Act 1998

If it is true that RIPA offers only minimal protection to employees, the same cannot be said of the Data Protection Act 1998 (DPA). The DPA replaces the 1984 Act of the same name and implements the EU Directive on Data Protection.[30] The DPA sets out various rules for the processing of personal information and applies to some paper records, as well as information held on computers.[31] The main requirement contained in the DPA is that personal data must be processed in accordance with a set of principles that are set out in the Act.[32] 'Processing' is defined as 'obtaining, recording or holding ... or carrying out any operation or set of operations on the information or data'. This definition is sufficiently wide that it includes the monitoring and recording of communications, as well as whatever use is made of any information that has been obtained by monitoring and recording.

There are eight data protection principles laid down in Part I of Schedule 2 to the Act. The most important is the first: that personal data shall be processed lawfully and fairly. In particular, data shall not be processed unless (a) at least one of the conditions in Schedule 2 is met, and (b) in the case of sensitive personal data, at least one of the conditions in Schedule 3 is also met. Schedule 2 sets out a number of conditions, the most common of which is that the individual concerned has given his consent to the processing.[33] In addition to this, data must be processed in accordance with the fair processing code set out at paragraphs 1 to 4 of Part II of Schedule 1. Essentially, this requires that data should not be obtained in a misleading or deceptive way. It also states that data will not be processed fairly

---

29 Oliver, *op cit* fn 12, p 339.
30 No 95/46, adopted 24 October 1995.
31 For further discussion of the provisions of the Data Protection Act, see Wong, Chapter 12.
32 DPA, s 4(4).
33 Paragraph 1.

unless the employee has been given certain information about the processing, the purpose for which the data is being processed and any other information in the circumstances that will enable fair processing.

Additional protection exists under the DPA in respect of information which is classified as 'sensitive personal data'. This refers to information concerning:

- racial or ethnic origin;
- political opinion;
- religious beliefs or beliefs of a similar nature;
- trade union membership;[34]
- physical or mental health or condition;
- sexual life;
- the commission or alleged commission of any offence; or
- proceedings for any offence, the disposal of such proceedings or the sentence of any court in such proceedings.

This type of data must not be processed at all unless, in addition to the conditions outlined above, a condition in Schedule 3 is met. Again, explicit consent is one of the Schedule 3 conditions. Generally, the Schedule 3 conditions are narrower in their scope than those in Schedule 2.

The DPA is a statute of very considerable complexity. It is clear that the Act does not prohibit employee surveillance, but it does regulate the way in which employers monitor their staff and the use that employers make of any information that they collect. In an attempt to provide employers with some clear guidance on how to comply with the Act, the Information Commissioner published a series of Codes of Practice. Part III of the Code on Monitoring at Work is the most relevant for our purposes.[35]

The Information Commissioner's Code of Practice on Monitoring at Work

On 11 June 2003, the Information Commissioner[36] published the third part of the Employment Practices Data Protection Code, entitled Monitoring at Work.[37] The Code aims to provide practical guidance to employers on how they should comply with the DPA and to encourage them to adopt standards of good practice. The Code also aims to strike an appropriate balance between the legitimate expectations of workers that information about them will be handled properly and the legitimate

---

34 Within the meaning of the Trade Union and Labour Relations (Consolidation) Act 1992.
35 The Employment Practices Data Protection Code also deals with recruitment and selection, employment records and medical information.
36 Formerly known as the Data Protection Commissioner. The role of the Information Commissioner is to be the independent public champion of public openness and personal privacy. The Information Commissioner has various specific responsibilities set out in the DPA 1998, the Freedom of Information Act 2000 and other legislation.
37 The Code was introduced under the DPA, s 51.

interest of employers in deciding how best to run their businesses. The Code does not impose any new legal obligations and is intended to be consistent with both the HRA and RIPA.

The Information Commissioner states that:

> Monitoring in the workplace can be intrusive, whether examining emails, recording phone calls or installing CCTV cameras. Employees are entitled to expect that their personal lives will remain private and that they have a degree of privacy in their work environment. The fundamental message is that, where monitoring does take place, employees should be aware of its nature and extent and the reasons for carrying it out. Only in exceptional circumstances will it be appropriate for employers to monitor their employees without their consent.[38]

The Code sets out a number of core principles:

- It will usually be intrusive for employers to monitor their workers.
- Workers have legitimate expectations that they can keep their personal lives private and that they are also entitled to a degree of privacy in the work environment.
- If employers wish to monitor their workers, they should be clear about the purposes and satisfied that the particular monitoring arrangement is justified by real benefits that will be delivered.
- Workers should be aware of the nature, extent and reasons for any monitoring, unless (exceptionally) covert monitoring is justified.

The Code encourages employers to establish a policy on monitoring electronic communications. Such a policy should set out clearly the circumstances in which workers may or may not use the employer's telephone and email system for private communications. It should make clear the extent and type of private use that is allowed. As far as Internet access is concerned, the policy should specify the restrictions on material that can be viewed or copied. Simply banning 'offensive material' is unlikely to be sufficiently clear for people to know what is and is not allowed. The policy should also lay down rules for private use of the employer's communications equipment when used away from home or away from the workplace, eg the use of facilities that enable external dialling into the employer's networks. There should be an explanation of the purposes for which monitoring is carried out, the extent of the monitoring and the means used. Finally, the policy should state how it is to be enforced and the penalties that are likely to apply in the event of the policy being breached.

The Code says that covert monitoring of employees will only be justified in exceptional circumstances. Any use of covert monitoring should normally be authorised by senior management within the context of a specific investigation. The covert monitoring should stop once the investigation has been completed.

The Code also introduces the idea of an 'impact assessment' as the precursor to any monitoring activity. It says that the impact assessment is a process by which an

---

38 Press Release, 11 June 2003.

employer can make a justified decision as to whether monitoring is appropriate; adopt the most appropriate type of monitoring in a given context; and balance the adverse impact on workers against the business benefits. The monitoring arrangement should be a proportionate response to the problem it seeks to address. It appears from the Code that employers may seek to use the device of the impact assessment as a means of bypassing the issue of employees' consent. The Code states that employers who can justify monitoring on the basis of an impact assessment will not generally need the consent of individual workers.

An appropriate balance?

Employers have a legitimate need to monitor what their employees are doing at work. Some monitoring is clearly necessary to make sure that employees are performing their duties properly and to ensure that there is a safe and supportive working environment which is free from discrimination and harassment. Some monitoring is also necessary to protect the integrity of the employer's communications systems, for example, from viruses or fraudulent use. However, at the same time, there remains a compelling argument – and one accepted by Strasbourg case law and the Information Commissioner – that an individual's right to privacy does not stop when he goes to work. Individuals remain entitled to a degree of privacy, even in the context of their working environment.

The question that arises is whether the law in the UK strikes an appropriate balance between employers' legitimate needs to monitor and employees' entitlement to this measure of privacy. Certainly, the law has come a long way in the last few years, but it does lag some way behind the developments in surveillance technologies that have taken place during the same period. It would be fair to say that the legislation we have in the UK does not provide a coherent or straightforward system of regulation. Nor does it provide employees with a clear idea of how much privacy they can expect when they are at work. Instead, what we have is legislation that overlaps in places and conflicts in others. The Information Commissioner's Code of Practice on Monitoring at Work provides some useful practical guidance but, ultimately, it will be left to courts and employment tribunals to make sense of the new legislation by applying it to real situations.

At the moment, the balance of legal authority is certainly in favour of the employer's right to monitor. The employee's right to privacy at work remains an undeveloped and still relatively contentious idea. If it is to become a reality, it will have to be forged on an incremental, case-by-case basis. What we can probably expect in the next few years is litigation that tests the boundaries of employees' rights to privacy at work. It is only through the emerging case law that we are likely to gain a clearer idea of where the limits of lawful employee surveillance lie.

Chapter 14

Privacy, Surveillance and Identity
Mathias Klang

Surveillance technology

Throughout history, technology has been used to control the undesirable behaviour of others in a cost-efficient manner. Construction of walls such as Hadrian's Wall or China's Great Wall were motivated as cost-efficient defence systems. During the crusades, great castles were built to enable the defence of a territory using the minimum amount of manpower[1] and, more recently, barbed wire[2] has been used to control both persons and animals. Bentham's Panopticon was a creation aimed at the minimisation of the human costs of surveillance.[3] The costs of surveillance were transferred onto the individual and the architecture enhanced the levels of self-control among the inmates of the all-seeing prison. Taking this perspective, it is not surprising that camera technology today is being implemented and developed for use in surveillance.

This chapter looks at the merging of digital-optical systems currently being implemented to aid in the surveillance of socially undesirable behaviour. It will examine the legality of these systems and look at the level of preparation which the law has in meeting these systems currently in use. The chapter also examines the social implications of this development, which has led to the role of the camera as the unblinking, unforgiving eye in our urban environment. This will be done by looking at areas where digital technology has enabled major changes in the relationship between image and surveillance: facial recognition, pattern recognition, and number recognition.

Camera, self and image

Many societies make a strong connection between the image of a person and the soul. Primitive societies fear photography since it is believed that the camera will take with it something more than the image; it will also take part of the person or soul. In Oscar Wilde's *The Picture of Dorian Gray*, the image of Gray takes a central role. In his desire for eternal youth and beauty, Gray realises that his portrait will maintain its beauty while he himself will not: 'Why should it keep what I must lose?'[4] The permanency of the image robs Gray of his innocence and he wishes that his body be maintained while the image in the portrait decays. Wilde's tale of moral disintegration is an interesting play upon the connection between image and reality.

---

1 Runciman, S, *A History of the Crusades*, 1987, Cambridge: CUP.
2 Razac, O, *Barbed Wire*, 2002, Kneight, J (trans), London: Profile Books.
3 Foucault, M, *Discipline and Punish*, 1977, Sheridan, A (trans), Harmondsworth: Penguin.
4 Wilde, O, *The Picture of Dorian Gray*, 2003, Harmondsworth: Penguin Classics.

One of the major changes in photography was the introduction in 1888 of the Eastman Kodak 'Snap Camera'.[5] This camera 'freed' the photographer due to its revolutionary new film, which drastically shortened the time required for the camera shutter to be opened and therefore did not require a camera stand or that the photograph's subject remain motionless for a long period of time. These innovations were important steps towards the possibility of recording people's images without their consent. The portability and cheapness of the camera allowed it to develop further and become a leisure item, giving the photographer, or kodaker[6] as they were sometimes known, the ability to document and preserve images that would serve as proof that acts took place and give non-present onlookers the ability to share vicariously in the experiences of the photographer.

The dissemination and use of this technology re-interpreted our relationship between self and image. The new uses for the camera soon demanded social and legal reactions in order to curtail the ways in which this technology could and should be used. On the night of his death in 1898, two men entered his home and, without permission, photographed the body of Prince Otto von Bismarck. His heirs later sued to prevent publication of the photograph and to compel its destruction, along with all copies and the photographic plate. The court granted an injunction on the basis that the photographers should not profit from their illegal entry.[7] In 1907, the Law Regulating Copyright to Works of Portraiture and Photography[8] was enacted in Germany. This legislation granted individuals rights in their own images and created the possibility of preventing publication. In situations such as Bismarck, control is in the hands of the immediate surviving family for a period of ten years.[9]

In 1903, the New York State legislature created for the first time the right to sue for invasions of privacy after a young girl had been photographed without her knowledge and the image was used in an advertising campaign without her consent. The Rochester Folding Box Company was sued for using the image but the courts could not find that misappropriation of personality was protected by common law[10]. The court suggested that legislation needed to be enacted to protect individuals from similar occurrences, and in 1903 the New York Civil Law was amended at ss 50 and 51 to protect against individuals' images being used in commercial advertising.

---

5 See www.kodak.com.

6 Kerns, S, *The Culture of Time and Space 1880–1918*, 1983, London: Weidenfeld & Nicolson.

7 RGZ 45, Judgment of 28 December 1899, Bismarck, 170, 173, discussed in Helle, J, *Besondere Persönlichkeitsrechte im Privatrecht*, 1991.

8 Gesetz betreffend das Urheberrecht an Werken der bildenden Künste und der Photographie, or 'Kunsturheberrechtsgesetz' (KunstUrhG), of 9 January 1907 (RGBl 1907, 7), last amended 2 March 1974 (BGBl I, 469).

9 KunstUrhG § 22.

10 *Roberson v Rochester Folding Box Company*, 171 NY 538 (NY CA, 1903).

The growth of camera surveillance

Surveillance cameras (closed circuit television, or CCTV) have been used since the 1950s, a period which also saw the development of the video cassette recorder, which further lowered the expense and ease with which images could be recorded and stored. At the end of the 1960s, the first commercial systems for the surveillance of retail stores appeared in the UK.[11] Since then, the use of CCTV has exploded and is continuing to grow: today, surveillance systems are gazing at us in everything from small corner stores to large banks, in transport systems from taxis to the London Underground, from lonely footpaths to crowded streets and sports arenas. They are used to prevent accidents and crime, promote security and safety, and monitor critical systems and heavy traffic. CCTV has quickly become a necessary infrastructure with which to ensure health and safety at a cost-efficient level. Along with the spread of CCTV systems there has been a growing interest in the study of their social effects, their efficiency and their advantages and disadvantages in relation to issues of privacy and public surveillance.[12]

For those who previously maintained surveillance without CCTV, the advantages seem obvious. Once the initial infrastructure has been installed, the task of monitoring no longer requires a significant physical presence; instead, a large number of cameras may be monitored by a single controller. It is, however, important to remember that the cameras are only part of the system. The images are sent to a control room, where the collective images from many cameras are viewed by controllers working long shifts in front of several monitors 24 hours a day, seven days a week. In order to be able to cope with the huge amounts of information that the cameras produce, several choices must be made by the controllers. They decide which cameras are viewed on the monitor and which individuals to watch for any suspicious activity. In highly developed systems, cameras can be used to follow suspect individuals' movements over long periods of time. In such cases, the decision to follow certain individuals is based upon the previous experiences of the controller.[13]

In a study of the effects of CCTV in the cities of Newcastle upon Tyne, Birmingham and King's Lynn, the results showed a fall in property crime (for example, break-ins, vandalism and burglaries) directly after the installation of CCTV systems.[14] This seemed to show that the cameras had a preventative effect, since the risk of being caught increased. The effect of CCTV on violent crimes was less clear. The cameras were deemed to be an important tool in police investigations following crime, rather than having a strong preventative effect.

---

11 Moran, J, 'A brief chronology of photographic and video surveillance', in Norris, C, Moran, J and Armstrong, G (eds), *Surveillance, Closed Circuit Television and Social Control*, 1998, Aldershot: Ashgate.

12 See, eg, Norris *et al, ibid*; Painter, K and Tilley, N (eds), *Surveillance of Public Space*, 1999, Crime Prevention Studies Vol 10, Criminal Justice Press, or the Urbaneye Project, at www.urbaneye.net.

13 For information on the work of controllers see, eg, Norris, C and Armstrong, G, 'CCTV and the social structuring of surveillance', in Painter and Tilley, *ibid*.

14 Brown, B, *CCTV in Town Centres*, Police Research Group Crime Detection and Prevention Series, Paper 68, 1995, London: Home Office.

In a study carried out in Airdrie, the number of reported crimes fell by 21% during the two years following the installation of CCTV systems.[15] Property crimes fell by 52%, while violent crime fell by 19%. Not all crimes statistics fell, though: drink driving and disorderly behaviour increased substantially and drug related crimes during the same period increased by more than 1,000%. Studies in Doncaster,[16] Burnley,[17] Glasgow,[18] Southwark[19] and Crawley[20] all show that reported crimes fell after the installation of CCTV. The studies suggest, however, that the effect of CCTV on crime is not permanent. Crime in all areas tended to rise again over time. Other issues investigated in these studies were whether the criminal acts were transferred to areas beyond camera control or whether the changes in crime statistics could be attributed to factors other than the installation of CCTV. The general picture that appeared was that the effects of CCTV on crime prevention may be difficult to determine but that the material gathered from these systems was seen as an invaluable asset to police investigations. These results are not limited to the UK; they have been confirmed in tests in other countries, such as Sweden[21] and Norway.[22]

While the advantage may be that CCTV allows for more monitoring in a more cost-effective manner, it has brought with it a new problem, in the form of information overload. The electronic gaze of the surveillance system does not blink or rest, but it is dependent upon the prolonged attention spans and experience of its controllers. Studies of controllers have shown that they tend to observe certain groups of individuals to a much larger extent.[23] This naturally leads to corroboration of their preconceived ideas about these groups once a crime is committed. This human connection can be seen as the weak link in the surveillance infrastructure, and intelligent surveillance software is being developed in the hope of increasing the efficiency of surveillance systems. This has led to the development of systems which have the ability to automatically sort and analyse data collected

15 Short, E and Ditton, J, *Does Closed Circuit Television Prevent Crime?*, 1996, Edinburgh: Scottish Office Central Research Unit.

16 Skinns, D, 'Crime reduction, diffusion and displacement: evaluating the effectiveness of CCTV', in Norris *et al*, *op cit* fn 11.

17 Armitage, R, Smyth, G and Pease, K, 'Burnley CCTV evaluation', in Painter and Tilley, *op cit* fn 12.

18 Ditton, J *et al*, *The Effect of Closed Circuit Television on Recorded Crime Rates and Public Concern About Crime in Glasgow*, 1999, Edinburgh: Scottish Office Central Research Unit.

19 Sarno, C, Hough, M and Bulos, M, *Developing a Picture of CCTV in Southwark Town Centre*, 1999, Final Report: Criminal Policy Research Unit, South Bank University.

20 Squires, P, *CCTV and Crime Reduction in Crawley: Follow-up Study 2000. An Independent Evaluation of the Crawley CCTV System*, 2000, Health & Social Policy Research Centre, University of Brighton.

21 Blixt, M, *Kameraövervakning i brottsförebyggande syfte*, RAPPORT 2003:11, Brottsförebyggande rådet (BRÅ).

22 Winge, S, *Politiets fjernsynsovervåking ved Oslo Sentralstasjon – en evaluering av kameraenes effekt på kriminalitet og ordensproblemer*, PHS Forskning 2001:1.

23 See, eg, Norris and Armstrong, *op cit* fn 13.

by the cameras. Below I will consider two types of biometric[24] data (facial recognition and pattern recognition) and numberplate recognition as examples of intelligent surveillance systems. Where once the operators were mediators, values are now encoded and programmed into the system.[25]

Facial recognition

During 2002, six UK cities tested facial recognition software; of these, the London Borough of Newham, Tameside in Greater Manchester and Birmingham did so publicly.[26] Facial recognition software attempts to map the landscape of the human face and reduce this landscape to a unique numerical code. The purpose of this exercise is to create a database of faces that can be stored, compared and retrieved efficiently. The numerical code is based upon the angles and measurements of the face: there are about 80 distinctive measurements, known as nodal points, which can be made of each face. Examples include distance between eyes, width of nose, eye socket depth, cheekbones, and jaw line. In order to achieve maximum efficiency, the facial recognition software should be able to function in diverse conditions, observing individuals in motion, in various lighting conditions and from different angles.

Since its commercialisation in the 1990s, the use of facial recognition software has been steadily increasing. It is interesting to note that the software has not been an overwhelming success and yet, despite the disappointing results, it is still being implemented as part of surveillance systems in many countries. The American Immigration and Naturalization Service discarded facial recognition software after unsuccessfully attempting to use it to identify people in cars at the Mexico-US border.[27] In January 2000, the police in Tampa Bay, Florida used facial recognition software at Super Bowl XXXV to check people entering the arena against a database of individuals wanted for police questioning. No warning was given to the individuals entering the stadium. According to the American Civil Liberties Union, the system did identify 19 individuals; some of these were false alarms, the rest petty criminals.[28] Within the UK, the London Borough of Newham has implemented the technology and there have been several requests for more information from other councils interested in applying the technology.

The major drawback with facial recognition software is that it is too sensitive to environmental changes. Simple changes such as lighting, clothing, headgear, weight loss or gain, alteration of facial hair and sunglasses can fool the system. The sensitivity of the system in these cases results in two types of errors, called false positives and false negatives. False positives occur when the system wrongly alerts

---

24 Van der Ploeg, I, 'Biometrics and privacy: a note on the politics of theorizing technology' (2003) 6(1) *Information, Communication, Society*, pp 85–104.

25 Lianos, M and Douglas, M, 'Dangerization and the end of deviance' (2000) 40 *Br J Crim* 261.

26 Meek, J, 'Towns secretly testing "spy" software', *The Guardian*, 13 June 2002.

27 Stanley, J and Steinhardt, B, *Drawing a Blank: The Failure of Facial Recognition Technology in Tampa, Florida*, ACLU Special Report, January 2002.

28 ACLU, 'Q&A on Facial Recognition', at http://archive.aclu.org/issues/privacy/facial_recognition_faq.html.

that a person has been identified, ie a match has been made between the individual in front of the camera and someone stored in the database. False negatives occur when the system fails to identify an individual stored within the database as he or she appears in front of the camera. A study of facial recognition systems has found that most systems generate a high amount of errors even in so-called ideal conditions.[29]

The main arguments in support of facial recognition surveillance systems are based upon the premise of benevolent watchers preventing crime.[30] In order to be successful, though, two important conditions must be satisfied: first, those who are about to commit a crime must be entered into the database, and secondly, the system must be able to identify the individuals in the database. Although evidence suggests that current technology is not sufficiently advanced to fulfil these conditions, facial recognition surveillance systems continue to be installed.

Pattern recognition

The majority of surveillance systems are used reactively. At best, they alert the user to an act in progress which can be stopped if human reaction is swift; at worst, they statically collect evidence of an act and provide the basis for further investigation and evidence to be used when prosecuting the act. The reactive use of surveillance is also useful as a deterrent, as the systems increase the risk of a perpetrator being identified. The installation of surveillance systems for crime prevention is often heralded as a success, since installation is often followed by a decrease in crime within the field of vision of the camera.[31]

There are attempts, however, to use surveillance systems more proactively. This means not only that surveillance systems can be used to prevent acts through their deterrent effect, but that they can actually be used to attempt to determine when an act is about to take place. This information can then be used to prevent the act from occurring. The main thrust of research and development in this area has focused on security and safety in London Underground stations, where surveillance systems are being used to do more than passively record images.[32] Surveillance technology is here being used in an attempt to deal with a diverse set of problems such as overcrowding, passengers standing too close to the edge of the platform or falling onto the tracks, unattended luggage, intrusion into forbidden areas, and even unusual movements in passageways.

---

29 Blackburn, D, Bone, M and Phillips, P, *Facial Recognition Vendor Test 2000*, 2001, Evaluation Report, sponsored by DoD Counterdrug Technology Development Program Office, Defense Advanced Research Projects Agency & National Institute of Justice, at www.dodcounterdrug.com/facialrecognition/DLs/FRVT_2000.pdf.

30 Norris, C and Armstrong, G, *The Maximum Surveillance Society*, 1999, Oxford: Berg.

31 *Ibid*.

32 See, eg, Boghossian, B, *Motion-Based Image Processing Algorithms Applied to Crowd Monitoring Systems*, 2000, PhD thesis, Department of Electronic Engineering, King's College London; Fuentes, L and Velastin, A, 'Assessment of image processing techniques as a means of improving personal security in public transport', Second European Workshop on Advanced Video-based Surveillance, AVBS 2001, Kingston upon Thames, 4 September 2001.

Pattern recognition systems are based on the fact that many human activities follow predictable patterns. The actions which are of greatest interest to the observer are deviations from the pattern rather than the constant flow of ordinary behaviour. A good example is the movement of crowds within Underground stations, where the ebb and flow of commuters can be quickly recognised as a pattern of behaviour where few individuals deviate from the norm.

In order to analyse the movements of crowds and individuals within the field of vision of a surveillance camera, the first step is to eliminate non-essential information from the analysis. Non-essential data is actually that which is permanently within the field of vision, ie the background or, to put it another way, the stage upon which the actions will take place. This is done because what is important within this analysis is the movement or non-movement of non-permanent fixtures within the field of vision. After this is done, everything new within the camera's field of vision is analysed by the system. Movement is therefore seen as a 'blob' moving across a background.[33] The next stage is to enter material with which the system can compare any actions that are irregular and which may need investigation. Within public transport areas, most people move in regular, fixed patterns, and as a result the system can be programmed to compare the movements of a crowd with the actions of an individual who does not follow regular patterns of movement. Irregular patterns of movement can then be classed as being suspicious and a call to investigate can be automatically sent to security officials. Such technology is used in the area of suicide prevention: the behaviour of someone planning suicide differs from that of the commuter; they tend to 'wait for at least ten minutes on the platform, missing trains, before taking their last few tragic steps'.[34]

Pattern recognition surveillance systems are presently being tested in London Underground stations[35] and have been seen as relatively successful implementations of surveillance technology. The ability of such systems to detect unusual behaviour raises new questions. Surveillance systems are no longer passively monitoring what is being done; they are now also making assumptions about normality of behaviour, where deviation from the established norm of behaviour is seen as undesirable and questionable.

Numberplate recognition

At the beginning of the 20th century, the number of cars in the UK was on the rise and it was realised that a system of identification was necessary. The Motor Car Act 1903 required all vehicles to be registered with the authorities, and to carry numberplates.[36] The Act was passed in order that vehicles could easily be traced in

---

33 Fuentes, L and Velastin, A, 'People tracking in surveillance applications', Second IEEE International Workshop on Performance Evaluation on Tracking and Surveillance, PETS 2001, Kauai (Hawaii), December 2001.

34 Graham-Rowe, D, 'Warning! Strange behaviour' (1999) 164(2216) *New Scientist*, 11 December.

35 Henderson, M, 'CCTV to spot "odd" behaviour on Tube', *Times Online*, 10 July 2003.

36 The Act entered into force on 1 January 1904.

the event of an accident or contravention of the law. By 1930, numberplate numbers were running out and a new scheme was introduced, which consisted of three letters and three numbers. By the beginning of the 1960s, a further change was made, adding the year of issue or 'registration'. This information was useful for car buyers, in that they could immediately ascertain the age of a vehicle. In 2001, the numbering scheme was significantly altered, allowing for more easily recognised and remembered numbers and using the font known as Charles Wright. The standardisation of car numberplates is intended to minimise the risk of error and to maximise legibility. An additional advantage created by standardisation is that the numbers can be made machine readable. This is the first step on the way to automated numberplate recognition and to the implementation of camera surveillance in recording and tracking vehicle movements.

Within the UK, Scotland is leading the way in implementing the widespread use of Automatic Number Plate Recognition (ANPR) systems. These systems use cameras to capture registration numbers and automatically check them against various databases containing 'details of vehicles of local and national interest eg driven by persons wanted for questioning, seen in suspicious circumstances etc. Work is in hand to ensure that the most is made of what is already proving to be a useful crime fighting tool'.[37] ANPR systems are particularly useful when placed in key positions, for example on bridges, and at present the Scottish ANPR system is being expanded to cover the Forth and Tay Bridges.[38] In 2002–03, police forces in England and Wales invested £4.65 million to implement ANPR surveillance; the pilot project has been heralded as a great success, resulting in an increase in arrest rates.[39]

Another large scale implementation of ANPR can be seen in the London congestion charging zone. In 2003, London initiated its experiment into urban road pricing. The equipment involved in the congestion charge system is a network of 203 camera sites that monitor every entrance into and exit from the congestion charging zone.[40] Travel by car into the charging zone costs £5 if payment is made by 10 pm on the day of travel; an additional £5 surcharge will apply if payment is processed between 10 pm and midnight on the day of travel. Failure to pay by midnight will trigger the sending of a Penalty Charge Notice of £80 to the registered keeper or hirer of the vehicle.[41]

The growth and dissemination of ANPR systems may eventually lead to an ability to search and track any car travelling on the road network. As a result of

---

37 Cameron, R, *Annual Report of Her Majesty's Chief Inspector of Constabulary for Scotland 2002–2003*, laid before the Scottish Parliament by Scottish Ministers, September 2003.

38 Scottish Executive, 'Smart cameras for Forth and Tay Bridges', SEJD News Release 195/2003 (2003).

39 Police Standards Unit, *Automatic Number Plate Recognition (ANPR)*, Home Office, at www.policereform.gov.uk/psu/anprnew.html.

40 Transport for London: www.cclondon.com.

41 This is reduced to £40 if paid within 14 days and failure to pay the penalty charge within 28 days will result in the penalty being increased to £120.

successful local tests[42] of ANPR systems, the Police Standards Unit is preparing to launch a national ANPR surveillance system in 2005. With the advent of national ANPR, the area within which the individual remains unobserved shrinks substantially. Naturally, the reduction of crime is an important social value and it cannot be efficiently upheld without limitations on the individual's freedom. It is, however, important to ensure that safety measures are taken to provide for the privacy of the individual. The concept of privacy as a human right applies even to those who are guilty of crimes. The limitation of a criminal's privacy must be proportionate to the severity of the crime committed. Constant supervision should only be implemented if the crime warrants it – not because technology enables us to do so.

Law, CCTV and smart surveillance

When attempting to assess the legal effects of CCTV and the implementation of smart surveillance programs within Europe, it is important to identify the distinct legal approaches developed by individual states. Some European countries, such as Sweden and Norway, have chosen to enact specific legislation with regard to camera surveillance, while other countries, such as England and Finland, have chosen not to regulate in this manner.

The Swedish law on camera surveillance deals mainly with the rules relating to permits for the installation and use of surveillance systems in places to which the public has access.[43] Sweden has set itself apart from other countries by its attempt to control the use of surveillance systems through the implementation of a permit system. There is a clear set of rules governing situations in which CCTV systems may be implemented and how they may be used. The provisions pay a great deal of attention to the balance between the need for surveillance systems and the loss of integrity which these systems entail.

However, the existence of this legislation in no way negates the importance of the legislative instrument which applies to all European Union Member States: the Data Protection Directive.[44] In fact, whereas the Swedish law on camera surveillance applies only to surveillance in places where the public has a right of access, the rules created by implementation of the Data Protection Directive apply even to surveillance systems installed in places to which the general public has no right of access.

The UK Data Protection Act 1998 (DPA)[45] states that one of the functions of the Information Commissioner is to:

---

42 According to the Police Standards Unit, the first part of Project Laser involved nine police forces stopping 39,429 vehicles and resulted in 3,080 arrests. The second phase ran between June 2003 and June 2004: www.policereform.gov.uk/psu/anprnew.html. The system is expected to be implemented nationally in 2005.

43 Lagstiftningen om (allmän) kameraövervakning.

44 Directive 95/46/EC of the European Parliament and of the Council of Europe of 24 October 1995 on the protection of individuals with regard to the processing of personal data and the free movement of such data.

45 For a more detailed discussion on the Data Protection Act, see Christie, Chapter 13 and Wong, Chapter 12.

promote the following of good practice by data controllers and, in particular, so to perform his functions under this Act as to promote the observance of the requirements of this Act by data controllers [where] the Commissioner considers it appropriate to do so ... [T]he Commissioner shall, after such consultation with trade associations, data subjects or persons representing data subjects as appears to him to be appropriate, prepare and disseminate to such persons as he considers appropriate codes of practice for guidance as to good practice.[46]

Through these powers, the Commissioner has developed a CCTV Code of Practice in which the importance of the growth of facial recognition systems is recognised and the importance of protecting the integrity of individuals is noted.[47] The principles contained within the Code include recommendations designed to maintain an acceptable level of privacy protection in the light of camera surveillance. Under the heading of Standards we find Recommendations 7–10, which are discussed below:

7   Cameras should be situated so that they will capture images relevant to the purpose for which the scheme has been established.

Recommendation 7 was created as a direct response to the Third Data Protection Principle, which states that 'Personal data shall be adequate, relevant and not excessive in relation to the purpose or purposes for which they are processed'. Since surveillance systems are regularly placed in public spaces, it is important to ensure that they intrude as little as possible into the lives of individuals who are in no way connected to the purpose of the surveillance systems. If cameras are installed to prevent crimes in specific areas, then the cameras should be limited to those areas and not be used in an overly invasive manner:

8   If an automatic facial recognition system is used to match images captured against a database of images, then both sets of images should be clear enough to ensure an accurate match.

This Recommendation is based on the Third and Fourth Data Protection Principles. The Third Principle states: 'Personal data shall be adequate, relevant and not excessive in relation to the purpose or purposes for which they are obtained.' The DPA does not elucidate on the meaning of these words; however, the Principle explicitly refers to the importance of collecting no more data than is necessary for the given purpose. The task of ensuring that no more than the necessary amount of data is collected is complex in relation to CCTV surveillance. The Third Principle is closely linked to the Fourth Principle, which states that 'Personal data shall be accurate and, where necessary, kept up to date'. Data are considered to be inaccurate 'if they are incorrect or misleading as to any matter of fact'. The data controller must take all reasonable steps to ensure the accuracy of the data:

9   If an automatic facial recognition system is used, procedures should be set up to ensure that the match is also verified by a human operator, who will assess the match and determine what action, if any, should be taken.

---

46 DPA, s 51.
47 CCTV Code of Practice, July 2000, at www.crimereduction.gov.uk/dp98cop.doc.

This is based upon the First and Seventh Principles. The cornerstone principle of the DPA is Principle 1, which states, 'Personal data shall be processed fairly and lawfully and, in particular, shall not be processed unless at least one of the conditions in Schedule 2 is met, and in the case of sensitive personal data, at least one of the conditions in Schedule 3, is also met'. A recurring concept in Schedule 2 is that the data processing is 'necessary'; in this situation 'necessary' is intended to ensure two features: first, that the collection of the data itself is necessary, and secondly, that the data processing should involve the minimum (necessary) amount of personal data. In terms of CCTV surveillance, this must mean that cameras should be used only when they are necessary for the prevention of crime and that in this pursuit the amount of information gathered should be kept to a minimum:

> 10 The result of the assessment by the human operator should be recorded whether or not they determine there is a match.

A great deal of the focus in the Code of Practice is on the importance of ensuring quality within automated decision-making systems; this is done to a large degree by taking into account individuals' rights and also by ensuring that the systems are checked by human operators. The involvement of human operators in the final decision-making stage is to ensure that the system remains accountable and is not arbitrarily unjust.

Individual rights

Human rights are today an integral part of political discourse; they are accepted and rarely questioned, and most states profess a belief in them despite any actions which contradict these proclaimed beliefs – in this manner they are truly hegemonic. Despite this almost universal belief in the importance of such rights, practical recognition of human rights is far from universal and uniform. The major drawback in human rights discourse is that such rights do not have an independent existence: they come into existence by virtue of the conscious social decision to create, and to believe in, the concept of inalienable human rights as an inherent part of human nature.[48] Despite rhetoric to the contrary, human rights are a social construct. The fact that the rights are socially constructed does not make them arbitrary or conventional, but it does contain within it the most important weakness of human rights and this is the fact that they require justification through contextual interpretation.[49] Creating and maintaining rights of privacy is especially difficult in the light of new technologies and in Europe the area of advanced CCTV surveillance must pay special attention to two particularly relevant European Conventions that create rights to privacy, namely the Convention for the Protection of Human Rights and Fundamental Freedoms (ECHR)[50] and the Charter of Fundamental Rights.[51]

---

48 Donnelly, J, *Universal Human Rights in Theory and Practice*, 2nd edn, 2003, Ithaca, NY: Cornell UP.
49 *Ibid.*
50 Council of Europe of 4 November 1950 (ETS No 5), at www.echr.coe.int/Eng/BasicTexts.htm.
51 Proclaimed by the European Council in Nice on 7 December 2000 (2000/C 364/01), at www.europarl.eu.int/charter.

The ECHR and the Charter are very similar with respect to privacy,[52] and this chapter, for the sake of brevity, will look only at the text of the ECHR. It is important to note that the Charter does not bind Member States of the European Union but obliges the European Council, European Commission and European Parliament to observe its content in their legislative work. The ECHR, however, has become substantive law in the Member States. Article 8 states:

(1) Everyone has the right to respect for his private and family life, his home and his correspondence.

(2) There shall be no interference by a public authority with the exercise of this right except such as is in accordance with the law and is necessary in a democratic society in the interests of national security, public safety or the economic well-being of the country, for the prevention of disorder or crime, for the protection of health or morals, or for the protection of the rights and freedoms of others.

The purpose of this Article is to ensure that privacy is protected. Naturally, there cannot be unlimited privacy, and the issue becomes one of balancing the right of the individual to privacy with the needs of the state.[53] What is important to note is that the use of surveillance systems is a *prima facie* invasion of an individual's right to privacy and as such it must be supported by adequate legislation to be justified under the ECHR. It should also be noted that the right to privacy is not only applicable against the state and therefore state-controlled surveillance. The ECHR, through the interpretation of the European Court of Human Rights, obliges the state to act positively and provide privacy even if the surveillance equipment is operated by a private actor.[54]

Loss of privacy is one of the main social costs of the massive implementation of CCTV: the gaze of the camera follows and records the innocent as well as the guilty and it is important to ensure that the systems in place do not burden individual privacy unnecessarily. The question is therefore one of proportionality. The implementation of CCTV to prevent crime or enhance security has a detrimental effect on an individual's privacy, and therefore the advantages of the system must be appraised in relation to these losses. This need for proportionality is reflected in Article 8 of the ECHR. The main arguments against intelligent surveillance systems fall into three categories: (1) system error; (2) function creep; and (3) privacy.

System error

Errors occur within any system, and it is important to attempt to keep them to a minimum. The most common faults are false positives and false negatives generated by the system, and all false responses should be minimised since they generate mistrust amongst users of the system. From the privacy perspective, false positives are the most damaging systems error as they can lead to the identification of an individual on false grounds. This identification and the actions resulting from it add to the loss of privacy of the individual identified.

---

52 Explanatory text to the Charter of Fundamental Rights: http://ue.eu.int/docCenter.asp?lang=en.

53 See Wong, Chapter 12.

54 See, eg, *X and Y v Netherlands* (1985) 8 EHRR 235; *Hatton and Others v UK* (2002) 34 EHRR 1.

Function creep

Function creep can occur in two ways: first, the system can be used for purposes other than for that which it was designed. This is prohibited by the DPA, which states that data may only be used for the purpose for which it was collected.[55] The second form of function creep occurs where individual operators use the system in an unauthorised manner. The frequency with which such occurrences take place shows that legislation on its own is not enough to prevent individual users looking at unauthorised parts of the system.

In Sweden, following the murder of the Swedish Foreign Minister in September 2003, most rules set to safeguard privacy against function creep failed. Since 1975, hospitals have been taking DNA samples from all children born in Sweden. This biobank is to be used for specific purposes regulated under the Swedish law overseeing DNA databases.[56] The purposes of access listed in the law are medical treatment and purposes such as quality control, education, research, clinical testing, and development work. After the murder of Anna Lindh, Huddinge University Hospital in Stockholm gave DNA samples to the police. The hospital claimed that its actions were legal since the police have the right to seize evidence while investigating serious crimes (Rättegångsbalk, Chapter 27). In this pressed situation, the interpretation of a conflict of legal obligations, ie to obey the police or to protect the integrity of the individuals whose data is stored in the DNA Database, requires great strength on the part of the responsible doctor. The law, it appears, did not provide adequate protection of the individuals' integrity as the law concerning the use of biobanks was easily ignored in favour of the efficiency of the Police investigation.

However, the creation of clear laws is not enough to guard against function creep. In an enormous display of function creep by individual operators using a system in an unauthorised manner, more than 200 policemen across Sweden are now suspected of unlawful access (*dataintrång*) after the murder of Anna Lindh. None of them were involved directly in the investigation; they were indulging their curiosity by using police systems to access information on the murder enquiry.[57] The creation of databases and the linking together of databases and surveillance facilities is one of the greatest privacy concerns today.[58] Connecting databases allows for data which is stored and collected for legitimate purposes to be compared in an illegitimate manner. Such illegitimate use of data must be an issue of great importance for the bodies concerned with the data protection of individuals.

Privacy

As previously shown, CCTV in general and smart surveillance systems in particular pose a great threat to the individual's right to privacy. The loss of privacy via

---

55 Data Protection Principles Two and Three.
56 Lag (2002:297) om biobanker i hälso- och sjukvården m.m.
57 Brottsbalk (1962:700) 4 Kap § 9c.
58 Norris and Armstrong, *op cit* fn 30.

surveillance should only be permitted if the benefits created by such systems greatly outweigh the sum of an individual's loss of privacy. This utilitarian argument is morally appealing, and is supported in legal philosophy and in substantive law. Its foundations lie in the realisation that the individual's right to privacy is not, and nor should it be, an absolute right.

However, arguments in support of smart surveillance are based firmly on arguments of criminal deterrence – an effect which, on the whole, has not been proven either in theory or in practice. The deterrent effect is seen to come from the fact that the criminal justice system can use smart surveillance as an important tool in its efforts to identify criminals. Even if the deterrent effects of smart surveillance have not manifested themselves in tests, it would be acceptable to implement such systems if the crimes themselves were serious enough to motivate that every possible effort should be made in an attempt to prevent, or solve, them. However, in most cases, the greatest effects of smart surveillance have been seen with lesser crimes or crimes against private property. The question which needs to be asked is whether the right to privacy should be curtailed in this manner in an effort to prevent these types of crimes, or whether it would be better to use economic resources on other crime prevention initiatives.

Privacy is a fundamental human right, meaning that it is granted to all individuals and can only be removed or reduced in a limited set of circumstances. The use of surveillance systems comprising of databases and cameras deployed in public spaces prior to the commission of any crime is a substantial limitation on the right of privacy of individuals within the database. Details of known criminals stored within a database connected to a surveillance system which actively searches for them without a crime being committed, following them in case a crime is committed, is neither an efficient use of resources nor a legitimate limitation on the individuals' rights of privacy. If we see certain rights as inherent and privacy as such a right then the system of monitoring even before an offence has been committed is a serious limitation on privacy and the storing of potential suspects' profiles can be seen as dehumanising. This trend is further supported by the adoption of pattern recognition systems that limit the individuals' right to deviate from the given norm, as shown in the section on pattern recognition.

Conclusion

The subject of surveillance is a large area to deal with in a single chapter. The task is made particularly difficult since we stand only at the precipice of large scale dissemination of smart surveillance systems which are commonly justified on the grounds of combating evils (such as terrorism). Despite the novelty of widespread CCTV and smart surveillance, there is much opposition to its deployment. It is not currently seen as a panacea for criminal activity.

When it comes to judging smart surveillance from a legal perspective, it is important to consider the whole data processing process and to be aware that legal safeguards are not capable of creating fault-free systems: the potential for systems abuse must be acknowledged and striven against. When using the DPA to ensure individual privacy against intrusions by smart surveillance systems, the weaknesses of this legislation must be considered and prepared for.

Within the European Union, data protection legislation is seen as a great advantage and a step forward in the protection of individuals' privacy. However, it is important to remember that the legislation was produced prior to the development of advanced smart surveillance and should not be the only piece of legislation that can be effectively used to defend individuals' privacy. The human rights instruments are also important tools, but have not been used effectively and proactively to ensure that the individual retains their privacy, which is so often taken for granted. Presently, the world is involved in a quest to minimise criminality and terrorism. While these are worthy causes, they must not become ultimate goals in themselves.

Chapter 15
Should States Have a Right to Informational Privacy?

Andrew D Murray

Introduction

As has already been said elsewhere in this book, digital technology is a double-edged sword.[1] It provides great freedoms, empowering the user to meet virtually with people they would otherwise never encounter, to address large gatherings and to assemble and manage large amounts of data, allowing them to learn, research and direct complex operations. Equally, digital technology can, in an Orwellian fashion, monitor, manage or control the actions of the user.[2] Commentators have unfortunately tended to focus on the second, controlling, aspect of digital technology,[3] and within this the focus tends to be on the ability of the *state* to control or manage large amounts of personal (or private) data.[4] Such commentators frequently overlook the corresponding privacy interest of the state. This is in part due to the conditioned response of the civil rights movement. It is hard for a commentator schooled in the civil rights tradition to imagine the rights of the state as being under threat, and in the rush to ensure individual informational privacy, by which is usually meant freedom from state interference, the assumption is that the state can look after itself. This in turn is due in part to the persistence of the erroneous image of the state as Orwellian State with the ability in the digital (or informational) age to control all information types and thereby control citizens through information management.[5] It is also a reaction to the outdated image of secrecy, even paranoia, which so defined the relationship between the state and the

---

1   See, eg, Klang, Chapter 14; Christie, Chapter 13.
2   See Klang, Chapter 14; Christie, Chapter 13. See also Westin, A, *Privacy and Freedom*, 1967, New York: Atheneum, Prologue.
3   See Wong, Chapter 12; Klang, Chapter 14. See also Raul, A, *Privacy and the Digital State*, 2002, Norwell: Kluwer; Cate, F, *Privacy in the Information Age*, 1997, Washington, DC: Brookings Institution Press, especially Chapter 7.
4   Throughout this chapter, states will be labelled 'the Orwellian State' when discussing such empowerment of the state through digital technology.
5   This image is nourished in the work of civil rights campaigners such as Cyber-rights and Cyber-liberties (UK), in particular through the work of its founder Dr Yaman Akdeniz; see, eg, Akdeniz, Y, Taylor, N and Walker, C, 'Regulation of Investigatory Powers Act 2000: bigbrother.gov.uk: state surveillance in the age of information and rights' [2001] *Crim L Rev* 73. It is, though, erroneous as the power to control information lies not with the state but with the fourth estate. This may be seen in the recent Hutton Inquiry hearings in London. While the state was required, by public expectation and media scrutiny, to hand over all documentation relating to the Inquiry, media compliance with Lord Hutton's requests was rather less forthcoming. Many key journalists refused to hand over any documentation on the basis of 'journalistic privilege'. Thus, the power to control information may be seen in this case to lie clearly with the media, not the government. For a full report on this, see *Private Eye*, no 1088, 5 September 2003, p 4.

individual during the Cold War years.[6] In fact, it may be argued that the advent of digital technology has empowered the citizen in a way that George Orwell could not have imagined. With the advent of the Internet, citizens may now access volumes of government data hitherto deemed impossible to circulate. The development of digital radio and television has led to televised, live parliamentary coverage, and the advent of 24-hour rolling news. Finally, powerful search engine technology means that a citizen may subject their local representative or any government Minister to scrutiny in a way unimaginable ten years ago.[7] It may reasonably be argued that digital technology, rather than trapping the citizen within the web of state control, has empowered the citizen while enmeshing the apparatus of state in a culture of informational freedom. The aim of this chapter is to ask whether our obsession with cultures of freedom (when discussing the state) and privacy (when discussing the individual) are healthy. Are there times when states should be allowed to rely on a particular concept of state privacy (in addition to the already recognised concept of National Security or secrecy)? More simply: should states have a right to informational privacy?

Information gathering

Digitisation of information has caused a seismic shift in the management, sharing and processing of data which has brought about important social and societal changes. These changes lie at the heart of this chapter and therefore a short excursus into digitisation and information management is necessary to demonstrate why informational privacy, a recent and potent concern for most individuals,[8] is proving to be a growing concern for states.[9]

Before the widespread adoption of digital information management, sometimes called the computer age, but more correctly the information age, information was held in discrete and often poorly catalogued packets. To give but one example, medical records were usually held on manual filing systems and each hospital had an individual set of records for each patient. Thus, a patient who regularly attended three different hospitals would have at least four sets of medical records – one at

---

6 Outdated as may be seen through strong freedom of information movements in almost all developed nations. See, eg, the UK Freedom of Information Act 2000, the US Freedom of Information Act, 5 USC § 552, the French Loi no 78-17 du 6 Janvier 1978 relative à l'informatique, aux fichiers et aux libertés, and the Canadian Federal Access to Information Act (RS 1985, c A-1).

7 In a very unscientific experiment I carried out such a search, on Google, relating to my local MP. I found that the MP has been campaigning to have a convicted killer excluded from the area upon his release from prison; has recently addressed the local cricket club; and has asked whether the Leader of the House would 'arrange a debate on the report that the Home Secretary intends to introduce compulsory identity cards and on the implications of that in terms of both cost and the freedom and liberty that we have enjoyed for so long in this country' – House of Commons Hansard Online.

8 Raul tells us that informational privacy, ie, the ability to control information about oneself, is one of the defining concerns of the American public at the beginning of the 21st century. See Raul, op cit fn 3, p 1.

9 The remainder of this chapter will use the current experience in the UK to examine the privacy concerns of modern democratic states. The experiences of the UK government and the UK state are, though, not unusual.

each hospital and one held by their GP – meaning that no one set was complete or definitive. Further, as all data was manually recorded and indexed, searching the patient's file would be a time-consuming exercise and, as indexing was a skilled job and therefore expensive, only key information would be indexed in any event. The development of information technology[10] has allowed for a single record, which can be accessed by all carers contemporaneously and which may, instantly, be searched by any keyword. This example illustrates the power of digital informational management and retrieval. This is developed further by Fred Cate, in his book *Privacy in the Information Age.*[11] Here, Cate offers four generic reasons for the growth of digital information and digital information management. The first, which may be clearly seen from the example above, is that it is easier to generate, manipulate, transmit and store information. Individuals with simple database programs such as Microsoft Access can manage and manipulate more data on a simple home PC than a medium-sized organisation such as a school or small business could do in the analogue era. Secondly, the cost of collecting, manipulating, storing and transmitting data is lowered. Cheap storage media such as CDs and DVDs, the advent of cheap Internet access and the development of file sharing systems such as KaZaa mean that, for a few pence, thousands of pages of data may be uploaded, downloaded and stored. Thirdly, electronic information, due to its very nature, has developed an intrinsic value not found in analogue information. Because digital information is cheaply processed and stored, it attracts a premium in the marketplace. This market advantage encourages gatherers of information to favour the collection of digital information over analogue information, leading to vast increases in the volume of digital information available. Finally, Cate notes that the operating parameters of computer systems and networks generate additional digital information through back-up copies and cache copies. Due to these four factors, Cate records that 'we are witnessing an explosion in digital data'.[12] While this is undoubtedly true, and while it is equally the case that Cate has identified four key contributors to the increased volume and trading of digital information through networks, I want to focus here on a fifth contributor, which has had a far greater impact on our media and culture over the past five years, and which as a result is the major challenge to state privacy: convergence.

The effect of convergence upon the generation, management and manipulation of digital data has long been overlooked, but there is no doubt that with the convergence of traditional media providers such as telecommunications, radio, television and traditional print media, the crossover effect of convergence has encouraged greater media intervention and commentary on nearly all aspects of everyday life. This can clearly be seen in the digital media operations of major UK media providers: the archetypal case being the UK state broadcaster, the BBC. Over the past ten years the BBC has proven to be most adept at exploiting digital content

---

10 The key aspect of IT or information technology is in its ability to harness the power of information. Too often commentators focus on what the technology can do, not on what the information allows. This is a critique levelled by Richard Susskind in his book, *Transforming the Law*, 2000, Oxford: OUP.

11 *Op cit* fn 3, pp 14–15.

12 *Op cit* fn 3, p 16.

cross-subsidisation: this being the re-utilisation of content such as a single news or current affairs story across several formats with little marginal costs. A single news story filed by a reporter is often distributed across several analogue and digital formats, such as digital and analogue television (BBC News, BBC News 24); digital and analogue radio (BBC Radio News); on-demand digital video and audio (BBCi real video); and digital text (BBCi News, Digital Teletext). The incremental costs of each re-use are minimal, with the only significant outlay being transcription costs for the textual services. This cross-subsidisation of news gathering costs allows the BBC, and others, not only to gather data cheaply,[13] but also to variably distribute across networks. As a result, there has been an explosion of outlets for such information through an increasing number of digital news services. In 1984, news stories in the UK were reported via the two main television news services, BBC News and ITN News (which also supplied content to Channel 4 News), two major radio news providers, BBC Radio News and Independent Radio News, and via broadsheet and tabloid press. There was no 24-hour service. Anything occurring overnight would first be reported in the breakfast news (radio and TV) and in the first editions of the press. Twenty years later, convergence has led to a world of constantly streaming news and information. We have several 24-hour TV news channels available in the UK, including general content channels such as CNN, CNBC, Sky News, BBC News 24 and ITN News. In addition, we have many specialist news channels such as Sky Sports News, Eurosport News, Bloomberg, Star News, Al-Jazeera and SAB TV. Furthermore, we have dozens of digital radio news stations and thousands of news and current affairs websites. The amount of raw current affairs information available is mind-boggling. Equally mind-boggling is the speed with which information can be transmitted in our digital world. When Pan-Am flight 103 was blown from the sky above Lockerbie in December 1988 it took two to three hours for the news to circulate Europe and North America, and two to three days for it to circulate the world; on 11 September 2001, news of the first plane hitting the World Trade Center travelled so quickly that by the time the third hijacked plane hit the Pentagon, some 58 minutes later, viewers across the world were already following events live on digital television and via the Internet. These two factors – increased information gathering through the cross-subsidisation of content, and the instant, always-on transmission of information – have changed the relationship between states and individuals. This new relationship sits very uneasily. Governments, who in democracies must appeal to popular opinion, are in their dealings with the electorate less concerned with policy or substance and instead focus on image and presentation. In the UK, this has led to endless debates on political 'spin' and media manipulation.[14] The UK is not the only country to suffer – it is apparent also in the US and in other countries – but the UK government does appear, to the British people at least, to be particularly obsessed by spin. It is the contention of this chapter that this is due to the above changes in our informational environment caused by digitisation and convergence. The contract

---

13 Reflecting Cate's second reason for greater information gathering. *Op cit* fn 3, p 14.
14 See below: 'The social dimension'.

between the state and the people[15] has been rendered void by our apparently insatiable thirst for political news and comment. The state is paralysed by fear. It may be that the only way to protect the state, and thereby restore the balance between the state and the people, is to afford privacy to the state so that it may make its mistakes in private and without fear.

States and informational privacy

All organisations, including states, require time out of the public gaze to allow them to engage in relaxed and open discussion, experimentation and risk analysis. As noted by Cate, 'constant scrutiny can cause organisations never to get away from public posturing and image control'.[16] Thus, the current political obsession with spin may be seen as a direct result of a lack of suitable privacy for states in democratic societies. This effect had previously been predicted by Robert Luce[17] and Alan Westin.[18] Westin's work in the privacy field is highly regarded and forms arguably the most complete classical definition of privacy.[19] Westin approaches privacy from both zoological and anthropological perspectives. He claims that 'man's need for privacy may be rooted in his animal origins',[20] finding that 'the animal's struggle to achieve a balance between privacy and participation provides one of the basic processes of animal life. In this sense, the quest for privacy is not restricted to man alone, but arises in the biological and social processes in all life'.[21] Such a definition of privacy suggests that the need for individual and group privacy is a bio-social function: in part a biological response to certain stimuli such as a reaction to bereavement or a precursor to procreation. In addition, it is societal, reflecting the social norms of the community, family and individual. As Westin says, 'limits are set to maintain a certain degree of distance at certain crucial times in … life'.[22] This definition seems to offer little scope for extending protection to non-human actors such as states. As non-biological actors, states do not possess the necessary biological element. This suggests that an exceptional social demand, or accepted social norm, would be needed to extend privacy protection to states. Although historically there appears to be little demand to do so,[23] it is the

---

15 The contract between the state and the people is a manifestation of Rousseau's Social Contract. Rousseau defined his 'Social Pact' in Book I, Chapter 6 of *The Social Contract* (1998, Ware: Wordsworth Classics) as follows: 'Each of us puts in common his person and his whole power under the supreme direction of the general will; and in return we receive every member as an invisible part of the whole.' In modern democratic states this contract underwrites the relationship between state and individual and throughout this chapter this contract will thus be referred to as the 'social contract'.

16 Cate, *op cit* fn 3, p 25. For further discussion see below: The social dimension'.

17 Luce, R, *Congress, An Explanation*, 1926, Cambridge, MA: Harvard UP, pp 12–13, as quoted in Cate, *op cit* fn 3, p 25.

18 See Westin, *op cit* fn 2, p 45.

19 The classical definition of privacy is rooted in the human condition and draws heavily upon anthropology, sociology and biology. This is discussed in detail in the following text. For further discussion of Westin's work, see Wong, Chapter 12.

20 *Op cit* fn 2, p 8.

21 *Op cit* fn 2, p 11.

22 *Op cit* fn 2, p 13.

23 As demonstrated in the texts referred to in fn 3 above.

contention of this chapter that it may be time to reconsider our social contract with the state. As Westin himself noted, there is a need for privacy protection to be offered to organisations as well as individuals.[24] In particular, privacy is necessary during the early stages of policy formulation, or in Westin's terminology 'staging processes'.[25] The danger is that with the changes to society brought about by digitisation, discussed above, we may now not be affording the necessary level of privacy protection to state actors to allow them to properly carry out this staging process.

Prior to the advent of digital media, the relationship between the state and its citizens was well defined by a clear social contract. Representatives were elected to carry out the wishes of the public. These representatives were primarily scrutinised by other elected, and in the case of the House of Lords unelected, representatives. External scrutiny came from a variety of sources, all of which were to a greater or lesser degree in a symbiotic relationship with representatives. Primarily, this external scrutiny was effected by the fourth estate. Media organisations, be they print or broadcast media, employed lobby correspondents; the relationship between representatives and lobby correspondents being a closely defined one.[26] Also, a variety of home correspondents, sketch writers, political editors and leader writers would convey to the public the key aspects of government initiatives and policy implementation. All journalists, though, were required to cultivate a relationship of trust with representatives. If a journalist failed to respect the privacy of any representative, particularly a member of the government, sanctions would quickly follow. As editors had a duty to protect their lobby correspondents, they would often self-censor any story which breached this relationship of trust. In this fashion, the social contract was respected by both the state and the media.[27] Secondly, a degree of information would be put into the public domain through publications such as *Hansard* and through official reports and papers. Such reports and publications, though widely available in public libraries, were little read. Expensive to buy,[28] individuals wishing to read such documents usually had to obtain them through their library, frequently encountering a delay should the report prove popular. In effect, these reports were mostly only read by two sets of interested parties. The first of these were journalists, who as already discussed were required

---

24 'Privacy is necessary so that organizations may do the divergent part of their work out of public view.' Westin, *op cit* fn 2, p 45.

25 Westin, *op cit* fn 2, p 45.

26 See Negrine, R, *Politics and the Mass Media in Britain*, 2nd edn, 1994, London: Routledge, pp 136–37. See also Franklin, B, *Packaging Politics*, 1994, London: Edward Arnold; Kuhn, R, 'Spinning out of control? New Labour and political journalism in contemporary Britain', paper presented to the Political Journalism: New Challenges, New Practices Workshop, European Consortium for Political Research, 2000, Copenhagen, at www.essex.ac.uk/ecpr/events/jointsessions/paperarchive/copenhagen/ws17/kuhn.pdf. For an alternate view, see Schlesinger, P, 'Rethinking the sociology of journalism: source strategies and the limits of media-centrism', in Ferguson, M (ed), *Public Communication*, 1990, London: Sage, p 61.

27 In the event that any newspaper or broadcaster broke rank, the state could choose to 'brief against' that reporter or publication. In effect, a breach of privacy led to media management or 'spin'.

28 Such publications are produced by The Stationery Office, formerly HMSO, which holds a monopoly on publication of official reports. To purchase a 100 page report a cost in excess of £20 would not be unusual.

to respect the privacy of representatives in order to cultivate access. The second were academics. Scholarly comment on government initiatives and policy implementation would in time follow from professors of politics, sociology, government and law. Such comment was, though, to have little impact upon the privacy rights of the state for three reasons. First, they were usually generated by reference to such publicly available documents as those discussed above: thus the data carried little privacy implications. Secondly, the extended time delay before publication of such reports usually meant that the 'staging process' had long since concluded. Finally, they were overwhelmingly comment written by academics for academics, the readership of such commentaries being on the whole extremely narrow.

In the event that information needed to be kept from the public domain, the state could rely upon laws of state secrecy.[29] Although strong secrecy provisions remain in place in the UK, and in most Western democratic states, it is important to note that secrecy is not a substitute for privacy. This point was forcefully made by the eminent political sociologist Edward Shils, who noted that in relation to secrecy, law forbids the disclosure of information, while control of simply private information is at the discretion of the possessor of information. Although privacy protections may provide sanctions against 'coercive acquisition' of private information, secrecy protects the information itself, however obtained.[30] For a modern democracy to function we must achieve what Shils refers to as a 'state of political civility'.[31] This is a condition in which there is enough privacy to nourish individual creativity and group expression; enough publicity of government affairs to let the public know the facts necessary to form judgments in political matters; and a small area of secrecy for government to preserve the integrity of certain secret information and the privacy of internal policy-making processes.[32] Thus, it is clear that privacy and secrecy offer quite distinct protections, and for complete protection states need to enjoy both.

Before the advent of digital media the relationship between the state and the media, academia and HMSO, assured privacy as well as secrecy. However, as outlined above, digitisation has led to a breakdown of these relationships. Digitisation of the media has caused a decentralisation of media power, meaning that it is by degrees more difficult for the state to cultivate and manage its relationship with the fourth estate. With this in mind it may now, as previously suggested, be time to question the current formulation of our social contract with the state.[33]

---

29 In the UK the Official Secrets Acts 1911 and 1989.

30 See Shils, E, 'Privacy: its constitution and vicissitudes' (1966) 31 *Law and Contemporary Problems* 281, p 284. See also Shils, E, *The Torment of Secrecy*, 1956, London: Heinemann, p 26.

31 See Shils, E, 'Civility and civil society', in *The Virtue of Civility*, 1997, Indianapolis: Liberty Fund.

32 See Westin, *op cit* fn 2, p 26 (discussing the work of Shils). See also Shils, *The Torment of Secrecy*, *op cit* fn 30, pp 21–27, 154–60.

33 By 'us' I mean all citizens of the state, not only those active in the media. This is because as consumers of media content we are all complicit in this redrafting of the social contract.

The social dimension

In challenging the accepted status quo, it is advisable to begin by examining the foundations of the current position. To begin, therefore, we need to look more closely at the social foundations of privacy and how this fits into the wider definition of privacy and our relationship with the state. Alan Westin defines the essence of privacy by reducing it to a quasi-proprietary right 'to determine when, how and to what extent information is communicated to others'.[34] He goes on to suggest that the right to privacy performs four narrow functions within modern democratic societies. It provides personal autonomy, emotional release, self-evaluation and limited and protected communication.[35] Ken Gormley instead focuses on four wider definitions of privacy.[36] These are: (1) 'an expression of one's personality or personhood, focusing upon the right of the individual to define his or her essence as a human being';[37] (2) 'within the boundaries of autonomy – the moral freedom of the individual to engage in his or her own thoughts, actions and decisions';[38] (3) 'citizens' ability to regulate information about themselves, and thus control their relationships with other human beings, such that individuals have the right to decide when, how, and to what extent information about them is communicated to others';[39] and (4) the essential components approach which breaks down privacy into 'components, such as Ruth Gavison's secrecy, anonymity and solitude'.[40] Gormley, by placing Westin's definition of privacy within a wider context, brings to the fore the social dimension of the definition. Gormley demonstrates how Westin's right to control forms part of a wider web of rights and duties which also encompass individual expression, autonomy and solitude. Westin may argue that the original construction of his definition also encompasses these expressions of personality, but his definition focuses on the anthropological foundations of the privacy rather than its social constructs.[41] By contextualising Westin's definition, Gormley demonstrates the predominant role of contemporary society in defining community standards of privacy. Thus, we may define privacy within a modern social democracy as: 'the protection afforded by social and legal norms within a given society which allow individuals to determine when, how and to what extent information is communicated to others.' This modified version of the Westin definition emphasises the dominant function of the social aspect within the bio-social definition of privacy. In doing so I hope to give effect to the values of autonomy, individuality and solitude which form the core of the works of Pound, Henkin and Gavison. Also, by placing the emphasis on social and legal norms it is

---

34 Westin, *op cit* fn 2, p 7. It may be noted that this is in many regards closer to Shils' definition of secrecy rather than privacy. See *The Torment of Secrecy, op cit* fn 30, Chapter 1.

35 *The Torment of Secrecy, op cit* fn 30, p 32.

36 Gormley, K, 'One hundred years of privacy' (1992) *Wisconsin L Rev* 1335, p 1337.

37 This definition arises from Pound, R, 'Interests in personality' (1915) 28 *Harv L Rev* 343 and Paul Freund's Address to the American Law Institute on 23 May 1975.

38 This comes from Henkin, L, 'Privacy and autonomy' (1974) 74 *Columbia L Rev* 1410.

39 This is the socio-biological definition described by Westin, and by Fried, C, 'Privacy' (1968) 77 *Yale LJ* 475.

40 See Gavison, R, 'Privacy' (1980) 89 *Yale LJ* 421.

41 Westin, *op cit* fn 2, Chapter 1.

to be hoped it sufficiently narrows the definition of thus avoiding the risk of 'pure privacy'.[42]

Applying the modified version of the Westin definition of privacy to the current situation within the UK, the need to debate a clearly defined state privacy right becomes apparent. As privacy is in itself a reflection of social as well as legal norms, we must identify what the norms of that society are. Before doing so, though, we must note that with regard to such norms society tends to see privacy merely as a tool to achieve some result rather than as an end in itself.[43] Thus, in order to measure norms in relation to privacy we must measure the results of privacy rights and not seek to identify the right itself. In so doing we find ourselves returning to Westin's four functions of privacy, these being (1) personal autonomy, (2) emotional release, (3) self-evaluation, and (4) limited and protected communication.[44] All four of these functions are applicable to states as well as individuals, but for the purposes of this chapter I wish to focus on the first two of these: autonomy and emotional release. These two functions in particular were protected by the informal relationships of trust cultivated between the government, media and academia. As a result they are the functions most threatened by the breakdown in these relationships caused by the growth of digital media.[45]

States, like individuals and other organisations, value personal autonomy. Autonomy represents the right of the individual to protect their 'inner space', that ultimately private space where they can be alone with their ultimate fears and thoughts. Westin described this space as being crucial to the exercise of independent judgment as such judgment 'requires time for sheltered experimentation and testing of ideas for preparation and practice ... without fear of ridicule or penalty and to alter opinions before making them public ... Without such time for incubation and growth many ideas and positions would be launched into the world with dangerous prematurity'.[46] Governments (and other political parties) in digitised Western democracies are being systematically stripped of this inner space by a ravenous digital media. With more space (both physically and temporally) to fill, every snippet of potential government policy is being reported as fact, or at least as a policy position. Government Ministers in the UK spend almost as much media time today rebutting reports and denying what is not government policy as they do

---

42 Westin has been criticised as providing an overbroad definition of privacy, a right which at its fullest extent could lead to 'pure' or unrestricted privacy. See Gerety, T, 'Redefining privacy' (1977) 12 *Harv Civil Rights-Civil Liberties L Rev* 233.

43 As recorded by Cate, 'a society's interest in protecting privacy reflects that society's interest in the result, not in privacy'. See Cate, *op cit* fn 3, p 23.

44 See discussion above.

45 Although states also need time for self-evaluation, this is (arguably) less important with regard to the state than it is with regard to the individual, as within our democratic society we may, through the media, take part in 'deliberative democracy' through the functioning of the 'public sphere'; see Habermas, J, 'Diskursethik: Notizen zu einem Begruendungsprogramm', in *Moralbewusstsein und kommunikatives Handeln*, Frankfurt am Main: Surhkamp (translated by Lenhardt and Nicholsen as 'Discourse ethics: notes on a program of philosophical justification', in *Moral Consciousness and Communicative Action*, 1990, Cambridge, MA: MIT Press); Benhabib, S, *The Claims of Culture*, 2002, Princeton: Princeton UP. Further, should the state truly require protected communication, it may choose to make use of secrecy provisions.

46 Westin, *op cit* fn 2, p 34.

positively promoting actual policy. As a result, the effectiveness of the government in carrying out its primary duty is compromised by this methodical and continuous invasion of privacy. This has had a most deleterious effect on the relationship between the state and the individual, as will be examined below. In addition, the government of the day requires periods where it can find release from the constant scrutiny of its public role. Some may challenge this statement as being something of an anathema, as the very role of the government and the state is to carry out a public function in public.[47] A government is, however, no more than a collection of individuals, selected by the electorate to represent their wishes. Even within a sphere of deliberative democracy we must recognise that the human components of the government, and therefore the state itself, need an opportunity for emotional release. They must be afforded the chance to express their anger and frustration without fear of consequence, else they internalise it with potentially dangerous repercussions. If members of the government are not afforded this opportunity, their emotional frustration may affect their ability to carry out their duties in the service of the state. Thus, the individual and the state have a mutual, and valuable, need for privacy protection. Here too the breakdown of the relationship between state and media which is symptomatic of the process of digitisation is having a deleterious effect. In particular, the 'always-on' nature of 24-hour news means that Ministers of State, through their offices, must always be ready to answer any charge at any time of the day or night. The release afforded by the overnight media 'blackspot' is no longer there. The combined effect of these developments has been the creation, within many states, of a government 'Office of Communications' or 'Office of Information'.[48] In the UK, a *de facto* Office of Communications was set up by the incoming Labour administration in 1997. This office, officially the Prime Minister's Press Office,[49] headed by the Prime Minister's Press Secretary and later Director of Communications, Alastair Campbell,[50] has been the focus of intense public and media scrutiny. It is the contention of the UK media that this government in general, and this office in particular, is obsessed with a presentation culture, or, as it is usually referred to, a culture of 'spin' or media manipulation. The media charge that this office is quite unlike that of the Prime Minister's Press Secretary of previous governments. Whereas previous incumbents in the role of PM's Press Secretary, such as Sir Bernard Ingham, dealt predominantly with enquiries directed to the Prime Minister, the Office of Communications oversees and co-ordinates the government's response to any media or public enquiry, whichever government department is the focus of the enquiry. The charge presented by the media is that this administration is less focused on policy as a result of this obsession with image. I would suggest that in this regard the media are

---

47 This is an application of 'deliberative democracy'. See Habermas, *op cit* fn 45; Benhabib, *op cit* fn 45, Chapter 5.

48 For example, South Korea, India, Oman, Singapore, Saudi Arabia and Guyana all have either Ministries or Offices of Information, while Canada, Hungary, the US and the UK have official Communications Offices.

49 From 2002 the PM's Press Office split into the Communications Office and the PM's Strategy Unit. Until September 2003, Alastair Campbell headed both offices.

50 Alastair Campbell served as Press Secretary to the Prime Minister from 1997 to 2001, and as Director of Communications and Strategy at 10 Downing Street from 2001 to 2003. He was replaced in this post in late 2003 by David Hill.

quite incorrect. Although there is no doubt that the current administration does place a far greater emphasis on media management and co-ordination of information, this is a result of the development of the unrelenting media culture found today in the UK. The government are required to co-ordinate all responses to all enquires wherever and whenever lodged as they have become aware that failure to do so will inevitably lead to inconsistent or contradictory statements being released to the media from different offices of the state. This is inevitable, as modern media demands mean that all offices of the state are continually inundated with requests for information: eventually some conflicts must occur. In addition, an Office of Communications is needed as it would be impossible for individual departments to deal with the weight of enquiries while continuing to undertake their primary role. Further, the advent of 24-hour news requires a dedicated team working round the clock to respond to all enquiries. Thus, the creation of an Office of Communications may be seen as an inevitable response to the changing media environment. The government is required to enter into an extensive information management policy in order to be able to respond to the demands of the modern digital media environment. This is overwhelmingly due to the fact that the government must now carry out all its affairs in a public setting. Any policy of media management or 'spin' is merely a supplementary effect of the loss of privacy that has been suffered by the government. With no opportunity to make its mistakes in private, and with autonomy and emotional release stripped away by the modern media, the government has fought back with a policy of media manipulation and management. In a very real sense, with the removal of the informal barriers which used to protect the privacy of our public officials, a smokescreen has had to be erected by these officials in order to afford them the privacy they require.

Conclusion: re-evaluating social norms

The development of spin politics is not in itself a good reason to suggest rebuilding the barriers removed by the development of a converged, digital, media environment. The removal of these barriers is seen by several commentators as a natural and positive evolution of our relationship with the state – their removal forcing the government to engage in a more candid discourse with its people.[51] Other commentators believe spin politics may be dismissed as a short-term response to this new challenge: a challenge which will eventually lead to a more settled relationship between the state and the media where the news agenda will be set by pronouncements of the political elite.[52] If, though, we return to our earlier definition of privacy within a modern social democracy – 'the protection afforded

---

51 In particular, it is suggested that elected leaders and the policies they pursue are more responsive to public opinion. See Page, B and Shapiro, R, *The Rational Public*, 1992, Chicago: University of Chicago Press; Shapiro, R and Jacobs, L, 'Who leads and who follows? US Presidents, public opinion and foreign policy', in Nacos, B *et al* (eds), *Decisionmaking in a Glass House*, 2000, Boulder, CO: Rowman & Littlefield.

52 See Bennett, W, *News*, 2000, New York: Longman; Dorman, W and Farhang, M, *The US Press and Iran*, 1987, Los Angeles: University of California Press.

by social and legal norms within a given society which allow individuals to determine when, how and to what extent information is communicated to others' – we can immediately see the weakness in taking such a view. This defines privacy as being a reflection of social and legal norms. Thus, if a norm, social or legal, requires privacy protection in a particular situation, we, as a society, extend such protection. In this case there is a divergence in the UK between legal norms, which currently focus on freedom of state information and personal privacy,[53] and social norms which appear to be seeking a more balanced relationship between the two.[54] Evidence of a balanced social norm is apparent in the public response to the politics of spin and political reporting. Surveys continually demonstrate that the public have lost faith in the current political system, political parties and their elected representatives.[55] Within the UK, participation in party politics is at an all-time low and, more worryingly, electoral turnout has fallen consistently since 1992 and is now at an all-time low for any period where there has been universal suffrage.[56] When asked why they are not participating in the political system of the UK, most non-voters respond that in the modern media-driven era, all parties seem the same, and most tellingly they are fed up with the culture of spin and lies now seen across UK politics.[57] Society has therefore conclusively rejected the politics of spin. If this is the case, we must ask what alternative society we would like to put in its place. Although it is too early to state definitively that a formal recognition of state privacy is the best reflection of current social norms, it is suggested that the present malaise felt by the public with regard to the current political settlement demonstrates the weakness in continuing to develop the culture of openness in political reporting seen over the last seven years. What is called for is an open and intelligent debate on all possible settlements, including the possibility of privacy protection for states in the digital environment. Only by a full, frank and open discussion will acceptable norms be identified. It is to be hoped that this chapter provides a catalyst for such a discussion.

---

53 Legal norms codified primarily in the Freedom of Information Act 2000 and the Data Protection Act 1998 ensure such a balance.

54 Where the two are in conflict it is suggested that we follow social norms. Due to the high degree of flexibility of social norms over legal norms, social norms will usually better reflect the current demands of society.

55 A recent ICM Survey (5 October 2003) 'found widespread disillusionment with the traditional parties, with almost three-quarters (74%) of those questioned agreeing that "none of the parties seems to have any really new or attractive policies for tackling problems in the country"'. Source: Ananova, at www.ananova.com/news/story/sm_826095.html. MORI statistics (www.mori.com/polls/trends/trust.shtml) show that in 2003 only 2% of respondents described themselves as 'very satisfied' with the way politicians and the government do their jobs, and only 26% (with regard to politicians) and 24% with regard to the government were 'fairly satisfied'. This may be compared to lawyers (11% very satisfied, 43% fairly satisfied); teachers (33% very satisfied, 51% fairly satisfied) and accountants (12% very satisfied, 45% fairly satisfied).

56 'Turnout at 80-year low', BBC News, 8 June 2001. The turnout figure of 59.38% at the 2001 general election was the lowest since the 57% turnout at the 1918 general election.

57 See fn 55 above.

Chapter 16
Code, Access and Control
Jon Bing

'Computer-conscious law making'

The phrase 'Computer-conscious law making' was the title of a contribution by Professor Herbert Fiedler in 1973.[1] The phrase is the English version of the more elegant German phrase 'Automationsgerechten Rechtssetzung', which was introduced by Fiedler and others in the early 1970s.[2] Professor Fiedler was a founding father of computers and law, and combined a deep insight in information technology with his interest in designing legal provisions for computerisation.

The new information technology at this time (1960s) offered the ability to computerise certain procedures and decisions.[3] These may be considered rather trivial compared to the potential of current technology, but do – it is suggested – offer some valuable insights. Take, for instance, the first example of a legal provision explicitly amended to allow for computerisation. This was an amendment of 18 July 1958 regarding a certain deduction employees could claim against their tax.[4] The amendment changed the sum which could be deducted from 562 DM to 564 DM. The reason was simply that 562 could not be divided by 12; therefore, the system had to retain data on how much had already been deducted during the year in fractions of Deutschmarks in order to make the monthly sum exact. As 564 can be divided by 12, it became unnecessary to retain data on the sum already deducted – it was the same amount each month. In this way, the regulation[5] was adapted in order to make the use of information technology more efficient. Perhaps this example is so trivial that it obscures the point, which is the interdependency between the computerised systems and the regulation.

In public administration, computerised systems have been phased in to become an integral part of the decision-making process. Starting in the 1960s, systems have become an increasingly important part of the administration of regulations, especially in sectors dealing with mass-administrative tasks, like social security, tax

---

1 Data Processing in Government, Luxembourg, 1973.

2 There are many examples; an important paper is Herbert Fiedler's 'Wandlungen der Automationsgerechten Regchtssetzung', DVR 1972–73.

3 This was the age of the IBM 360-series, when computers become important tools in engineering the European welfare states.

4 'Pauschbetrag für die Werbungskosten', cf Haft, F, *Elektronische Datenverarbeitung im Recht, EDV und Recht* Bd 1, Berlin 1970:75; Steinmüller, W, *EDV und Recht – Einführung in die Rechtsinformatik*, Juristische Arbeitsblätter, Sonderheft 6/1970:56 and Herbert Fiedler *op cit* fn 1, p 8.

5 In this paper the term 'regulation' will be used in a generic sense, to include both statutes and regulations issued under the authority of statutes. Obviously, categories of legal sources will differ between jurisdictions, but this paper does not require any sophistication in the terminology.

and unemployment. They started out as rather simplistic systems, exemplified by the early German amendment, but became gradually more sophisticated. Though terms like 'artificial intelligence' or 'knowledge-based systems' were alien to this development, the systems nevertheless computerised decisions that had previously been made by humans. It falls outside the ambit of this essay to characterise this process,[6] but we should not underestimate the degree to which legal regulations were contained in computer programs. The rules were not elegantly represented in a modern programming language, but by plodding along in COBOL or similar traditional languages.

An example which has been well researched is the early Norwegian system for housing aid.[7] This was programmed in COBOL as early as 1972. The system decided whether an applicant was entitled to a social benefit to reduce housing costs. As input, the applicant only gave his or her personal identification number.[8] The system then made automatic requests to the national personal register, tax and social security administration systems, and databases on building costs, etc. The data collected in this way was processed by the system, and the output was either a form letter explaining why the applicant was not entitled to the benefit, or a cheque for the benefit due. The system made approximately 100,000 decisions annually when in operation, and appeals were limited to a check of whether the data on which the decision was based was correct. In this way, a trivial type of legal decision had been fully automated, obtaining what has been the objective of many knowledge-based systems in the legal domain, though nobody would like to characterise this very conventional system as an example of artificial intelligence.

Computerised legal decisions

Examples such as those above stimulated research into the interdependence between law and the systems representing legal regulations. In Europe, studies relating to the 'informatisation of society' (an inelegant phrase) have been carried out, often by social scientists – the interest being the reshaping of public administration by the introduction of computerised systems. Within this tradition, there are also legal studies, and two major studies from the Scandinavian countries may be mentioned. One is Dag Wiese Schartum's doctoral thesis of 1993.[9] In this, he includes research where he has taken part of the source code for certain systems and compared them in detail with the regulations governing the same decisions. He discloses how the programs may deviate from the law: amendments to the regulations have not been implemented in the programs, interpretations of the regulations reflected in the programs are not correct, the regulations are too general

---

6   A somewhat more detailed discussion is offered in Bing, J, 'Three generations of computerized systems for public administration' (1990) 3(2) *Ratio Juris* 219, though that paper is now dated.

7   Bing, J, 'The emergence of a new law of public administration: research issues related to the Norwegian housing aid system', in Kaspersen, HWK and Oskamp, A (eds), *Amongst Friends in Computers and Law*, Computer/Law Series No 8, 1990, Deventer: Kluwer, pp 229–40. The paper contains further references to prior analysis of the housing aid system.

8   In Norway, each person is assigned a unique PIN.

9   *Rettssikkerhet og systemutvikling i offentlig forvaltning*, 1993, Oslo: Scandinavian UP.

or vague to be directly implemented, and the programmers have acted as regulators on a low and specific level. The thesis compares the legal rules as they are represented in a programming language with certain semantics, and in the natural language of regulatory texts, where the semantic is more uncertain, and the meaning has to be argued on the basis of the principles governing the interpretation of legal sources. Where the principles allow more than one valid interpretation of the regulations, the programmer will have to make a choice. This choice is generally not made by a person with a legal background, and not governed by the principles on the interpretation of regulations; the choice will often be based on what is 'efficient' or 'appropriate' within the framework of the system being developed. The result is the replacement of the somewhat uncertain norms represented by regulations with the certain norms implemented in programming language.

The other major work is Cecilia Magnusson Sjöberg's doctoral thesis of 1992,[10] where similar issues are addressed, including the legal status of a computer program representing legal rules which goes beyond what follows from the statutes and regulations formally adopted.

It will be appreciated that when legal rules have been represented by computer programs, they will work in a way that is *different* from conventional regulations. The programming language has a well-defined semantic, different from a regulation in natural language, which may be interpreted differently by different persons – something which is central to the argument of lawyers, and subject to methods developed for arguing what interpretation should be seen as correct. There may be cause to argue the interpretation of a certain regulation – but when this regulation is represented by a computer program, an interpretation in the semantics of the programming language has been made once and for all, and any argument must now address the program as such rather than the application of the regulation in a certain case.

This has many consequences; one is that the traditional review of decisions will be inadequate. An appeal is traditionally made in a single case, the decision being reviewed by an administrative body, a tribunal, or a court – depending on the field of law and national regulations – and the decision may be confirmed or amended. Such an approach is nearly meaningless to the extent that a decision has been made by a computerised system. Of course, one may check that the data (the variables) are correct or 'true'. If this is not the case, they will be corrected and the case is processed by the system again, producing a new decision, which will differ from the first decision if the correction of data is relevant to the result. However, the review can hardly include the assessment of whether the program represents the regulations in a proper way. This would presume the review to examine the source code, and compare this to the regulations being implemented – a task that reviewing lawyers are hardly competent to do. If they set out to do this, and if they conclude that the programs are a misrepresentation of the regulations, the result could hardly be confined to the case on appeal: *all* cases processed by the system would have been imprinted by the same error, and the consequence would seem to

---

be that all cases[11] would have to be processed again. One would surely hesitate to create such a consequence.

With respect to the Norwegian housing aid system mentioned above, approximately 100,000 decisions were made annually. In the first year of operation, approximately 10% were appealed. The public agency in charge did not have capacity to review 10,000 cases manually. The regulation was amended, abolishing general review, replacing this with a check of whether the data on which the decision was based had been correct.

It may be maintained that we still have no appropriate solution for judicial review or corresponding routines with respect to automated systems. Indeed, it would seem that the attention of lawyers is not attracted to these systems. There may be several reasons for this. One may be that decisions that are automated are typically mundane or trivial from a legal point of view, embedded as they are in mass administrative systems within the public sector – though we can find corresponding systems within the private sector, for instance within banking and financing. For the same reason, a practising private lawyer may rarely be concerned with such decisions, as the transaction costs of the 'lawyering process' easily exceeds the value involved in the decision, thus creating some sort of 'blindness' for these type of systems from the private lawyer's perspective. It is perceived as a matter for the public administration itself to guide its clients, or the responsibility of other services dispensing legal aid, typically social workers. A second reason may be that such decisions are not in all jurisdictions viewed as 'legal'. Decisions within public administration are – it is my impression – in some jurisdictions regarded as factual rather than legal, though the tradition of public law in the Scandinavian countries qualify them as legal and analyse them in the same way as a civil case.

Explaining automated decisions

Article 15 of the European Data Protection Directive[12] addresses automated decisions. The general principle in Article 15(1) prohibits member countries from making individuals:

> … subject to a decision which produces legal effects concerning him or significantly affects him and which is based solely on automated processing of data intended to evaluate certain personal aspects relating to him, such as his performance at work, creditworthiness, reliability, conduct, etc.

The Article goes on to provide some exceptions to this prohibition in the next paragraph. Among the requirements to qualify for one of the exceptions is the provision that measures to 'safeguard the data subject's legitimate interests' are included.

---

11 At least those falling within the stipulated time limit for possible review.

12 Directive 95/46/EC of the European Parliament and of the Council of 24 October 1995 on the protection of individuals with regard to the processing of personal data and on the free movement of such data.

Our concern here is not this Article as such, though it is a matter of interest that it relates to automated decisions.[13] Implementing the Directive into Norwegian law, the legislator introduced a new principle in s 22 of the Data Protection Act.[14] This stipulates that if a decision has 'legal or other important effects for the data subject', and is 'fully based on automatic processing of personal data', the data subject may demand that the processor[15] explains the content of the rules in the computer programs producing the decision. This is obviously a measure to safeguard the legitimate interest of the data subject.

In the context of this chapter it is an interesting provision, as it requires that an explanation of the rules contained within the program is set out for the data subject. It gave a right not to access the program itself in source code, but to be given an explanation. Norwegian law does not contain a similar provision for traditional regulations published in print, though the public administration has a general duty to guide members of the public in all relevant ways, including explaining regulations. This is due to traditional regulations being published in a language which it is presumed can be read by the subjects of the law, and reminds us of one of the dilemmas in drafting legislation – making the natural language text sufficiently precise to be used in applying the law by courts and other experts, but at the same time retaining readability so that the general public can understand the rules.

A computer program producing a decision obviously cannot be read by members of the public in the same way, and making a copy of the source code available would hardly help.[16] Therefore, it would seem a proper solution to require an explanation to be made. The snag is, however, that in those cases where researchers have tried to disclose the rules embedded in computer programs, it is often difficult to find someone within the organisation of the processor that can provide such an explanation. Often, what is available is the regulation in conventional text form; the computer programs are the responsibility of those persons handling information technology, and they are often at a loss to explain the transition from regulation to code. This can be seen as a general problem in the documentation of complex computer programs, which is emphasised as the data subject does not need an explanation of the program but the rules embedded in them, and on a level of generality appropriate to understand the decision.

The provision has not yet been subject to much attention: there are no administrative or court cases that can illustrate how the provision will work in

---

13 It is believed that the Article was inspired by the practice of the French data protection authority, relating to a system employed by a bank to assess whether a client applying for a loan had the sufficient economic strength to service the loan. The bank used an automated system (an expert system), which was directed to make the advice of the system subject to human consideration before making a decision.

14 Act 2000:31 (Lov om behandling av personopplysninger).

15 The legal or physical person processing the data.

16 And might also disclose information which the processor (or right holder) has a legitimate interest in not making available to third parties.

practice.[17] Currently it remains almost a curiosity, but is an indication of the legislator perceiving the need to address the rules embedded in computerised systems.

Code as code

As mentioned above, studies of automated decision-making were peaking some years ago, having been followed by broader and more general studies. The tradition of 'informatisation of society' is less accentuated, perhaps because information technology became such a basic part of society after the deregulation of the Internet and the introduction of the World Wide Web in the early 1990s that the emphasis on computerised systems within the public sector became less appropriate.

However, we can recognise the ideas in an outstanding legal book published in 1999: Lawrence Lessig's *Code and Other Laws of Cyberspace*. Here Lessig argues that one should look at the structure of 'cyberspace'[18] as a sort of regulator. Like a legislator, its structures force users to follow certain rules. However, unlike conventional regulations, the 'code' of the computer programs does not permit the user to violate these rules: if the user does not follow the rules of cyberspace, the systems or services will not function. If legal regulations are mapped onto this structure, we will have self-enforcing legal regulations, and if rules are implemented that do not correspond to legal rules, the user still has to follow them. Of course, this summary does not justify Lessig's arguments but, in the context of this paper, the point may be appreciated.

Joel Reidenberg has coined the phrase *lex informatica* to characterise this type of regulation.[19] The point is really rather similar to the issue discussed in the studies made by, for instance, Schartum (see above). The legal rules are taken as design criteria for an information technology solution, and are embedded into that solution as computer programs (or hardware). The result is a system that only permits the user to follow the rules. Obviously, the system will only be appropriate if the rules are represented in an adequate way – and the lesson learned from the studies of systems within public administration is that even when the objective is to implement the rules as carefully and loyally as possible, the result is bound to include elements which are controversial, due to uncertainty in interpretation, the pragmatics of a complex, real world context in which the system has to work, or simply human errors.

A major difference between the latter and former studies is that the emphasis has changed from public sector systems to those within the private sector. An example is systems implemented for digital rights management (DRM). Simple versions of

---

17 I am not aware of any cases in which a data subject has actually asked for an explanation according to s 22.

18 A term first used by US science fiction author William Gibson in his novel *Neuromancer* (1984, New York: Ace Books).

19 Reidenberg, J, '*Lex informatica*: the formulation of information policy rules through technology' (1998) *Texas L Rev* 553.

such systems are well known. One is conditional access control, which scrambles television broadcasts through cable networks or from satellites[20] that are designed to ensure that the broadcasts are only received by subscribers, who are issued with smart cards containing a chip that includes the code needed to unscramble the broadcasts.

The Audio Home Recording Act[21] requires the inclusion of a 'serial copy management system' (SCMS) in all digital audio recording devices manufactured, imported or distributed in the US. The SCMS permits the making of an unlimited number of first generation copies of a recording, but precludes making further copies from the first generation copies.

A third example is the Content Scrambling System (CSS) for movies distributed on DVD. Movies can only be performed on players with CSS, produced on the basis of a licence issued by the DVD Copy Control Association Inc. The licensing regime is open, in the sense that anyone may acquire a licence to produce a player for an annual fee. The licensee is assigned player keys and agrees to protect them by encryption. In addition to encryption, the system consists of a mechanism for authentification, which is designed to deny access to the key material on the DVD to an unauthorised player. The authentification implies that components must recognise each other before the movie is played. This protection scheme was corrupted by people trying to develop a player for the Linux operating system, who did not accept the licensing terms of the DVD CCA. One of these was a Norwegian youth, who was prosecuted for posting a program on the Internet that allowed users to bypass the protection scheme and play movies. The case has attracted some international attention, although the legal provision invoked was a provision in the Norwegian criminal code designed to make hacking a crime, and which is rather particular to the jurisdiction. The youth was acquitted by the appellate court, which found that he was not guilty of an unlawful act.[22]

International action has been taken to create a legal basis for DRM systems. The World Intellectual Property Organization Copyright Treaty of 1996 (WCT) includes obligations on countries to implement legal protection of technical protection mechanisms in national legislation (Article 16) and laws on tampering with copyright management information (Article 17). These Articles form the basis of some of the provisions in the US Digital Millennium Copyright Act[23] and provisions in the European Directive on Copyright and Related Rights in the

---

20 Cf Directive 98/84/EC of the European Parliament and of the Council of 20 November 1998 on the legal protection of services based on, or consisting of, conditional access.

21 17 USC Chapter 10.

22 The decision is available in an unofficial English translation from several sources, for instance www.jus.uio.no/iri/english/law/the_norwegian_dvd_case.html. Its importance is lessened as the relevant provisions will be changed, partly due to the Council of Europe Cybercrime Treaty, and partly due to the implementation of the WCT through the directive mentioned later in the text.

23 17 USC § 120(k).

Information Society. The policy issues relating to this development will be with us for many years to come.[24]

But before cyberspace, there also were spaces ...

The integration of legal rules with technological solutions is not novel. In the excitement of examining the relationship between computerised systems and regulation, we should not forget that the interrelationship between physical arrangements and law is a very old one.

Some believe that the creation of physical barriers around land formed the origins of ownership of real property; certainly, the phrase 'fencing in' is still used to indicate that someone has the physical means to enforce what is believed to be his or her rights. There are numerous instances of such strategies operating in the physical world in order to make the enforcement of man-made rules mandatory, or at least more efficient. A locked door makes it necessary to force one's way into a house in order to steal jewellery or a stereo. Locking a car is a simple strategy for making theft more difficult – the laws of many jurisdictions have taken this into account, and distinguish between the unlawful use of a car that is locked and one that is not locked, indicating that in the latter case the owner is 'tempting' the criminal to misuse the car. 'Sleeping policemen' in the road encourage drivers to stick to the legal limit, as exceeding the limit may bring serious harm to the car. And so on.

There are also related versions of this. Road traffic law provides many examples. The law in many countries states that a car's speed should be relative to the road conditions, requiring the driver to slow down on slippery roads in winter or when driving in heavy mist. In addition, the authorities use road signs making maximum speeds explicit: if the sign stipulates the maximum speed is 50 km/h, one cannot argue that the conditions were excellent, and that a speed of 70 km/h was appropriate for the road condition. Indeed, we populate our environment with signs, making us aware of the legal regulations restricting our freedoms, like 'no smoking' signs, the number of passengers permitted in a bus, etc.

These examples serve to remind us of the obvious; the implementation of regulations in computer programs, and the introduction of technical protection mechanisms and other similar developments related to information technology (some of which are mentioned below), are not radical, new ways of forging links between the physical world and law. It is rather part of a continuum that stretches far back in the history of man, to the very origins of law itself. But information technology offers us ever more subtle means and more sophisticated possibilities than before. It may not be a matter of gradual development: the new means may be different in quality which justifies them to be set apart and considered as something new within the regulatory continuum.

---

24 Directive 2001/29/EC of the European Parliament and of the Council of 22 May 2001 on the harmonisation of certain aspects of copyright and related rights in the information society.

'Click wrap licensing' and DRM systems

A common regulatory strategy is to introduce into legislation default provisions for standard types of contracts. Many contractual arrangements are rudimentary; the purchase of a Coke and a hamburger in a shop does not really necessitate the negotiation of the contractual terms to govern the transaction. Default legislation may in such cases replace a contract. Through the procedures of the regulatory process, such provisions are presumed to be drafted in a way which balances the interests of the parties in the perspective of a typical transaction of the category addressed.

One of the areas of law where this is predominant is intellectual property. Physical carriers of copyrighted works, like a book or a record, combine two types of legal regimes. The carrier is a type of goods, and its purchase follows the rules of sale of goods: if, for instance, the book is damaged, or pages are missing, the purchaser can argue that the book is defective, and claim a replacement or his or her money back. At the same time, the literary work printed in the book is governed by copyright law. The purchaser does not meet any representative of the right holder, and the legal position of the purchaser with respect to the work is wholly determined by the default provisions in the legislation. It would be futile for the purchaser to try to negotiate a right for reproduction of a limited edition of the work with the salesperson in the bookshop, as this person is not authorised to make contracts on behalf of the right holder. Likewise, it is futile for the right holder to attempt to limit the legal position of the purchaser by incorporating unilateral statements in the book, claiming that these are to be considered accepted when the purchaser buys the book.

The legal recognition of such unilateral clauses incorporated into a physical carrier of a copyrighted work may vary between jurisdictions, and also be relative to the situation in which the transaction takes place. Much attention has been paid to 'shrink wrap licensing', where the clause is printed on the box containing the carrier of the computer program (or other works in a machine-readable format). There have been instances where a distinction is drawn between cases where the clause can be read without 'breaking the seal', and where it is printed in the accompanying documentation and is thus only available after the seal has been broken. In Norwegian law, it is stated rather generally that such unilateral clauses are not sufficient to form a binding contract – this has been compared to allowing the seller to 'print his or her own law'. The point has been confirmed by several court decisions; a recent one is the 'DVD case',[25] in which the court held that labelling a DVD carrying a movie would not restrict the right to make private copies according to the default provision of the Norwegian Copyright Act.

In the traditional situation, the balance between the parties is struck and maintained for two reasons. One is the introduction of default provisions in the

---

25 Decision by Borgarting Appellate Court, 22 December 2003, at www.jus.uio.no/iri/english/law/the_norwegian_dvd_case.html.

legislation, which stipulate the legal position obtained by the purchaser when buying the physical carrier of the copyrighted work. The other reason is the pragmatic situation in which the purchase takes place, where there is no practical possibility for the right holder to negotiate an individual contract.

In the digital environment, the second reason changes, with major consequences for legal policy. If the purchase is made by accessing a service on the Web, the order and contract are made by the purchaser clicking on appropriate elements, typically ticking off alternatives in a pre-defined form on the screen. In this environment, the right holder may require that the purchaser accepts contractual terms that restrict the legal position obtained with respect to the work which are different from the position defined by default legislative provisions.

One may argue that the situation is similar to that of unilateral provisions in the conventional situation, and that the doctrine sketched above for shrink wrap licensing should also prevail for 'click wrap licensing', but the consequence of this may be that it would be very difficult to conclude a valid contract across the Web. Therefore, this consequence is not drawn. Rather, legislation confirms that valid contracts may be formed in this way.[26]

The situation is still developing, but one can see the possibility of default provisions in the legislation being forced out by the contractual terms stipulated by right holders. It is also probable that the right holder would draft such terms in order to protect their interests. This may lead to losing the balance struck by the default provisions of the legislation, which have been considered fair legal policy. However, the situation is dynamic: a negative response by potential purchasers to contractual terms that may be perceived as unacceptable may result in revision of the terms,[27] or the terms may become important in the competition between right holders, and therefore converge towards a balance. Or there may be further legislative initiatives, for instance mandatory provisions protecting the legal position of consumers.

This development should not be considered alone. It should be considered in the perspective sketched in the discussion, above, on the introduction of DRM systems. Not only will the purchaser have to accept the terms on which the protected work or material is offered, but he or she will also have to accept an associated DRM solution. This may be a generic DRM system residing in the purchaser's equipment, governing the use of the material purchased. The DRM system will identify the terms in the licence agreement, and will enforce them. The user will typically not be able to use the material in other ways than agreed; *lex informatica* will rule the situation. Of course there will be examples of circumvention, but this is of little importance in assessing the normal and typical situation.

---

26 The major European example is Directive 2000/31/EC of the European Parliament and of the Council of 8 June 2000 on certain legal aspects of information society services, in particular electronic commerce, in the Internal Market (Directive on electronic commerce), in which s 3 governs 'Contracts concluded by electronic means'.

27 One may consider the unfavourable user reaction to restrictions represented by the zoning of DVDs.

A trade in legal positions with respect to protected material

The fusion of contracting in the digital environment with computerised systems for enforcing the terms of the contract gives an interesting perspective on legal policy. One will appreciate that in the discussion of DRM systems above, the examples of the computerised systems were rather static. For instance, control of conditional access to a television broadcast is binary: either the viewer pays for the smart card and has access, or he or she does not. Also, the even more conventional examples of computerised decision systems within public administration are static: once the programming has been done, the system works, with the exception of maintenance for error correction and amendments due to changes in the regulatory environment.

The discussion above on interaction between online contracting and DRM systems may open a more dynamic perspective. In the negotiations, a large number of possibilities are open to the purchaser. For instance, the purchaser wants to use a certain piece of music. In conventional terms, the purchaser's legal position was determined by the default provisions of the legislation. Now, the legal position to be obtained is open to negotiation. The user may want to purchase the track for use in his or her home, for one time performance, for a limited period, or for an unlimited period. The user may want to incorporate the track in a commercial or a multimedia work which he or she is constructing. The user may want to use the music as background in the elevator at his business premises. The user may want to broadcast the track – again qualified with respect to how many times, at what time of the day, etc. The possibilities are in principle endless, but business practices will probably combine standard bundles of rights and limitations corresponding to the typical demands in the marketplace. This we recognise from the traditional market – for instance, a 'publishing right' contracted between the author of an original literary work and the publisher bundles the right of reproduction with the right to distribute the reproduced copies. The possibilities for constructing bundles are so much larger in the digital environment; consequently, one may expect a diversity which makes the situation qualitatively different from a comparable transaction in the conventional marketplace.

It will also be appreciated that the DRM system is not something built in one way with a 'take-it-or-leave-it' label, like the current CSS for movies carried by DVDs. Rather, the contract will specify which features are to be incorporated in the DRM – the contractual clauses also become specifications for the computerised system's properties. The DRM will still enforce the contracted licence, but the situation may be considered rather different from that often implied when discussing the legal policies of digital rights management – there is not a unilateral imposition of a set of terms by the right holder; the DRM is constructed to reflect the contracted licence, the user having influence on the system's properties through negotiating for the desired use.

There will still be a need to consider other aspects of the situation further. The difference in negotiating power between the right holder and the user may need to be reflected in legislation by mandatory consumer protection provisions. In addition, there may be a need to consider legislation that makes it possible to revise a contractual arrangement which, from experience, is clearly unfair to one of the parties. Furthermore there may still be a need for legislation authorising circumvention, etc, of the protection mechanisms of the DRM system in certain cases where such systems prohibit the lawful use of protected material.[28]

When talking about transactions relating to intellectual property, there has to be a change in the legal terminology used in order to reflect the new situation. In the traditional market, we would talk about the purchase of a 'book' or a 'record', the rental or purchase of a 'video' or 'DVD', etc. As indicated above, lawyers are familiar with the dual nature of the subject of such purchases: not only is a physical carrier purchased, but also a right to use the protected material carried by that object. The purchaser's legal position with respect to the protected material, however, is defined by default provisions in the legislation, and therefore the most visible characteristic of the purchase is the goods changing hands.

In the digital environment, the physical carrier has obviously disappeared, and one will therefore tend to characterise the transaction as the purchase of a service. This is often described as the purchase of a 'file': for instance, when purchasing music, one purchases an MP3 file. In my opinion, this easily leads to the metaphor of the 'file' replacing the 'record', and the 'service' replacing the 'goods'. Such a metaphor is misleading, as it implies the conventional situation in which the purchaser's legal position is defined by some accessory provisions behind the scenes. It would be more appropriate to describe the transaction as the *purchase of a legal position* with respect to the protected material. This position is defined by the contract and implemented in a DRM system. The 'file' may be identical for the consumer purchasing a track for home use and the agency purchasing it for use in a television commercial, but the legal position purchased in the two instances will be different and one would also expect the payment to the right holder to reflect this difference. Describing this as the purchase of a 'file' would mask the real nature of the transaction.

In this discussion, it has been presumed that there are two parties: the purchaser and the right holder. Obviously, 'the right holder' is generally not one legal or physical person, but has a more complex nature. For the purposes of negotiating and contracting the use of protected material, there will in practice have to be one person representing the rights; traditionally this would be the 'producer'. The 'producer' will have acquired rights from others, and there will be a net of contractual relationships authorising the 'producer'. In relation to music, the producer will have contracted with the composer, the author of the lyrics, and the different performing artists (singers, musicians, conductor, etc). The contractual relationships will be different, but often require the 'producer' to share with the others some of the income or profit made from marketing the protected material, in the form of royalties or otherwise. Traditionally, this requires extensive accounting,

---

28 Such provisions are implied by Directive 2001/29/EC of the European Parliament and of the Council of 22 May 2001 on the harmonisation of certain aspects of copyright and related rights in the information society; Article 6(4). Implementation of this Article in Norway is proposed by a new s 53b of the Copyright Act, where it is proposed that if a user is not given the access to the work to which the user is entitled, an appeal may be made to a tribunal, which decides whether or how access is to be given.

payments of accumulated fees on an annual basis, etc. In the new, digital environment, the payment to the 'producer' by the purchaser may instantaneously be distributed according to the contractual terms. Such an arrangement, it is claimed, will not import higher transaction costs.[29] It may be argued that the new technology will also make possible or probable a re-definition of the roles between the parties making up the 'right holder' in the conventional situation, where the 'producer' becomes a dynamic networked organisation (or virtual company). However, this is left just as an indication; there is no room here to pursue this argument further.

A complex electronic marketplace

In the sketch above, purchasers negotiate with right holders a legal position with respect to the protected material. One may find that this implies a rather cumbersome procedure for the purchaser – perhaps sitting in front of his or her computer screen, reading complex legal provisions defining different licensing terms or situations, making choices by ticking off predefined alternatives, etc.

There are alternatives. Before the Web caught our attention, considerable legal discussion revolved around the use of systems for electronic data interchange (EDI), which has gained acceptance in such schemes as EDIFACT.[30] These systems rely on messages generated by computers based on a strict syntax, which enables receiving computers to interpret the message and act upon its content without the intervention of human users. A simple example is a retailer-wholesaler system: when the stock of a certain item sinks below a certain level, the retailer's computer system generates a message, placing an order at the wholesaler, and the wholesaler's system will include the ordered items in the list to be picked from the stock when the next truckload sets off in the direction of the retailer.

Today, structured messages are replaced by XML documents. In the future, we can expect such systems to be realised by autonomous electronic agents. Such agents would be rather sophisticated: they would not only order what the purchaser wants, but also negotiate the conditions. Without going into great detail, consider the example of a company wanting to purchase some music by Mantovani to be played in the background in one of its showrooms. There are several commercial recordings of his music, and the purchaser is not too concerned with which orchestra performs. An electronic agent is activated; in this agent is pre-recorded data about the purchaser, such as its location, average annual turnover and other data which may be relevant for the transaction. The order is sent to the agent, which uses pre-defined databases containing data on music rights to contact several right holders (reproducing itself for simultaneous negotiations), and identifies itself to the agents representing the right holders. Negotiations are

---

29 The information is based on a presentation by Netaccount, Norway; the firm itself has terminated its operation.
30 Electronic data interchange for administration, commerce and transport.

initiated, and the purchaser's agent tries to obtain the necessary legal position with respect to one of the possible suppliers for as low a price as possible. The agent has some leeway; for instance, it may accept an offer which is not the lowest in price, but which extends the licence to several showrooms. Using electronic signatures and certificates, and relying on encryption, the deal is closed, money is transferred, and the supplier seals the music in an appropriate DRM licence (after having assured itself of the existence of an appropriate DRM system in the purchaser's system).[31]

This may appear to be a complex procedure. And it is complex, if we lift the curtain and look behind the stage. From the purchaser's perspective, however, it is simplicity itself: the purchaser just calls up an appropriate electronic agent, specifies the objective and initiates the procedure. The result is nearly immediate.

Perhaps we can liken this scenario to using a search engine on the Web, for instance Google, which may appear as a toolbar in a browser's header. Specifying what one is looking for brings back a list of possibly relevant sites. This is simple from the user's perspective, but again, if we were to lift the curtain and look at what's going on behind the stage, we would find something rather complex.

We can appreciate that, in the negotiation, the agent would need to be able to distinguish between different legal positions. These would have to be defined in a way that can be interpreted by a program, and therefore a formalism would be needed which could express the legal positions in a coherent and logical way. Current developments include such attempts, though it may be argued that they do not map sufficiently accurately to the 'bundle of rights' necessary for a trade in protected material.[32] There are some indications that rules written in a form to be interpreted by computer programs are given legal recognition, comparable to the recognition given to contractual terms. A major example is the Directive on Electronic Commerce, which in Article 13(1) specifies conditions for the operator of a caching service to avoid liability. This substantive issue is itself of little interest in this context, but we can note that according to Article 13(1)(b) and (c), a condition for avoiding liability is that the provider of the caching service complies with the conditions of access and the rules for updating – regarding the latter it is indicated that this should be 'specified in a manner widely recognised and used by the industry'. The preamble to the Directive does not explain what types of 'manners' the Article refers to, but it can be argued that the wording implies that certain elements included for interpretation of computer programs only have been made relevant for determining the liability of the providers of a cache service. Such elements will typically be meta-tags in HTML coding or robot.txt instructions in the root of a database.

---

31 For a more detailed discussion of such issues, see Bing, J and Sartor, G (eds), *The Law of Electronic Agents*, CompLex 4/03, 2003, Oslo: Norwegian Research Center for Computers and Law/UniPub.

32 Interesting developments include XrML (eXtensible rights Mark-up Language), Resource Description Framework (RDF) and HTML meta-tags. It is my belief that a formalism based on modal logic and definitions of normative positions will be necessary. See for instance Jones, A and Demolombe, R, 'Actions and normative positions – a modal-logical approach', in Jacquette, D (ed), *The Blackwell Companion to Philosophical Logic*, 2002, Oxford: Blackwell.

What material is to be stored in the cache of a proxy server is not decided on a case-by-case basis by the operator; this is obviously not feasible. There are programs which analyse the traffic flow, and which – according to the criteria in the program – 'decide' what is to be stored. The provider of a caching service will have to ensure that the program observes the rules specified at the original site, for instance for updating, in order to benefit from the limitation of liability.

The operator of the original site, and the right holder, will know, of course, that the Web includes proxy servers and that the material may be reproduced and accessed on a server outside his control. There may be situations in which the operator wants to ensure that such intermediary storage does not continue beyond a certain date. This may be written in clear text in the document, but the operator will know that the program deciding to reproduce the material on a proxy server will not be able to interpret natural language, and that no human is involved in the decision. Therefore, there are possibilities to address the program itself, using the appropriate meta-tags in HTML or other recognised formats.

The future of digital rights will emerge in the digital environment itself. The current examples of technical protection measures, which are part of access control or simple DRM systems, are often discussed from a perspective which is limited to their current use. There has been justified criticism of this *lex informatica*, which is the continuation of a long tradition of enforcing rights through computerised systems – indeed, through even more crude solutions like the 'sleeping policemen' to tame speeding cars.

If we project the possibilities onto the emerging electronic marketplace, we may see some more dynamic and sophisticated DRM systems, and see how rights themselves are defined in the terms of programming language. The introduction of such instructions addressed to programs rather than humans seem to have gained a certain legal recognition already. And the perspective opens up to scenarios of marketplaces of electronic agents, both more complex and sophisticated than what are currently the case, and more simple to use for prospective purchasers. At the same time, the actors may re-organise themselves, using the possibilities of dynamic networking organisations to find new patterns for interaction and co-operation.

This chapter therefore ends on an optimistic note, rather than echoing some of the justified critical voices commenting on current international recognition of technical protection mechanisms as part of DRM, but the legal policy issues involved are not to be belittled – there are bound to be interesting and controversial stretches of road ahead of us in the near future.

Chapter 17
Biotechnology and Rights: Where are we Coming From and Where are we Going?

Roger Brownsword[1]

Introduction

Biotechnology, like information technology, or indeed any other form of technology, promises certain distinctive benefits but, at the same time, presents its own particular set of hazards or risks. It follows that an adequate regulatory framework needs to have the profile of the technology-to-be-regulated clearly in its sights; in particular, insofar as the regulatory framework is intended to play a protective function, the risk side of the profile needs to be in focus.[2] This being so, we can agree with Francis Fukuyama that we should distinguish between technologies that are low-risk and those that are high-risk.[3] We can also agree that the risks associated with some technologies are more transparent, identified, and better understood than is the case with others. For example, whilst we understand that nuclear technology is high-risk (at any rate, relative to the severity and scale of the physical and environmental damage that it might do), we do not yet have a settled view about the nature or the order of risk presented by nanotechnology – we are not sure whether the utopian vision of a benign nanosphere or the apocalyptic vision of a nano takeover is right, or whether a more accurate risk-profile lies somewhere between these extremes.[4] What, then, should we make of the respective risk-profiles of information technology and biotechnology?

Fukuyama suggests that information technology is relatively low-risk. Thus, speaking of computers and the Internet, Fukuyama says:

---

1   I am grateful to the Leverhulme Trust for its support, which has enabled me to complete this paper.

2   For seminal work on the modalities of regulation, see Lessig, L, *Code and Other Laws of Cyberspace*, 1999, New York: Basic; for analysis of the breadth and depth of the regulatory range (in its legal modality), see Brownsword, R, 'Regulating human genetics: new dilemmas for a new millennium' (2004) 12 *Med L Rev* 14.

3   Fukuyama, F, *Our Posthuman Future*, 2002, London: Profile. However, it should be noted that the judgment that a particular technology is 'low-risk' or 'high-risk' as the case might be is relative to three key considerations, namely: (1) the *kind* of harm (physical, environmental, social, economic, moral, political, and so on) to which the risk pertains; (2) the *severity and scale* of the harm if the risk eventuates; and (3) the *probability* of the risk materialising. On the first consideration see Jasanoff, S, 'Product, process or programme: three cultures and the regulation of biotechnology', in Bauer, M (ed), *Resistance to New Technology*, 1995, Cambridge, CUP, p 311; on the second and third considerations, see Bauer, M, 'Resistance to new technology and its effects on nuclear power, information technology and biotechnology', *ibid*, especially 8–11. So, eg, at 19, Bauer is able to say: 'Information Technology imposes small damage with high probability ... Nuclear power is characterised by high damage potential with relatively low probability [and, thus, is 'technically' low-risk (at 8)]. The risks of biotechnology are still largely unknown.'

4   See, eg, Radford, T, 'Nanotech moves the future to a new level', *The Guardian*, 28 July 2003, p 5; McKibben, B, *Enough: Genetic Engineering and the End of Human Nature*, 2003, London: Bloomsbury, p 121.

[T]hese new forms of information technology (IT) promised to create wealth, spread access to information and therefore power around more democratically, and foster community among their users. People had to look hard for downsides to the Information Revolution; what they have found to date are issues like the so-called digital divide (that is, inequality of access to IT) and threats to privacy, neither of which qualify as earth-shaking matters of justice or morality.[5]

No doubt we can debate (along with Lawrence Lessig[6] and the contributors to this volume) whether Fukuyama has fully appreciated the rights-related risks presented by information technology; this is a matter to which we will return briefly at the end of this chapter. For present purposes, though, it is what Fukuyama says about the risk-profile of biotechnology that is of particular interest. Without yet giving away the plot, Fukuyama warns that regulators should keep a very careful eye on biotechnology because it is much more risky than we might suppose. What might this mean?

To many, and especially to those who evaluate biotechnology in utilitarian cost/benefit terms, Fukuyama's warning will sound like a reminder that short-term benefits may be outweighed by much longer-term latent consequences (for example, costs that do not manifest themselves until several generations on down the human chain). In fact, though, this is not at all what Fukuyama is saying. Thus:

> While it is legitimate to worry about unintended consequences and unforeseen costs, the deepest fear that people express about [bio]technology is not a utilitarian one at all. It is rather a fear that, in the end, biotechnology will cause us in some way to lose our humanity – that is, some essential quality that has always underpinned our sense of who we are and where we are going ...[7]

However, what kind of fear is this? What Fukuyama could be saying – and he would not be alone in saying this – is that some applications of biotechnology will fatally compromise the context in which we make sense of individual achievement, personal identity, individual right and responsibility, and the like, as well as in which we are able to experience the full gamut of human emotions.[8] If this prognosis is accurate, we will come to regret the relentless drive for autonomy that impels us towards expanding the range of biotechnological options. *Paradoxically, this means that the hidden danger of biotechnology is not so much an accident waiting to happen when the technology goes wrong but a contextual catastrophe that happens when the technology works – that is, when the scientific assessment is that the technology is 'safe' and 'reliable', we are most at risk.* Alternatively, some might interpret the risk in terms of compromising human dignity itself, each new application of the technology representing a further assault on fundamental values, with the danger being not so much ahead of us as clear and present. If such fears are well founded, biotechnology offers an unusual risk-profile: the most serious risks are not so much associated with accident and abuse as with successful use, and what is most

---

5 *Op cit* fn 3, p 182.
6 *Op cit* fn 2.
7 *Op cit* fn 2, p 101.
8 *Op cit* fn 2, pp 172–73.

threatened is either human dignity itself or the context in which humans can give meaning to the idea that they have intrinsic dignity.

The fact that Fukuyama might not mean what we first think he means suggests that our judgments concerning the rapid developments in biotechnology, particularly with regard to human genetics, originate in several different value perspectives. Accordingly, in the first part of the chapter, we can focus on the question of where, as it were, we are coming from in judging biotechnology. What are our guiding perspectives? Later, the perspectives so identified enable us to reflect on where we are likely to be going with biotechnology.

Perspectives on biotechnology: where are we coming from?

How should we address the challenges, both legal and ethical, presented by modern biotechnology? According to Baroness Mary Warnock:

> Technology has made all kinds of things possible that were impossible, or unimaginable in an earlier age. Ought all these things to be carried into practice? This is the most general ethical question to be asked about genetic engineering, whether of plants, animals or humans. The question may itself take two forms: in the first place, we may ask whether the benefits promised by the practice are outweighed by its possible harms. This is an ethical question posed in strictly utilitarian form. ... It entails looking into the future, calculating probabilities, and of course evaluating outcomes. 'Benefits' and 'harm' are not self-evidently identifiable values. Secondly we may ask whether, even if the benefits of the practice seem to outweigh the dangers, it nevertheless so outrages our sense of justice or of rights or of human decency that it should be prohibited whatever the advantages.[9]

In modern bioethical debates, the two approaches identified by Warnock – one utilitarian, the other reflecting a sense of justice, rights, or human decency – yield *three* competing perspectives. The first perspective is utilitarian pragmatic in nature; the second, defending human rights based on respect for human dignity, particularly emphasises the importance of autonomy and informed consent; and the third, pressed by the 'dignitarian alliance',[10] simply demands that human dignity should not be compromised.

In this part of the chapter, we can elaborate each of these three perspectives, clarifying how they operate with their own interpretations of such key ideas as consent (which may feature in the first two perspectives) and dignity (which may feature in the rhetoric of all three perspectives and which is particularly important for both the second and third perspectives), as well as sharpening our understanding of how they would read Fukuyama's warning.

---

9   Baroness Mary Warnock, 'Philosophy and ethics', in Cookson, C, Nowak, G and Thierbach, D (eds), *Genetic Engineering*, 1993, Munich: European Patent Office, p 67.

10 See Brownsword, R, 'Bioethics today, bioethics tomorrow: stem cell research and the "dignitarian alliance"' (2003) 17 *Notre Dame Journal of Law, Ethics and Public Policy* 15.

Utilitarian pragmatic

There are many variations on the utilitarian theme but the general approach prescribed by a utilitarian perspective is that, having reviewed our options (and taken stock of their consequences), we should follow whichever course promises to maximise the balance of benefit over risk or cost (or, if distress cannot be avoided, whichever course promises to minimise it). Typically, the starting point is that modern biotechnology has the potential to bring benefits of various kinds, improving the quality of human life. In practice, once such benefits are glimpsed, even on the far horizon, one senses a utilitarian presumption in favour of moving ahead in order to capture the benefits in question.[11] Because nothing (not even those techniques that tend to provoke a reaction of disgust, say, human reproductive cloning or recovering eggs from the tissue of an aborted foetus) is ruled out as a matter of principle, utilitarianism encourages a thoroughly pragmatic approach: to be sure, so long as such techniques continue to provoke distress and disgust, and so long as there are not massive countervailing benefits, utilitarians are unlikely to argue for pushing ahead; once the moral panic dies down, however, the only thing that will stand in the way is a negative consequential calculation.

For the utilitarian, the risks or costs will be measured by reference to the negative impact on the preferences and interests of humans or the pain and suffering of sentient beings (human or non-human). In this light, Fukuyama's warning will be read as underlining the danger of restricting the risk assessment to short-term, direct and obvious negative impacts – that is, as a reminder that biotechnology may have unanticipated effects. However, unless there is widespread fear concerning such possible longer-term effects, the utilitarian pragmatic response will be to monitor the impact of the technology rather than to curtail its development and application.

As is well known, modern biotechnology has posed difficult legal issues in the patent system. Put simply, where patent applications are brought forward, the applicant must satisfy the examiners that the process or product in question is inventive and capable of industrial application. These are technical questions which the patent community regards as the principal issues for a patent examination. However, modern biotechnology has activated a degree of ethical concern which is encouraged by those patent regimes that explicitly provide for exclusion against patentability where patenting would be contrary to morality. In Europe, the jurisprudence of the morality exclusion clusters around Article 53(a) of the European Patent Convention in which it is provided that European patents are not to be granted where commercial exploitation of the invention would be 'contrary to *ordre public* or morality'. The potential significance of this provision was first highlighted by the *Harvard Onco-mouse* case, where the question concerned the patentability of a genetically engineered test animal for cancer research.[12] The

---

11 Cf, eg, Holm, S, 'Going to the roots of the stem cell controversy' (2002) 16 *Bioethics* 493, p 497: 'These very large and very likely benefits of stem cell research indicate that prohibition of certain kinds of stem cell research needs strong justification.'

12 OJ EPO 10/1992, 590. For discussion, see Beyleveld, D and Brownsword, R, *Mice, Morality and Patents*, 1993, London: Common Law Institute of Intellectual Property.

examiners responded in two stages. First, they declined to treat the products or processes of genetic engineering as unpatentable *per se*, judging a case-by-case consideration to be more appropriate. Secondly, in conducting the particular case-by-case assessment – the so-called 'balancing' approach – the examiners drew up what they saw as the competing interests. On the one side, there were the interests of humans in understanding more about the development of tumours and, thereby, bringing forward improved treatments for cancer. On the other side, there were the interests of humans in maintaining a safe environment (should onco-mice escape from laboratories there might be some environmental hazard) and the interests of the mice (to whom distress would be occasioned). All things considered, the examiners judged that the former interest (in relieving human suffering) outweighed the latter; hence, the balance indicated that it would not be contrary to morality to grant a patent on the onco-mouse.

Although the balancing approach evokes a picture of the various interests being placed in the utilitarian scales with their respective utility and disutility being measured, the fact of the matter is that a utilitarian calculus cannot be checked against any unproblematic metric. The weights attached to particular interests are not self-evident. Opponents of the onco-mouse patent might object, for example, that the interests of the mice were not given full value, that the *certain* imposition of pain and suffering should not so easily have been outweighed by *prospective* (and speculative) relief of pain and suffering. Indeed, one might suspect a speciesist bias in favour of human interests. However, this would not be the full story: there is indeed a bias in the patent system, but it is not so much a bias in favour of human interests as a bias in favour of granting patents.[13]

The approach of the examiners in *Harvard Onco-mouse* is pretty straightforwardly pragmatic utilitarian. The first stage refusal to exclude modern biotechnology as such is clearly pragmatic, and the balancing approach at the second stage is textbook utilitarian. There is, however, a deeper sense in which the patent regime is informed by a pragmatic utilitarian approach, this reflecting the patent community's general attitude towards the morality jurisdiction. Surprisingly (at any rate, to those outside the patent community), it was felt that the examiners in *Harvard Onco-mouse* had taken their moral jurisdiction *too seriously*, shifting the focus of the patent regime from the technical to the moral, from matters in which the examiners had the appropriate expertise to matters in which they did not. From this critical standpoint, if the morality exclusion should figure at all, its role should be marginal, excluding patents only in the most exceptional case where patenting would be inconceivable (given an overwhelming consensus that the invention is morally repugnant). Accordingly, since *Harvard Onco-mouse*, the European patent regime has been working hard to marginalise the morality question.[14] The upshot of

---

13 See, eg, Beyleveld, D, Brownsword, R and Llewelyn, M, 'The morality clauses of the directive on the legal protection of biotechnological inventions: conflict, compromise and the patent community', in Goldberg, R and Lonbay, J (eds), *Pharmaceutical Medicine, Biotechnology, and European Law*, 2000, Cambridge: CUP.

14 Most recently, at the European Patent Office, see LELAND STANFORD/Modified Animal [2002] EPOR 2, para 51; at the ECJ, see *Netherlands v European Parliament and Council of the European Union*, Case C-377/98 [2000] ECR I-6229.

this, therefore, is that the patent regime first espouses pragmatic utilitarianism to discourage operating the morality exclusion in relation to modern biotechnology and, secondly, where the morality exclusion is taken seriously, the governing approach is again pragmatic utilitarian.

As previously remarked, ideas such as respect for dignity and the need to obtain informed consent may feature in more than one perspective. From a pragmatic utilitarian perspective, respect for human dignity is likely to be appealed to in support of the idea that human distress is to be avoided, which, in turn, becomes an argument for moving ahead with biotechnologies that promise to relieve human suffering. More interestingly, the modern commitment to human rights and, concomitantly, the attachment to the importance of informed consent have to be weighed (*qua* contemporary human preferences) in any utilitarian calculation; however, respect for rights and consent is not categorically required but entirely contingent on the relevant preferences persisting (as well as on the costs incurred). We can give a couple of illustrative cases of the utilitarian approach to consent, one concerning property rights in body parts, the other concerning genetic databases.

The vexed question of whether it is appropriate to recognise proprietary rights in our own body parts[15] has some parallels with the question of how far networked space should be carved up in accordance with property entitlements – for example, with the question of whether property rights in domain names should be recognised and, if so, what weight they should be given alongside values such as freedom of expression.[16] Of course, the attraction of property rights is that they confer on the proprietor the right to control as well as the right to capture whatever commercial value the property has. Hence, when biotechnology or information technology develops in a way that points to a potential commercial value, the rush to establish relevant proprietorial control begins. In the case of biotechnology, the rush – in California, appropriately enough – was announced in the famous case of John Moore.[17] This story began in 1976 when Moore started having treatment for leukaemia. Moore's doctors realised at an early stage that a cell-line established from his T-lymphocytes might be valuable commercially. However, the doctors did not disclose this to Moore and his consent to the removal of his spleen together with the taking of blood and tissue samples was seriously under-informed. In 1981, the University of California obtained a patent on the cell-line duly developed, with the doctors listed as the inventors, and with the value of the potential products thought to be several billion dollars. When Moore discovered what had happened, he took legal action against the doctors and the University of California, pleading: (1) breach of fiduciary duty or lack of informed consent; and (2) conversion (wrongful interference with his property), with the object of asserting a claim to a share in the profits generated by the patent.

---

15 For discussion, see Beyleveld, D and Brownsword, R, *Human Dignity in Bioethics and Biolaw*, 2001, Oxford: OUP, Chapter 8.

16 For discussion, see Murray, A, 'Regulation and rights in networked space' (2003) 30 *JLS* 187.

17 *Moore v Regents of the University of California* (1990) 271 Cal Rptr 146; (1990) 793 P 2d 479.

By the time that the case reached the Supreme Court of California, it was pretty clear that Moore had a good claim for breach of fiduciary duty (and, in the event, this part of his claim was settled out of court). However, the claim for conversion, presupposing that Moore had proprietary rights in his own (removed) spleen, blood and tissue samples, was much more controversial. By a majority, the Supreme Court ruled against Moore on this head of his pleadings, reasoning *inter alia* that recognising such a property right would inhibit medical research.[18]

At first sight, this reluctance to recognise property rights in the source of tissue having commercial potential is puzzling when the same legal regime is perfectly happy to grant (intellectual) property rights to those who use the tissue to take forward inventive and commercially valuable work.[19] However, the pragmatic utilitarian assessment is that the recognition of proprietary rights in the sources of human tissue would give the sources a degree of control and bargaining power that would slow down the research work and make it more expensive. Just imagine, utilitarian pragmatists reason, what might have happened if Moore's doctors had been required not only to obtain his informed consent but also to pay him a release fee or an agreed royalty.

We can also see pragmatic utilitarian thinking chipping away at consent in relation to the terms set for the development and operation of genetic data banks. In a number of countries, perhaps most famously in Iceland, steps are being taken to build national gene data banks with a view to improving the understanding of how genes and environment interact to generate serious diseases. Unlike the Icelandic scheme, which has adopted an opt-out procedure (a notoriously weak signalling requirement for consent), the United Kingdom's Population Biomedical Collection, the so-called UK Biobank,[20] will draw on the DNA samples, lifestyle details, medical information and so on contributed by as many as 500,000 volunteers – in other words, the UK scheme is strictly opt-in. However, the funders of UK Biobank apparently favour participants being brought in on the basis of giving a *general* consent to their data being used. If this practice is adopted, it is conceivable that there might be some disjunction between a volunteer's understanding that the data will be used exclusively for research purposes and the terms of the general consent, which authorise use for research as well as commercial exploitation.

If, in contrast to utilitarian pragmatists, we find ourselves suspicious of opt-out procedures (because they do not unequivocally indicate that a reflective, free and informed consent has been given) and uneasy about the limited control enjoyed by data sources over access to (and the use made of) their genetic information, then we are looking for a perspective that takes consent and autonomy more seriously: such is the human rights perspective.

---

18 (1990) 271 Cal Rptr 146, pp 161–63.

19 Cf the critique of *Moore* in Boyle, J, *Shamans, Software, and Spleens*, 1996, Cambridge, MA: Harvard UP, especially pp 21–24 and 99–107.

20 See 'The UK Biobank', Parliamentary Office of Science and Technology: Postnote Number 180, July 2002. Details of the proposed ethics and governance framework for the UK Biobank are now available at www.ukbiobank.ac.uk/ethics.htm. From the perspective of participants, the proposals are weak on property but relatively strong on consent. For a careful assessment of the Icelandic database, see Vilhjálmur, Árnason, 'Coding and consent: moral challenges of the database project in Iceland' (2004) 18 *Bioethics* 27.

Human rights

It is widely accepted that the benefits of modern biotechnology should be pursued only so long as research and development and commercial exploitation are fully compatible with respect for human rights. This is the standard mantra of modern Conventions, declarations and codes in this field of technology. It is of the essence of this second perspective that individual autonomy should be respected by recognising the right of individuals to make their own choices, to consent or refuse as they choose, and to exercise control over their own person, property and privacy. As for Fukuyama's warning, this will be read as a caution against allowing the excitement generated by the supposed benefits of biotechnology to override respect for individual rights and, equally, the importance of having proper informed consents in place.[21]

Within this second perspective, one of the principal functions of consent is to preclude (or estop) a rights-holder from complaining about what would otherwise be an infringement of a particular right. Thus, if A acts in a way that is a *prima facie* violation of B's right R, it is a complete answer for A to show that the act infringing R was done with B's consent.[22] So viewed, it will be understood that consent is not a free-standing requirement or response, and that it is material only where A's action is a *prima facie* violation of some right held by B. As the much-debated *Source Informatics*[23] case illustrates, the fundamental question is not whether A acts with B's consent but whether B has a relevant right.

In *Source Informatics*, the applicant company's plan to collect anonymised data about the prescribing habits of general practitioners ran into difficulty when the Department of Health issued guidance advising that, because collection would occur without the knowledge or consent of patients, anonymisation alone would not suffice to obviate a breach of confidence. The company sought a declaration that this guidance was in error. At first instance, Latham J dismissed the application, taking a strongly protective approach towards any unauthorised use of confidential information. Even if anonymity could be guaranteed for the patients, even if there was no obvious harm to patients, Latham J was troubled by the prospect of unauthorised processing. Whilst some of Latham J's comments[24] might be interpreted as implying a longer-term and pragmatic utilitarian calculation, a great deal of what he says indicates a concern with the rights of patients. Even if patients cannot be harmed in the sense that another will have identifiable information about them, Latham J is reluctant to allow that there is, therefore, no breach of right (and, concomitantly, that their consent is not an issue). However, what right might this be? The obvious answer is that it is some species of proprietary right (in which case, use without the patient proprietor's consent would indeed be a *prima facie* violation of right).

---

21 To this extent, there is considerable similarity between rights debates in relation to information technology and in relation to biotechnology.

22 Cf Fletcher, G, *Basic Concepts of Legal Thought*, 1996, Oxford: OUP, p 109. However, this does not go as far as saying that consent is also a *necessary* justification. A may be justified in violating B's right in order to protect a more compelling right of B (or C).

23 [1999] 4 All ER 185 (Latham J); [2000] 1 All ER 786 (CA).

24 Eg, his comments concerning the public interest: [1999] 4 All ER 185, p 196.

On appeal, the Court of Appeal reversed Latham J's decision, saying that, once the information was anonymised, no harm could be done to the patients, and so no rights could be violated. Having reviewed the case law on breach of confidence, Simon Brown LJ articulated the focal question as follows:

> To my mind the one clear and consistent theme emerging from all these authorities is this: the confident is placed under a duty of good faith to the confider and the touchstone by which to judge the scope of his duty and whether or not it has been fulfilled or breached is his own conscience, no more and no less. One asks, therefore, on the facts of this case: would a reasonable pharmacist's conscience be troubled by the proposed use to be made of the patients' prescriptions? Would he think that by entering Source's scheme he was breaking his customers' confidence, making unconscientious use of the information they provide?[25]

With the qualifier 'reasonable' signalling that this is not simply a matter of a clear conscience, subjectively speaking, the question becomes: relative to what would a pharmacist reasonably so believe? The answer to this is: if the processing of the information infringes no rights (or interests) of the patient, then the pharmacist could reasonably believe that, even without the former's consent, no wrong is done to the patient. It is at this stage of the reasoning that Simon Brown LJ departs most obviously from the line taken by Latham J. In response to the question, 'What interest of the patient is the law seeking to protect?', Simon Brown LJ says:

> In my judgment, the answer is plain. The concern of the law here is to protect the confider's personal privacy. That and that alone is the right at issue in this case. The patient has no proprietorial claim to the prescription form or to the information it contains. ... [The patient has] no property in the information and no right to control its use provided only and always that his privacy is not put at risk.[26]

According to Simon Brown LJ, therefore, because privacy (construed narrowly) is the relevant right, anonymisation sufficiently protects the patient's interests, and their lack of knowledge or consent is immaterial.

This decision has attracted considerable criticism.[27] If (contrary to the Court of Appeal) we were to take a proprietary approach, such as we might attribute to Latham J, we would need to distinguish between information that fell within a person's proprietary right and information that fell without that right. If a person has a proprietary right in the information first put into circulation, then the patient must have the right to control the subsequent use of that information, *including the right to control whether or not the information is anonymised*. To say, as Simon Brown LJ holds, that the patient cannot be harmed once the information is anonymised may be correct where a restricted right of privacy is premised; however, where a proprietary right is premised, it is quite incorrect – if information which is subject to a proprietary right is anonymised without the patient's consent, the right has been infringed and the harm has already been done.

---

25 [2000] 1 All ER 786, p 796.
26 *Ibid*, p 797.
27 See, eg, Beyleveld, D and Histed, E, 'Betrayal of confidence in the Court of Appeal' (2000) 4 Medical Law International 277; Laurie, G, *Genetic Privacy*, 2002, Cambridge: CUP, pp 225–26.

Correctly understood, in the human rights perspective, consent (or its refusal) is a function of particular human rights (and the scope thereof); equally, human rights are themselves a function of a deeper principle of respect for human dignity. Recently, the Human Genetics Commission (HGC) in England adopted the principle of respect for persons as fundamental to its thinking on the matter of personal genetic information, articulating the principle in the following (dignity-referring) terms:

> Respect for persons affirms the equal value, dignity and moral rights of each individual. Each individual is entitled to lead a life in which genetic characteristics will not be the basis of unjust discrimination or unfair or inhuman treatment.[28]

Such a linkage between human dignity, human rights and respect for persons has an impeccable pedigree, reaching back to the Universal Declaration of Human Rights 1948, and its partner Covenants on Economic, Social and Cultural Rights 1966, and on Civil and Political Rights 1966. In each instrument, the Preamble provides that 'recognition of the inherent dignity and of the equal and inalienable rights of all members of the human family is the foundation of freedom, justice and peace in the world', and Article 1 of the Universal Declaration famously proclaims that 'All human beings are born free and equal in dignity and rights'. From this base, in the name of respect for human dignity, we find it demanded that there should be respect for one's capacity as an agent to make one's own free choices, respect for the choices one so makes, and respect for the context and conditions in which one can operate as a source of free and informed choice.[29] However, we should not make the mistake of supposing that this autonomy-centred perspective has a monopoly on conceptions of human dignity – this would be to reckon without our third perspective, that of the dignitarian alliance.

The dignitarian alliance

The fundamental axiom of the dignitarian alliance is that human dignity must not be compromised. It is an 'alliance' because there is more than one pathway to this ethic – Kantian and communitarian as well as religious. So, for example, if we were to express the dignitarian perspective in communitarian terms, we would say that human dignity is a good which must not be compromised by our actions or practices and that any action or practice that compromises this good is unethical, irrespective of welfare-maximising consequences (contrary to utilitarian pragmatism) and regardless of the informed consent of the participants (contrary to human rights thinking). According to this third perspective, Fukuyama's warning is a wake-up call to open our eyes to the dignity-compromising impact of biotechnology.

However, there is plenty of evidence that in international circles, and particularly in Europe, Fukuyama is preaching to the converted. The influence of the dignitarian

---

28 See *Inside Information*, May 2002, London: Human Genetics Commission, para 2.20.

29 As the HGC puts it (*ibid*, para 2.13): 'The principle of respect for persons requires that we acknowledge the dignity of others and that we treat them as ends in themselves and not merely instrumentally as means to ends or objectives chosen by others. This means that we must respect the autonomy of others.'

alliance can be seen both at home[30] and abroad, notably in regional and international accords such as the Convention on Human Rights and Biomedicine 1997, UNESCO's Universal Declaration on the Human Genome and Human Rights,[31] and the EC Directive on the Legal Protection of Biotechnological Inventions.[32] Insofar as such declarations in favour of human dignity simply reinforce the demand that human rights should be respected, they say little that is new. However, as Deryck Beyleveld and I have suggested elsewhere,[33] it is in these most recent appeals to human dignity that we find the new turn in bioethics.

Somewhat confusingly, both the dignity-based human rights perspective and the perspective articulated by the dignitarian alliance can claim to be rooted in the writing of Immanuel Kant,[34] for, in Kant's work, we find not only the idea that humans have intrinsic dignity (albeit duty-driven rather than rights-driven)[35] but also the idea that human dignity has no price and that humans owe themselves a duty of self-esteem. In these seminal remarks, modern writers find support for a variety of supposed applications of Kantian morality, including the claim that commercialisation of the human body is an affront to dignity (by putting a price on something that is beyond price). However, commodification of the human body – whether in the form of commerce in human organs or tissue, prostitution, surrogacy for profit, or patenting human genes – is just one of a number of practices that are regularly cited as instances of human dignity being compromised. Typically, the dignitarian alliance also condemns sex selection and positive (eugenic) gene selection, germ-line gene therapy, embryo research and abortion, euthanasia and assisted suicide, genetic discrimination, and (perhaps top of its current list) human reproductive cloning. The list, though, is hardly closed, and there will surely be additions as technology opens up new bio-options and opportunities.

One way of trying to disentangle the second from the third perspective is to fix on two different reference points for human dignity. One reference point is the idea that human dignity speaks to what is special or specific about humans, that is to say, what is intrinsically and universally distinctive about humans. This reference point is to be contrasted with the idea that human dignity speaks less to what is special about humans *qua* humans and more to what is special about a particular community's idea of civilised life and the concomitant commitments of its members. Here, appeals to human dignity draw on what is distinctively valued concerning human social existence in a particular community – indeed, on the values and vision that distinguish the community as the particular community that it is and relative to which the community's members take their collective and

---

30 Cf Hilary and Steven Rose, 'Playing God', *The Guardian*, 3 July 2003, p 25 (on harvesting eggs from aborted foetuses and the erasure of 'the human dignity claims of the potential child').

31 Adopted at the 29th Session of the General Conference, 11 November 1997.

32 Directive 98/44/EC; OJ L 213, 30 July 1998, 213.

33 *Op cit* fn 15.

34 See, in particular, Kant, I, *The Metaphysics of Morals*, Gregor, M (trans and ed), 1996 [1797], Cambridge: CUP, p 209.

35 For the significance of this distinction, see Beyleveld, D and Brownsword, R, 'Human dignity, human rights, and human genetics', in Brownsword, R, Cornish, WR and Llewelyn, M (eds), *Human Genetics and the Law*, 1998, Oxford: Hart, p 69; Beyleveld and Brownsword, *op cit* fn 15.

individual identity. Whereas the former tends to be closely associated with the human rights perspective and the aim of giving individuals the opportunity to flourish as self-determining authors of their own destinies, the latter (as expressed by the dignitarian alliance) combines a (Kantian) view of what is distinctive about humans (their dignity) with views about what defines life as civilised (and, thus, respectful of human dignity) in a particular community.

The dignitarian alliance, as we have said, has sought to turn back the biotechnological tide on several fronts, *inter alia* opposing the patenting of human gene sequences (or copies thereof),[36] the licensing of embryonic stem cell research,[37] and permitting tissue typing of embryos for the sake of saviour siblings.[38] In each case, the alliance rejects the pragmatic utilitarian argument that the promotion of general benefit justifies biotechnologically-friendly regulation as it rejects the arguments made from the human rights perspective in which the primacy of autonomy and the justificatory significance of consent are relied on. For the alliance, the utilitarian pragmatists and the proponents of human rights are, quite simply, coming from the wrong place – the only place to come from is one in which it is understood that human dignity must not be compromised.

Where are we going?

If the three perspectives sketched above give us an indication of where we might be coming from in our thinking about the regulation of biotechnology, where are we likely to be going in the foreseeable future?

In the United Kingdom at least, there is a clear political will to push ahead with the development of biotechnology. The flavour of the prevailing political view comes through very obviously in the Prime Minister's Foreword to the recent Government White Paper, *Our Inheritance, Our Future:*[39]

> Our country has a remarkable scientific tradition. The extraordinary achievements of Newton, Darwin and a host of other eminent scientists have both greatly increased the understanding of our world and improved the quality of life for everyone.

> Our record continues to be outstanding; with just one per cent of the world's population, we receive nine per cent of scientific citations. Nowhere has this record been more notable in recent decades than in bio-science and bio-technology.

> The discovery in Britain of the structure of DNA 50 years ago – perhaps the biggest single scientific advance of the last century – marked the beginning of a golden age of bio-science in Britain which continues today. It is likely to have as big an impact on our lives in the coming century as the computer had for the last generation.

> The more we understand about the human genome, the greater will be the impact on our lives and on our healthcare. ...

36 See, eg, *Howard Florey/Relaxin* [1995] EPOR 541; for commentary, Brownsword, R, 'The *Relaxin Opposition* revisited' (2001) 9 *Jahrbuch für Recht und Ethik* 3.
37 See Brownsword, R, 'Stem cells, Superman, and the report of the Select Committee' (2002) 65 *MLR* 568.
38 See *R (Quintavalle on Behalf of Comment on Reproductive Ethics) v Human Fertilisation and Embryology Authority* [2002] EWHC 2785 (Admin); [2003] EWCA Civ 667. For discussion, see Brownsword, R, 'Reproductive opportunities and regulatory challenges' (2004) 67 *MLR* 304.
39 Cm 5791, June 2003.

I am proud to know that much of this ground-breaking work is already taking place in our country. I am also absolutely determined that the National Health Service should be able to respond to these advances so the benefits of genetics and the more personalised and improved healthcare it will bring are available to all.

It means we must prepare now for the future. We must invest in research and research facilities to drive further discovery. ...[40]

The White Paper continues in the same vein, declaring that the government 'want the NHS to lead the world in taking maximum advantage of the safe, effective and ethical application of the new genetic knowledge and technologies as soon as they become available'.[41] And, more generally, it underlines its commitment to supporting UK science and technology with an additional £1.25 billion set aside as part of a long-term support strategy.[42]

In some places, where the perspective of the dignitarian alliance prevails, politicians would face real difficulty in promoting biotechnology alongside a commitment to its ethical application. However, in the United Kingdom, the perceived ethical application of biotechnology is greatly facilitated by the relative weakness of the dignitarian view and by a working accommodation – the 'ruling synthesis' as it were – between the utilitarian pragmatic perspective and the perspective of human rights.[43] The effect of this synthesis is that there is a real momentum towards the greater availability of (what are perceived to be) socially beneficial biotechnological applications with human rights acting as a side constraint to ensure that new applications are simply options and that individual participation is still subject to personal choice, consent and control.

To a considerable extent, the recent White Paper echoes the ruling synthesis, its opening remark being that '[a]lthough there are difficult moral issues raised by genetics advances we see enormous overall potential benefits for patients'.[44] This theme is repeated several times.[45] Indeed, the general approach[46] is to balance the perceived benefits against the principle of respect for persons which, as we have said, the HGC has identified as fundamental to its thinking on the use of genetic information.[47]

Against this forward movement, it is only the perspective of the dignitarian alliance that proposes serious road-blocks. The difficulty for the dignitarians, however, is that their opposition is either seen as dogmatic, unreasoned, and unreasonable, or it is translated into a manageable objection within the ruling

---

40 *Ibid*, para 1.

41 *Ibid*, para 1.35.

42 *Ibid*, para 5.7, but cf *The Guardian (G2)*, 26 August 2003, p 9 for adverse remarks concerning the shortfall between the funding committed and the funding required to meet the government's aspiration.

43 On the ruling synthesis, see, further, Brownsword, *op cit* fn 2.

44 Cm 5791, June 2003, para 1.1.

45 *Ibid*, eg, at 1.34–1.39, 3.33–3.34, 6.1, and at 3.36 *et seq* where the benefits of genetic profiling at birth are mooted alongside the ethical and social concerns.

46 Signalled *ibid*, para 6.22.

47 See *Inside Information, op cit* fn 28.

synthesis. For example, religious objections (to the effect that biotechnologists are in danger of trying to play God) are translated as secular objections concerning safety; objections that condemn commodification or instrumentalisation as compromising human dignity are translated as concerns about obtaining informed consent; objections to the destruction of human embryos are translated into concerns that the special status of embryos should be respected; and any attempt to instate a community-defining ethic of respect for human dignity must reckon with the premise that this is a society in which a plurality of ethical perspectives demand recognition and respect. As if things were not already difficult enough for the dignitarian alliance, they also face a very obvious incrementalism with regard to the regulatory decisions that are made about biotechnology. In part, this incrementalism is assisted by a tendency to work from existing regulatory positions when contemplating changes in the regulatory framework; in part, it is forced on regulators by the development of a global marketplace for biotechnological applications. All the indications are, therefore, that – in the United Kingdom, at any rate – the destiny of the dignitarian alliance is to whistle in the wind.[48]

If the forward movement of biotechnology is to be retarded, it is suggested that this will be because restraint makes sense from the perspective of the ruling synthesis. On the utilitarian side of this synthesis, this implies that concerns about bio-safety might be so heightened that a precautionary approach is adopted. This is not inconceivable[49] and we know from the case of GM foods that public resistance can be effective even in the teeth of massive commercial and political pressure. However, there is another way in which the sense of moving ahead with biotechnology may come under closer scrutiny, but this time on the human rights side of the ruling synthesis.

As a number of writers, notably Francis Fukuyama,[50] Jürgen Habermas[51] and Bill McKibben,[52] have remarked, biotechnology seems to have the potential to compromise the context in which human social existence makes the kind of sense that we currently make of it. This is not the dogmatic conservatism of the dignitarian alliance. Rather, as McKibben puts it, having systematically 'traded context for individual freedom', we now find ourselves 'empowered, enabled, isolated, disconnected individuals'; if we go any further we may find that this is a world 'where consumption is all that happens, because there's nothing else left that means anything'.[53] In other words, it is not so much the compromising of human dignity that should concern us as the compromising of the context in which we give meaning to the dignity of individual choice, responsibility and achievement. If regulators take heed of this warning, they will face the difficult task of

---

48 Cf Brownsword, R, 'Stem cell research: culture, consent and dignity', in Mansel, A and Hauskeller, C (eds), *Crossing Borders*, forthcoming, 2005.

49 See, eg, Brown, P, 'GM crops fail key trials amid environment fear', *The Guardian*, 2 October 2003, p 1, and 'Birds and the bees: how wildlife suffered', *The Guardian*, 17 October 2003, p 4.

50 Fukuyama, *op cit* fn 3.

51 *The Future of Human Nature*, 2003, Cambridge: Polity.

52 *Enough*, 2003, London: Bloomsbury.

53 *Ibid*, p 47.

discriminating between those biotechnologies that are context-enhancing (or, at least, context-neutral) and those that are context-compromising. However, this is only half the story.

While regulators are grappling with the special problems presented by biotechnology, they are likely to deploy emerging technologies ever more widely in their general regulatory apparatus. Already, we see genetic profiling, CCTV, computer mapping of crime, monitoring and tagging, and so on, employed within the framework of traditional 'obey or pay' forms of regulation. Even though some of the technology is quite sophisticated, there is still the option of non-compliance and a chance that one will not be detected. However, we can imagine an 'all-seeing' 24/7 surveillance technology that enables the regulators not only to monitor our every action but also to identify *whose* action it is that they are monitoring. If we fail to comply, we will be seen and identified. We can elect non-compliance but we do so in the certain knowledge that we will pay. For regulators who are attracted by the idea of the technical fix, though, this is not the completion of the project. As a final step, traditional regulation (or 'East Coast Code' as Lessig would term it) may give way to technologically secured results, that is, to techno-regulation ('West Coast Code' as Lessig would put it).[54] In the ideal-typical case, techno-regulation *guarantees* compliance, whether by fixing the environment, human biology, or both. With such an ultimate technical fix, there is no such thing as the perfect crime; criminality is no longer an option.[55]

In the lead up to techno-regulation, we can anticipate that there will be concerns about the need to respect privacy and whether the technology adopted by regulators is necessary, proportionate, and justifiable, all things considered.[56] However, with techno-regulation, where the emphasis shifts to the elimination of choice, the concern is whether we can justify the treatment of subjects as though they lack the capacity to choose. The question that should give us all pause is quite simply this: how much techno-regulation can we take before the context in which we view ourselves as bearers of both rights and responsibilities is hopelessly compromised? If, no matter where we are coming from, we agree that this is a place that we do not want to go, then perhaps we can avoid doing so.

Conclusion

Biotechnology and information technology are increasingly interacting technologies, but the former has a distinctive risk-profile. Like other technologies, it may prove unsafe and it is open to abuse, but it is arguable that, distinctively, the risk presented by biotechnology is that it works and, in so doing, it is context-

---

54 See Lessig, *op cit* fn 2, pp 90–92, for some examples of 'West Coast' environmental or architectural thinking.

55 See, further, Brownsword, R, 'What the world needs now: techno-regulation, human rights and human dignity', in Brownsword, R (ed), *Human Rights (Global Governance and the Quest for Justice: Volume IV)*, 2004, Oxford: Hart, p 203. See, further, Brownsword, R, 'Code, control, and choice: why East is East and West is West' (2005) *Legal Studies*, forthcoming.

56 Again, with reference to information and communications technology, see Lessig, *op cit* fn 2.

compromising. This is the burden of Fukuyama's warning. It is a plea for conservation, but it is not cultural conservatism of the kind represented by the dignitarian alliance so much as a plea for a sustainable and meaningful social environment. As such, it is a plea that should strike a chord with each of the three perspectives and especially so with the human rights view.

With the political will being to maintain the United Kingdom's position in the vanguard of biotechnological research and development, Fukuyama's warning is no less relevant on this side of the Atlantic. Moreover, given a ruling ethical synthesis that presently recognises only a forward trajectory, it is difficult to see what might stop biotechnology in its tracks. One possibility is that the synthesis might reflect on its own presuppositions to appreciate the need for restraint, leading to acceptance of the importance of setting and holding regulatory lines (even provisional and precautionary regulatory lines). Another possibility is that there will be a reaction against regulators who over-rely on the technical fix; we might, indeed, come to see some value in a certain level of regulatory inefficiency. Putting these two possibilities together, we can go beyond Fukuyama to suggest that the future might be one in which the challenge is to draw context-sustaining lines in the face of the threat presented not only by the biotechnologists but also by the techno-regulators.

Index

Printed in the United Kingdom
by Lightning Source UK Ltd.
118644UK00002B/43-45